Political Ambition

Political Ambition

Who Decides to
Run for Congress

Linda L. Fowler
Robert D. McClure

Yale University Press

New Haven and London

Published with the assistance of the A. Whitney Griswold
Publication Fund.

Designed by Jo Aerne and set in Times Roman type by
Keystone Typesetting, Inc., Orwigsburg, Pennsylvania.
Printed in the United States of America by
Vail-Ballou Press, Binghamton, New York.

Library of Congress Cataloging-in-Publication Data
Fowler, Linda L., 1945–
Political ambition : who decides to run for Congress /
Linda L. Fowler and Robert D. McClure.
p. cm.
Bibliography: p.
Includes index.
ISBN 0–300–04405–4 (alk. paper)
1. United States. Congress. 2. Legislators—United
States—Attitudes. 3. Ambition. I. McClure, Robert D.
II. Title.
JK1021.F68 1989
328.73′077—dc19   88–22713
                                              CIP

The paper in this book meets the guidelines for
permanence and durability of the Committee on
Production Guidelines for Book Longevity of the Council
on Library Resources.

10 9 8 7 6 5 4 3 2 1

*To our teachers, Prof. Richard F. Fenno, Jr.,
and the late Charles S. Hyneman, who taught
us to appreciate legislative politics and democratic government and to value the men and
women who make them work.*

Contents

Tables and Maps

Tables

Maps

Preface

Political ambition is so deeply embedded in a democratic society that its presence is scarcely recognized and seldom appreciated. But the desire for governmental power should not be treated so lightly, because by ensuring that eager rivals call each other to account, it is the primary incentive for public officials to be responsive to public demands.

In the United States especially, ambitious individuals assume an unusually large share of the responsibility for organizing electoral contests. Because of the nation's decentralized party structures and weak partisan attitudes, American campaigns increasingly depend on the personal characteristics of the competitors, who woo the public on the basis of their particular qualifications to create their own personal coalitions of support. Such candidate-centered campaigns, however, require a level of commitment from the contestants that only the most politically motivated people can sustain. Thus the continued health of the electoral system in this country requires a sufficient supply of men and women who value public life, enjoy exercising political power, and are willing to pay the inflated price of elective office.

The presidential election of 1988, characterized by public dissatisfaction with the nominating process and widespread doubt that either party put forward its strongest candidates, dramatizes the questions that motivated our inquiry about the role of political ambition in House elections. Students of the Congress have recognized for some time the connection between electoral competition and the recruitment of individual candidates, and in puzzling over such issues as the effect of incumbency, the uncoupling of presidential and congressional voting, and the swings in partisan majorities in the House, they have posed the following questions: Why do some individuals run for office, while similarly qualified politicians remain on the sidelines? What produces a large field of likely contenders in one election year and a small crop in another? That observers of the presidential nomination process are now raising these issues, already so familiar to those who follow congressional elections, simply emphasizes how little we know about the incentives and disincentives that bring people in and out of public life.

In focusing today on what we call the unseen candidates—the men and women who could have run for Congress but chose not to—we hope to show our readers that election outcomes depend not only on the fall campaign, but also on the highly personal and private decisions made many months beforehand. We hope as well to make a cynical public aware of the values and goals of the individuals who offer the rest of us the luxury of choice on Election Day.

Since this project began, our separate thoughts about ambition in American political life have become so intertwined that it is no longer possible to distinguish where one author's work leaves off and the other's begins. This book is a genuine collaboration by two people who study Congress and parties, aimed at unraveling the role of political ambition in American politics.

Our partnership was enriched by the assistance of many of our colleagues. Richard F. Fenno, Jr., helped launch our investigation into congressional recruitment, encouraged us along the way, and provided careful criticism of various drafts. Others who generously read and commented on all or parts of the manuscript were Thomas E. Patterson, Kristi Andersen, and Jeff Stonecash at Syracuse University, Thomas Cronin of Colorado College, Lewis "Sandy" Maisel of Colby College, and Ronald Shaiko of Virginia Polytechnic Institute. In addition, David Rosenbaum of the *New York Times* and Alan Ehrenhalt of *Congressional Quarterly* checked our occasional tendency to wander from the realities of contemporary politics.

We also received research assistance from our students Rod Blackstone, David Goldstein, Elisa Koff, Jaqueline Domkowski, and Paulette Morgan, and secretarial support from the staff of the Political Science Department and the office of the dean of the Maxwell School of Citizenship and Public Affairs, in particular June Dumas, Judy Jablonski, and Theresa Shea. We thank them all for their hard work. We also want to acknowledge the support we received from Marian Ash at Yale University Press and from our editor, Fred Kameny, whose copyediting skills and literary judgment made our manuscript a better book.

Financial aid from the Graduate School at Syracuse University and the Dirksen Congressional Center helped us carry out parts of this project. In addition, sabbatical leave from Syracuse University enabled us to initiate the study, and we are grateful to the former dean of the Maxwell School, Guthrie Birkhead, and to the former chairman of the Political Science Department, Thomas Patterson, for making this possible.

Finally, we wish to thank the politically active men and women of New York's 30th Congressional District, who spoke so openly and intelligently about the recruitment of candidates in their community. We gratefully acknowledge that without their cooperation there would be no book at all.

Note on Interviewing Methods

This book is based to a large extent on interviews. The method used to conduct them, inspired by that employed by Richard Fenno in his studies of Congress, involved keeping to a minimum any distractions that might have inhibited or diverted the attention of those being interviewed. During the interviews we took no notes and used no recording devices; instead, we independently reconstructed the conversations immediately after they ended, then compared and reconciled our versions. The sources of the quotations appearing in this book are identified by name, except where the source has requested anonymity or is not a public figure.

Hidden Influences
and the Unseen Candidates

*The objects to be aimed at were to fill all offices with the fittest charac-
ters, and to draw the wisest and most worthy citizens into the legislative service.*

—*James Madison at the Constitutional Convention*

In every congressional district in the United States there are people who could
run for Congress but who choose not to when the opportunity arrives. Although
they are not without ambition and are fully aware of the advantages of service
in the world's most powerful legislature, these thoroughly political people
quietly consider running for Congress and then say no. Since they never formally enter the race and purposely sidestep the glaring limelight of the campaign, these "almosts" and "might-have-beens" are the unseen candidates for
Congress.

Most of these would-be candidates are well-known local officeholders believed ready by many in their communities to move up the political ladder.
Others who are not so obviously well positioned or lack comparable prominence are still well enough known to be viewed by community leaders as
holding promise as politicians. Among such lesser-known unseen candidates
are people who have worked behind the scenes in parties and campaigns or
have gained recognition through leadership in important, but not highly visible,
local organizations. Still others may be found on Capitol Hill, where they work
as aides to the members they hope to replace. Finally, there are those who have
spent most of their lives on the edges of politics but have long hankered for
public office. Suddenly this desire flames up under the heat of an explosive
public issue or the glow of a noteworthy career success. Overnight these fringe
participants are thrust into the public arena and discover a credible base for a
congressional campaign.

1

Given the wide array of backgrounds unseen candidates may have, the number lurking in any particular House district can be quite large. In some districts the pool may include as many as fifty people, in almost none is it below six or seven, and in the typical district it is roughly two dozen.

Whatever their number or background, unseen candidates share three essential traits. First, none is obviously a political crank. Second, each has given serious thought, at least briefly, to running for Congress. And third, each has some real prospect, however slim, of actually ending up there. As a result, all that first appears to distinguish the unseen candidates from the declared ones is that the latter publicly announce their intention to campaign for a seat in Congress, whereas the former confine themselves to private discussions within the elite world of political insiders.

Learning from the Unseen Candidates

In this book we try to bring into public view these discussions and the unseen candidates' private thinking, to make evident two basic facts about American politics: how individual ambition shapes the choices available to voters in congressional elections and how such ambition is affected by the nation's local traditions and its highly dispersed system of political and governmental power. The story we tell should not be read as just another chronicle of two elections. Instead it should be approached as an intimate account of how seasoned politicians reason about their ambitions and how their reasoning, and the actions that flow from it, shape congressional elections in important and sometimes unexpected ways.[1]

Ambition for a seat in the House, more than any other factor—more than money, personality, or skill at using television, to name just a few examples—is what finally separates a visible, declared candidate for Congress from an unseen one. Even among the declared candidates, it is the force of ambition that most often turns up as the critical difference between the winner and the losers, because only intense motivation can overcome the high political, personal, and financial hurdles that law and custom impose in a politician's path to a seat in the U.S. Congress.

The maze of constitutional federalism and political pluralism in the United

1. For the importance of political ambition in political recruitment see James A. Schlesinger, *Ambition and Politics: Political Careers in the United States* (Chicago: Rand McNally, 1966). For explicit treatments of how politicians calculate the costs and benefits of political opportunities see Gordon S. Black, "A Theory of Political Ambition: Career Choices and the Role of Structural Incentives," *American Political Science Review* 66 (March 1972): 144–159; David W. Rohde, "Risk-bearing and Progressive Ambition: The Case of the United States House of Representatives," *American Journal of Political Science* 23 (February 1979): 1–26; Jeffrey S. Banks and D. Roderick Kiewiet, "Explaining Patterns of Candidate Competition in Congressional Elections" (Paper prepared for delivery at the Public Choice Society, Tucson, Ariz., March 27–29, 1987).

States can divert even a strong ambition, if it is not narrowly focused on gaining a seat in the U.S. House of Representatives. More than any other modern democracy, the United States offers the politically motivated a cornucopia of public offices, spreading out in all directions and exerting substantial independent influence over many public questions. Energetic politicians can find real power in many places other than Washington and Congress. They can influence policy and achieve personal satisfaction in state and local government, in the hierarchy of American political parties, and even in some private organizations, such as the Chamber of Commerce and the United Auto Workers, which frequently comingle with state and national governments to define policy on many issues.

Given these diverse routes to political power, some people who enter politics with vague thoughts of going to Congress may be sidetracked along the way. After investing several years in public office, they may find that a seat in the U.S. House of Representatives offers no more influence or opportunity than the posts they already hold. In the short run, they might even see themselves losing political clout from the exchange of an established post in, say, state government, for the subordinate role of a junior legislator on Capitol Hill. Thus intense ambition alone is not sufficient to propel individuals to Washington: equally necessary is a highly focused desire for the distinctive life and institutional perquisites that are available in Congress—and nowhere else.

Single-minded ambition for a seat in the House not only keeps prospective candidates pointed in the direction of Capitol Hill, it also motivates them to think about their options and plan their tactics well in advance of making a race. The high cost of congressional campaigns and the complex network of political action committees (or PACs), parties, and individual activists that must be brought together to support a modern House election require individuals to weigh the pluses and minuses of running long before they actually enter a contest. In fact, more than a third of the candidates running in the congressional primary of 1978 had decided to run right after the election of 1976, and the remainder had reached their decision by the following fall.[2] As House races become increasingly expensive and sophisticated, it is likely that a highly focused ambition will become an even more important hallmark of congressional candidates.

The ambitious unseen candidates are interesting in their own right as politicians, but they claim our attention here because they have a direct impact on congressional elections. In the first place, the caliber of people who run for Congress is particularly crucial in House elections. Voters cast their ballots in these races primarily on the basis of their familiarity with the candidates' personal and political attributes. Party labels, economic issues, and the identity

2. Louis Sandy Maisel, *From Obscurity to Oblivion: Running in the Congressional Primary* (Knoxville: University of Tennessee Press, 1982), p. 20.

of presidential candidates do matter, especially when voters have little exposure to the congressional candidates on the ballot, but for the most part the candidates' personal reputations, their experience in office, and their perceived empathy with the community count most with the electorate.[3]

The impact of a politician's personal and political history is most obvious in House races in which incumbents seek reelection. In these contests, reelection rates of 90 percent or more are the norm, and the incumbent usually wins by a comfortable margin.[4] These outcomes reflect the approval most incumbents enjoy in their districts, but they are also testimony to the glaring political deficiencies of the candidates who typically end up running against sitting members of the House. In recent years strong politicians—the heavyweights— who could mount a tough challenge to incumbents have tended to vanish from the electoral scene, in most cases leaving the task of defeating sitting congressmen to unknown, untried politicians.[5] With most challenges to incumbents turned over to middleweights and lightweights, who fail to interest the news media and excite political activists, voters usually get little exposure to incumbents' weaknesses and learn even less about the challengers' strong points. Faced with such an imbalance between two contestants' credentials and with such a disparity of information about the options before them, voters tend to choose the known quantity, the incumbent, over the unknown quantity, the challenger. In this highly personal environment, even the issues and party differences that might work to the advantage of challengers lose significance in voters' decisions on Election Day.[6]

3. Thomas E. Mann and Raymond E. Wolfinger, "Candidates and Parties in Congressional Elections," *American Political Science Review* 74 (September 1980): 617–632; Thomas E. Mann, *Unsafe at Any Margin* (Washington, D.C.: American Enterprise Institute, 1978), pp. 66–67; Gary C. Jacobson, *The Politics of Congressional Elections*, 2nd ed. (Boston: Little, Brown, 1987), chap. 5; Glenn R. Parker, "The Advantage of Incumbency in House Elections," *American Politics Quarterly* 8 (October 1980): 449–464.

4. For a review of the extensive literature on incumbency see Jacobson, chap. 3.

5. Barbara Hinckley, "House Re-elections and Senate Defeats: The Role of the Challenger," *British Journal of Political Science* 10 (October 1980): 441–460; Linda L. Fowler, "The Electoral Lottery: Decisions to Run for Congress," *Public Choice* 34 (December 1979): 399–418, and "Candidate Perceptions of Electoral Coalitions," *American Politics Quarterly* 8 (October 1980): 483–494; Thomas A. Kazee, "The Deterrent Effect of Incumbency on Recruiting Challengers in U.S. House Elections," *Legislative Studies Quarterly* 8 (August 1983): 469–480.

6. A growing body of literature suggests that individual voters do not use congressional elections as referenda on policy and that the modest policy effects that are discernible are more likely to be found in presidential and senatorial elections than in House elections. See Roderick D. Kiewiet, *Macroeconomics and Micropolitics: The Electoral Effects of Economic Issues* (Chicago: University of Chicago Press, 1983); James H. Kuklinski and Darrell M. West, "Economic Expectations and Voting Behavior in United States House and Senate Elections," *American Political Science Review* 75 (June 1981): 436–447; Eric M. Uslaner and M. Margaret Conway, "The Responsible Congressional Electorate: Watergate, the Economy and Vote Choice in 1974," *American Political Science Review* 79 (September 1985): 788–803; Richard Born, "Strategic Politicians and Unresponsive Voters," *American Political Science Review* 80 (June 1986): 599–612; Gerald C. Wright, Jr., and Michael B. Berkman, "Candidates and Policy in United States Senate Elections," *American Political Science Review* 80 (June 1986): 567–588.

Congressional races often become so one-sided because many unseen candidates want no part in a bruising battle with an incumbent rich in resources. Weak challengers get congressional nominations because the stronger candidates tend to say no, and this leads members of the House of Representatives increasingly to turn their attention to activities aimed at keeping the strongest unseen candidates sitting safely on the sidelines.[7] Incumbents wage permanent reelection campaigns by creating a constant personal presence in their districts. Constituents are of course the primary beneficiaries of all this personal attention, but at the same time potential opponents are the targets of the trips home, the newsletters and questionnaires, and the press releases and media events. In all these contacts with the electorate, members stress their personal attributes as lawmakers: their independence inside the Congress, their identification with local problems, and their contact with individual constituents. All these maneuvers are aimed at neutralizing the unseen candidates by creating an aura of overwhelming personal support for the incumbent, which everyone begins to believe will in the future withstand adverse partisan tides and economic downturns. Thus representatives who run ahead of their party's presidential ticket, as most do, insulate their careers from the ups and downs of national politics by gaining the reluctant collaboration of many strong unseen candidates, who decide not to run against highly visible and seemingly unbeatable incumbents.

Contests in which no incumbent is seeking reelection attract stronger and more numerous contestants, but the unseen candidates affect the races for these open seats as well. While primaries are common in open districts, the battles in them over party nominations range in competitiveness from political free-for-alls to tightly controlled transfers of power. Sometimes the field is so crowded that extremists capture their party's nomination with a tiny fraction of the vote. In other instances primaries may be one-sided affairs, or they may occur in only one party.

During general elections, however, no more than half of all races for open seats involve two well-matched opponents who provide voters with a genuine choice. In 1984, for example, there were twenty-seven open seats; of these, ten were won by candidates who received 60 percent or more of the total vote, and seven others by candidates who received between 55 and 60 percent of the vote. Thus only ten races met the traditional standard of competitiveness (according to which the winner receives 55 percent of the vote or less). Furthermore, in only seven of these contests were the opposing sides equally matched in campaign expenditures.[8]

---

7. See David R. Mayhew, *Congress: The Electoral Connection* (New Haven and London: Yale University Press, 1974); Morris P. Fiorina, *Congress: Keystone of the Washington Establishment* (New Haven and London: Yale University Press, 1977).

8. See Michael J. Malbin and Thomas W. Skladony, *Campaign Finance, 1984: A Preliminary Analysis of House and Senate Campaign Receipts*, (Washington, D.C.: American Enterprise Institute, 1985).

In races for open seats as well as in challenges mounted against incumbents, the unseen candidates therefore directly influence voters' choices in House elections. The quiet calculations made by unseen candidates in February or March of a congressional election year, or even earlier, have as much to do with the eventual outcome in November as do the noisy fall campaigns. This suggests that the preoccupation of the public and press with strategies and symbols of overt electioneering may be misplaced. Although the polling, the rhetoric, and the financial resources employed by candidates during campaigns can marginally adjust the way politicians are perceived on Election Day, the electoral potential of most candidates and the competitiveness of most elections are usually set long before the media and the voters take notice of what is going on in the nation's House districts. It is the unrecognized, unexamined decisions not to run made by so many strong candidates in winter and spring that more firmly fix the voters' actual choices in November. The die simply is cast in many congressional races before the election campaign ever begins, and the decisions of the unseen candidates are the major reason.

This view of congressional elections does not mean that in every House race the strongest candidates always refuse to run. Unseen candidates can be weak vote-getters or strong ones, probable losers or potential winners. Whether strong or weak, the unseen candidates determine the number and kind of options placed before voters in congressional elections.

Not only do the unseen candidates influence electoral outcomes in individual districts, their collective decisions may add up to a decided partisan advantage in Washington. When one party fields a strong set of contenders in many parts of the country, as the Democrats did in 1974, the net effect may be formidable in terms of its overall majority in the House.

In recent years, however, it has become very difficult to ascertain what factors lure potential winners into the electoral arena in a particular year. Although national party organizations and interest groups have become more active in recruiting candidates to run for congressional office, at the same time their concerns with national issues and presidential policies seem increasingly divorced from the outcomes of House contests. These two apparently inconsistent trends have left many political observers puzzled over the meaning of particular elections.[9] They also encourage us to reexamine the structure of

9. See Dom BonaFede, "Midterm Election Puzzle," *National Journal*, October 18, 1986, p. 2503. For the increasing role of national parties and PACs in congressional elections see Gary C. Jacobson, "Parties and PAC's in Congressional Elections," in *Congress Reconsidered*, ed. Lawrence C. Dodd and Bruce I. Oppenheimer, 3rd ed. (Washington, D.C.: CQ Press, 1985), pp. 135–138; Larry Sabato, *PAC Power: Inside the World of Political Action Committees* (New York: W. W. Norton, 1984), p. 75; Paul S. Hernnson, "Do Parties Make a Difference? The Role of Party Organizations in Congressional Elections," *Journal of Politics* 48 (August 1986): 589–615. For the influence the national political environment can have on recruitment in congressional elections see Gary C. Jacobson and Samuel Kernell, *Strategy and Choice in Congressional Elections* (New Haven and London: Yale University Press, 1981).

political competition in the United States. In particular, we need to understand the relationship among party activists at the local, state, and federal levels as they winnow out prospective House candidates. We also need to consider how various members of interest groups and staffs participate in the deliberations of potential contenders for a House seat. As the unseen candidates decide whether or not to run for Congress, their experiences and perceptions thus provide an opportunity to examine the significant changes that have taken place in American political organizations over the last decade.

Picking a District

Most politics in this country, whether they involve decisions on great matters of policy or fundamental shifts in political attitudes and party dominance, are first of all local politics. And all politics, in the United States and elsewhere, are the product of real people, going about their business, not in some general, global environment but in a quite particular, local one. The men and women who go to Congress, as well as all the unseen candidates who do not, are mainly the products of hundreds of local political forces, each peculiar to a given time and place. Clearly national parties are playing ever larger roles in congressional elections, as are PACs (which contributed on the average 31 percent of a candidate's funds in 1982, compared with 6 percent in 1974), and the tides of national opinion can sometimes influence the strategies of House candidates; nevertheless these forces operate within the still stronger context of local history and local political structures.

A close look at a single congressional district can shed light on the inherent localism of congressional politics and have other benefits as well for a study of unseen candidates. In the first place, a thorough understanding of a community is the only way to uncover all the unseen candidates for a congressional race, because they are not immediately apparent to an outsider. The pool of elected public officials in each district is an obvious place to start, but many different types of people make it to Congress: teachers, priests, housewives, radio broadcasters, farmers. So our search for the unseen candidates must reach out beyond elected officeholders. And just as the unseen candidates surely include people who do not hold public office, not everyone who does hold an elected position is a legitimate candidate for Congress: indeed most politically active citizens and public officials never think about becoming one. In short, the unseen candidates for Congress are not easily identifiable. They can be discovered only with a detailed understanding of the political life of a specific congressional district.

There is a second reason our story is set in a single community: frequently it takes a long time for a would-be candidate to decide not to run for Congress. Circumstances may change, other potential candidates may intervene, or new information may surface. In the process, the would-be candidate may change his or her mind a number of times as new reasons for running or not running come to light. All this can be appreciated only if the people involved are followed from the time they start thinking about making the race to the moment when they irrevocably decide one way or the other.

A third reason why a sure knowledge of the community is needed if an accurate story of the unseen candidates is to be told is that observers of this unexamined political phenomenon need a yardstick for measuring the veracity and completeness of the unseen candidates' explanations for their actions. After all, their decisions are intensely personal and often difficult to discuss with strangers who plan to publish their findings. The decisions are also complicated enough that the unseen candidates are sometimes unable to pinpoint when or why they decided not to run, even when they try to be completely candid. Therefore the story of each unseen candidate needs to be verified by local political insiders—friends and foes who know the candidate well, and whose observations can help us decide whether the reasoning of the candidate rings true. Is this person being realistic about his or her strengths and weaknesses? How do other people see his or her future prospects? What do political insiders think his or her motivations are? To answer these questions a community's political pulse must be continually monitored, and such intense monitoring cannot be spread over more than one district at a time.

Not every local community could fully serve our purpose. The district chosen for examination had to pass three important tests. First, it had to be in the middle of an election to an open seat. Because elections for open seats usually are more competitive than those involving incumbents and because the nominations of both major parties are more likely to be prized, such a contest provides the greatest enticement to those in a position to run for Congress. We could reasonably conclude that politicians who turned down the chance to run for an open seat were rejecting a genuine opportunity and were therefore truly unseen candidates.

Second, to have a manageable yet complete story, one in which all the possible candidates were interviewed while they were still making their decisions, the race had to have a definite beginning as well as the obvious ending. Such a definite beginning could be an incumbent's suddenly dying, resigning, or announcing his or her intention not to seek reelection. Any of these circumstances would enable us to know when to begin talking to local politicians and to be present when the unseen candidates made their decisions, instead of having to rely on warmed-over recollections. We would also be much less likely to miss interviewing any of the potential candidates in a circumstance where the period for decision making was so definite, because we could talk to all the party leaders and political power brokers while they were actually working to influence the process.

Third, the district had to have the basic political characteristics found in most congressional districts. An intense investigation of the politics of a congressional district could not be defended if the district were obviously atypical. The district chosen for examination would therefore have to be largely middle-class, contain at least some suburbs, and have a moderate amount of competition between the two major parties, though not intense competition.

On February 6, 1984, when Congressman Barber Conable announced his intention not to seek reelection to his House seat from New York's 30th Congressional District, we had a race that met our standards. "Republicans, Democrats begin scramble for Conable's job after 20-year wait," read the local newspaper's headline the next day.[10] All the available data indicated that there would be an outpouring of interest in the newly vacant seat, and that the district encompassed most of the dominant social, economic, and political forces in modern American life.

New York's 30th Congressional District is mainly but not entirely a suburban district, and around its suburban core lie a string of rural, agricultural communities and a small piece of Rochester's central city. Although as solidly middle-class as its suburban character would dictate, the district is not without diversity, and includes blue-collar workers, middle-level managers, and business leaders, as well as some of Rochester's wealthiest and poorest communities. Its ethnic composition manifests a similar diversity, encompassing a sizable Italian community along with smaller numbers of Irish, Jewish, Eastern European, and black voters.

Economically the district neither escaped the effects of the national recessions of the 1970s and early 1980s nor felt their full force. Farmers in the district, particularly dairy farmers, were hard hit, but not as devastated as some of those in the Midwest. Unemployment edged up in Monroe County, but Rochester remained more prosperous than most northern cities because local employment is dominated by expanding technological companies, such as Eastman Kodak, Xerox, and Bausch & Lomb, and not by the declining smokestack industries represented by such companies as U.S. Steel. Nevertheless, although Kodak, the giant of the photography world, laid off no one during the Great Depression, it stunned the local community in the early 1980s by cutting its work force substantially. And in the town of Batavia, in an outlying part of the district, the major local employer, Sylvania, completely shut down its factory, causing hundreds of workers to lose their jobs permanently.

The district also took part in the economic recovery of 1983–85. The Rochester area did not experience the economic surge of many Sunbelt cities, but it did feel new economic vitality and renewed prosperity.

Politically the district has followed the national trend toward split-ticket voting and declining domination by one party. As the Republican party's organizational grip on the district has slipped so that only memories remain of the

10. *Democrat and Chronicle* (Rochester), February 7, 1984, Sec. A, p. 5.

machine assembled by the GOP after World War II, the Democratic party has gained supporters and organization. In other words the partisan balance of the 30th Congressional District now teeters, as it does in so much of the United States: one party has an advantage, but not an advantage on which it always can count.

Tracking Political Decisions

Inside this mainstream political environment of upstate New York we followed the election campaigns of 1984 and 1986, trying to track the thinking of every political insider who played a significant role in determining who would be the 30th district's congressional representative. Although the unseen candidates in the 30th were nominally of particular importance to us, the declared candidates in each of the races were in fact of equal interest; this was so because the strongest support for our views on ambition arises when the thinking and actions of the unseen candidates are contrasted with the strategies and behavior of the declared ones, especially with the strategy and behavior of the two candidates who ultimately won the two elections.

To make these critical comparisons more vivid and to sharpen our line of reasoning, we have divided the book into two parts. The first introduces the characters and themes of the book, then focuses on the reasoning that led the unseen candidates not to run in 1984, and contrasts this thinking with the immediate decision of the year's eventual winner to plunge ahead. In the second part we turn our attention to all the declared candidates in the elections of 1984 and 1986 and the factors that account for the final outcomes of both these contests; although we focus mainly on the winners of these two races and their declared campaign rivals, we also show how the decisions made early in the spring of each election year by the many unseen candidates influenced the general election campaign several months later. Finally, we illustrate how the decisions and outcome of one election can dramatically alter the political decisions and the voters' choice in the next election.

This form of comparative analysis forces us to view politics from a perspective slightly different from that of most contemporary observers. To see so much of politics through the eyes of the unseen candidates requires focusing on quiet events and on things that receive little coverage by the media rather than on exciting headlines and the campaign hoopla that normally claim the public's attention. We emphasize the electoral calculations that politicians made privately in March over the strategies and issues they publicly debated in October. And we concentrate on understanding the attitudes of a small group of activists rather than on analyzing the opinions on Election Day of the public at large.

This is a view of democratic politics that goes against the instincts of most modern political commentators, because it gives considerable weight to the private and elite aspects of American democracy, whereas most analysts are inclined to stress the importance of public behavior and mass attitudes. Our view also suggests that much of importance on the contemporary political scene is neither readily discernible to ordinary people, nor amenable to conventional methods of analysis and observation employed by the mass media and by empirically minded scholars.

Quite consciously we try to expand conventional thinking about how American politics and congressional elections work and how we should study and explain them. We hope that by calling attention to what usually goes unnoticed we can persuade students of American politics that elections can never be reduced only to mass, public behavior, and that by considering the implications of what might have been they will also come to appreciate the subjective, the intuitive, the capricious, perhaps even the random, elements that inevitably enter political fortune and must therefore be included in any proper understanding of democracy as a whole.

The evidence that prompts these views about House elections and American politics comes from the scores of personal interviews we conducted in New York's 30th Congressional District. Between February 1984 and January 1987 we conducted eighty-five interviews with sixty-eight people involved in the district's congressional races of 1984 and 1986. Included in this group was everyone who actually made a run, as well as everyone who seriously considered it. The group also included nearly all the people mentioned by knowledgeable political insiders as persons who could have been, or should have been, serious contenders for the congressional seat. We interviewed the leaders and key activists in the major parties, leading officials of interest groups, and personal advisers to the unseen candidates, as well as the eventual contestants. In addition we discussed the race with knowledgeable people in state government and Washington. We also conducted follow-up interviews with important participants several times as the story unfolded over three years. Interviews were conducted before, during, and after each campaign, and details of the whole story were checked as late as January 1987. To supplement these interviews we also attended public gatherings of the local parties, the Republican district nominating convention in 1984, press conferences, and other significant events that shaped people's perceptions of the decisions being made in the 30th Congressional District.

The personal stories these men and women told us—their views of Congress and of the district, their political ambitions and calculations, their private worries and fears—form the basis of our study.[11] We believe that these stories

11. Several studies of congressional recruitment were conducted during the 1960s. See Jeff Fishel, *Party and Opposition* (New York: David McKay, 1973); Leo M. Snowiss, "Congressional Recruitment and Representation," *American Political Science Review* 60 (September 1966): 627–639; Lester G. Seligman, "Political Recruitment and Party Structure: A Case Study," *American Political Science Review* 55 (March 1961): 77–86; James David Barber, *The Lawmakers: Recruit-*

and our conclusions about them range beyond the specific problem of congressional recruitment and raise many questions (and suggest a few answers) that touch on the conduct of contemporary American politics far more generally.

We have tried to write a book that can be read at several levels. First, we hope it is a good story with plot and action that accurately describes the events and people leading to the selection of two new members of Congress from New York's 30th district. We shall be pleased if the men and women about whom we write agree that this is the way it all happened. But the story can be read at a second level. We see it as providing graphic illustrations of important facts, theories, and trends about American politics. (Occasionally, it also calls into question some received truths.) In this respect the story bears witness to much of what we already know of political life in the United States, but we hope the people in the book who represent these larger concerns give them added life and immediacy. In every chapter we try to paint portraits of one or two politicians whose backgrounds, ways of thinking, and considered actions make them ideal, flesh-and-blood spokespersons for accepted theories or trends in the nation's politics. By using these local politicians in this way we try to show how abstract ideas have living referents who daily go about their communities making democracy work. There is still a third level. We hope our study offers a few clues about the future of American politics, prompts some new explanations for the way the system works, and puts forward some interesting speculations and a few hypotheses about things still unclear.[12] And in so doing we hope it charts a path for other studies of unseen candidates in other congressional districts.

---

ment and Adaptation to Legislative Life (New Haven and London: Yale University Press, 1965). Since then, there has been relatively little research on the decision to run for Congress, except for the studies by Maisel, Fowler, and Kazee cited above. The lack of more comprehensive research in this area is considered by many political scientists a glaring weakness. See Leroy N. Rieselbach, "The Forest for the Trees: Blazing Trails for Congressional Research," in Political Science: the State of the Discipline, ed. Ada W. Finifter (Washington, D.C.: American Political Science Association, 1983), 155–188; Donald R. Matthews, "Legislative Recruitment and Legislative Careers," Legislative Studies Quarterly 9 (November 1984): 547–586.

12. Because so little is known about congressional recruitment, we believe that a case study of the sort undertaken here is most appropriate to identify key variables and develop plausible assumptions and hypotheses about the process. Harry Eckstein delineates these heuristic aspects of the case method in "Case Study and Theory in Political Science," in Strategies of Inquiry: Handbook of Political Science, vol. 7, ed. Fred I. Greenstein and Nelson W. Polsby (Reading, Mass.: Addison-Wesley, 1975): 79–137.

Part One
Political Reasoning

1

Opportunity:
Two Political Puzzles

We must take man as we find him, and if we expect him to serve the public must interest his passions in doing so.
— *Alexander Hamilton at the Constitutional Convention*

The first lesson of congressional recruitment is that it takes the spark of opportunity to ignite the flame of congressional ambition. With no outlet for release, a politician's desire for congressional office simply smolders and sputters, half suppressed and only partially acknowledged. But when a real chance to contest a House seat finally presents itself—the kind of opportunity provided by Barber Conable's surprise announcement not to seek reelection in New York's 30th Congressional District—vague career plans suddenly become real possibilities and hazy speculations about some day become serious calculations about right now.

By kindling the ambition of waiting politicians, opportunity promotes genuine political competition and makes democratic elections meaningful devices for popular control of public officials. Thus the distribution of political opportunity and its subsequent effects on electoral competition have public consequences as well as private ones.

For most politicians who aspire to a seat in Congress, the wait for a chance to realize their ambition is a long one, because lengthy tenure in office is such a dominant pattern in the contemporary House of Representatives that in any given year relatively few genuine opportunities open up. (Although the mean length of service of the members of the House declined from six terms in 1971 to 4.6 terms in 1983, it has averaged five terms over the last three decades.)[1] Year after year, the high reelection rates and lopsided margins of incumbent House members indicate to most ambitious politicians how small a real chance they have to move to Congress, unless a drastic change occurs in the political environment of their own congressional district or the nation.[2]

1. Norman J. Ornstein et al., *Vital Statistics on Congress, 1984–1985 Edition* (Washington, D.C.: American Enterprise Institute, 1985), pp. 18–19.
2. As noted in the Introduction, the reelection rate of House incumbents has averaged more than 90 percent in recent years. The percentage of incumbents who have won at least 60 percent of the vote has usually been about 70. See Ornstein et al., pp. 50, 53.

15

For two decades Monroe County typified this trend. From 1964 Conable blocked the path of everyone with congressional ambitions in New York's 30th Congressional District. He was a Republican in a Republican area, and only once in his career, in 1974, had he been challenged seriously by a Democratic opponent. His reputation as an influential legislator and effective vote-getter made it unthinkable that any Republican would challenge him. As long as Conable remained in Congress, no other local politicians could aspire realistically to a career in the House of Representatives.

Nor was there any ready outlet for congressional ambition in the two other congressional districts of Monroe County. To the east, the 29th district was represented by another Republican, Congressman Frank Horton, who had served in Congress even longer than Conable. After eleven terms in office, he showed no sign of giving up his post and seemed every bit as unassailable as Conable. Therefore to politicians in the eastern half of Monroe County, who were growing old and restless waiting for Horton to retire, the unexpected vacancy in the neighboring district provided the first opportunity they had seen in a long time.

Politicians with congressional ambitions were equally frustrated by the impregnability of John LaFalce, a five-term Democrat, in the 31st district, which cuts into part of the west side of Monroe County and the city of Rochester. Not only did LaFalce enjoy the reputation of a well-financed incumbent who campaigned constantly, he was also hard to challenge because the design of his district put politicians from Monroe County at a great disadvantage. The 31st district stretches all the way from Buffalo to Rochester, and politicians from Monroe County were convinced that they could never win there, against LaFalce or anyone else, because the district's political center of gravity was too far from their own home base.

By all counts the vacant seat in the 30th Congressional District was the only game in town: the only genuine opportunity in recent memory for a politician from the area to go to Congress and the only one likely to occur in the foreseeable future. For most local politicians with congressional ambitions, the election of 1984 to replace Conable was probably a chance that would occur once in a lifetime.

The vacancy in the 30th district fanned the flames of political ambition for another, closely related, reason: the new representative was likely to be as permanent a fixture on the local scene as Conable had been. Local political leaders understood that service in the House was a career involving a long-term commitment. Indeed they expected Conable's successor to acquire seniority and build influence in Washington that could then be used to further the interests of the local constituency. Local politicians had grown accustomed to having important Republicans come to town as a mark of respect for "Mr. Conable," who was nationally esteemed and influential, and they valued the attention that local projects received from federal agencies because of the power Conable exerted from his seat on the Ways and Means Committee. This special treatment was prominent in the minds of influential people in the district, who wanted their new representative to make a political investment over the long run and, by acquiring seniority and influence, to continue Conable's tradition as a heavyweight. They presumed that whoever won the seat would have the skill to use an incumbent's resources toward this end.[3] Local politicians agreed with this assessment and thought that Conable's House seat would probably not be vacant again in the twentieth century. Obviously such reasoning gave the decision about running in 1984 added urgency. If politicians with congressional ambitions did not reach for the brass ring now, when would they ever get the chance again?

Although Conable's presence had barred the way to Capitol Hill for two decades, his career had also exemplified the personal and political opportunity that resides there. After serving one term in the New York State Senate, Conable gained his House seat in 1964 despite Lyndon Johnson's landslide victory over Barry Goldwater, which caused so many Republicans to go down to defeat. One of few newcomers among the decimated Republican ranks, Conable soon gained appointment to the Ways and Means Committee, where he built a reputation for expertise and legislative skill and eventually became the ranking minority member. Given the committee's longstanding tradition of internal cooperation and its emphasis on technical knowledge, his membership in the minority party did not prevent him from shaping legislation.[4] Every tax law in the last decade bore his stamp, and among insiders in the House he was known as a key figure in the extraordinary bipartisan effort in 1983 to rescue the Social Security system.[5] Shortly before he retired at the age of sixty-one, Conable was voted by his colleagues the most respected member of the House of Representatives.[6] By every measure, he had gone to Washington and made a difference, and his experience there was a beacon for other ambitious local politicians to follow.

Careers in the House of Representatives have not always been so alluring to politicians. During Congress's first century, most elected officials preferred the

3. Some literature suggests that constituent service and such perquisites as franking contribute to the success of incumbents. See for example Bruce E. Cain, John Ferejohn, and Morris Fiorina, *The Personal Vote: Constituency Service and Electoral Independence* (Cambridge: Harvard University Press, 1987); Diane Evans Yiannakis, "The Grateful Electorate: Casework and Congressional Elections," *American Journal of Political Science* 25 (August 1981): 568–580.

4. Richard F. Fenno, Jr., *Congressmen in Committees: A Comparative View* (Boston: Little, Brown, 1973); John F. Manley, *The Politics of Finance* (Boston: Little, Brown, 1970). In recent years the committee has become more contentious and partisan. See Steven S. Smith and Christopher J. Deering, *Committees in Congress* (Washington, D.C.: CQ Press, 1984), pp. 185–186.

5. Paul Light, *Artful Work: The Politics of Social Security Reform* (New York: Random House, 1985).

6. "Even Congress is Unhappy with Congress," *U.S. News and World Report*, April 23, 1984, pp. 37–39.

civilized life of their state capitals to the humid swamps of the nation's, and they also found the power and prestige of their state and local governments equal to or greater than those of the central government.[7] From this nineteenth-century point of view holding a seat in the House was often regarded as a chore—a duty that responsible citizens agreed to accept but hastened to lay down as soon as they could. Indeed voluntary retirements accounted for much of the turnover in Congress a century ago, as members gave up their seats to return to positions in state and local government.[8]

But twentieth-century changes in the salaries and electoral security of members of Congress, coupled with the growth in the responsibilities of central government, reversed the nineteenth-century pattern: now most politicians who get to Washington want to stay there. Throughout the 1950s and 1960s, for instance, retirements in each election averaged only about 6 percent of the membership,[9] and a joke circulated on Capitol Hill that "around here, people only leave feet first."

To those who understood these ways of Congress, Conable's retirement at first seemed inexplicable. Just when he had reached the pinnacle of his power in the House, and while he was still young enough to look forward to many more years of influence, he had quit. After the initial shock many local politicians saw Conable's decision as a signal that life in Washington was maybe not as appealing as the twentieth-century image suggested. Perhaps the demands on a member of Congress were becoming too great and the working conditions too frustrating.[10]

As local politicians reflected on Conable's decision to retire, many of them came to believe that his decision to leave the House was linked at least in part to his distaste for the new ultraconservative element of the Republican party and to his aggravation with the confrontational style of his junior Republican colleagues. To a legislative craftsman like Conable, the party's young Turks were a

7. See H. Douglas Price, "The Congressional Career: Then and Now," in Nelson W. Polsby, ed., *Congressional Behavior* (New York: Random House, 1971): 14–27; James Young, *The Washington Community, 1800–1828* (New York: Columbia University Press, 1966).

8. Samuel Kernell, "Toward Understanding 19th Century Congressional Careers: Ambition, Competition, and Rotation," *American Journal of Political Science* 21 (November 1977): 669–693.

9. Calculated from Ornstein et al., p. 52.

10. See Stephen E. Frantzich, "Opting Out: Retirement from the House of Representatives, 1966–1974," *American Politics Quarterly* 6 (July 1978): 251–273; Joseph Cooper and William West, "The Congressional Career in the 1970's," in Lawrence C. Dodd and Bruce I. Oppenheimer, *Congress Reconsidered*, 2nd ed. (Washington, D.C.: CQ Press, 1981), 86–91; John R. Hibbing, "Voluntary Retirements from the U.S. House: The Costs of Congressional Service," *Legislative Studies Quarterly* 7 (February 1982): 57–74. Among new members there is some indication that interest in a long-term stay in the House is declining. See for example David S. Broder, "Legislatures in Trouble," *Washington Post*, December 11, 1983, Sec. C, p. 7; John E. Bibby, ed., *Congress Off the Record: The Candid Analysis of Seven Members* (Washington, D.C.: American Enterprise Institute, 1983), pp. 13–14.

perpetual irritant because of their delight in fomenting partisan conflict and their scorn for political compromise. When an article appeared in the *New York Times* in early March that profiled Conable and five other senior Republicans who were leaving the Congress and that discussed the aggravations of service in the modern House of Representatives, earlier suspicions about the stresses of life, in Washington hardened into a firm conviction that the demands of the job were not for everyone.[11]

Still the personal nature of influence in the House of Representatives, which Conable's career perfectly illustrated, more than compensated for these drawbacks in the minds of most politicians in Monroe County. Republicans recognized that they were likely to serve as members of the minority if they went to Washington, but Conable's example made it plain that party label was not an insurmountable barrier to the exercise of real power. Particularly to those who had experience in the highly structured party system of New York's state legislature, the greater scope for independent action by minority members in Congress was appealing. Democrats, too, saw this personal power and independence from party as an advantage. One Democratic city councilman who weighed the possibilities of running in the 30th district commented: "I would never run for a seat in Albany. It's a waste of time. In Albany, only three people matter: the governor, the Assembly speaker, and the Senate majority leader; the rest of the legislature is a bunch of sheep. If you are a minority-party member you might as well go stand in a closet. And if you are a junior member of the majority party all you can do is get someone an appointment with somebody that does matter. I loathe the place. Congress, however, is different. I respect the congressional process. There the individual member with intelligence and hard work can have some impact."

Not only did local politicians respond to the personal power available in Washington, they were aware of the respect a member of Congress received at home. This was evident from the warm praise lavished on Conable at party and district functions after he announced his retirement. In the local newspapers a spate of articles appeared lauding his record in Washington. Who could ignore the adulation that Conable received during his final months in office or be indifferent to the prospects of enjoying a similar status in years to come? To politicians thinking about replacing him political power in Washington was made sweeter by the prospect of personal recognition in the district, and the frustrations of dealing with congressional colleagues balanced by a warm relationship with friends and neighbors back home.

Fierce competition to lay claim to such an alluring prize therefore seemed inevitable in the early months of 1984, and the expectations for a rough-and-

11. Martin Tolchin, "Why Six in Their Prime Will Leave House," *New York Times*, February 14, 1984, sec. B, p. 6.

tumble contest were heightened by the large pool of people in the district with a claim to Conable's mantle. As in most congressional districts, the large number of state and local offices so characteristic of American politics gave many local politicians a legitimate basis for a campaign for higher office. In Monroe County alone, there were 114 major elected offices serving city, town, county, or state functions, and a host of others on town and city boards fulfilling lesser responsibilities. A wide range of interest groups and an active community of business, professional, and civic organizations also gave some citizens who did not hold public office the necessary visibility and recognition to consider running for Congress. Service in party offices in the area also provided credible bases for an election bid.

On the afternoon of February 6, 1984, a few hours after Conable announced his intention to step down, all of the 30th Congressional District of New York braced for a real political donnybrook to find Barber Conable's successor. But to nearly everyone's surprise, one never materialized.

Two Puzzles

Instead of a brawl over the nomination in 1984, there was hardly a scuffle. Of more than twenty individuals mentioned publicly as potential replacements for Conable (and another ten or so mentioned by community and party leaders in private), only six formally announced their intention to seek his seat. Just three of the six were serious candidates with any chance of winning; the others—a retired airline pilot, a skimobile enthusiast, and a former state police trooper—all lacked political experience and seemed more interested in their own personal political causes than in representing the people of upstate New York in Congress. What this meant was that for every serious, declared candidate in the race, there were ten unseen, undeclared ones. Conable expressed the widespread bafflement in the late spring over the dearth of committed competitors for his seat. "I'm disappointed by so few candidates coming forth," he told us. "Evidently my performance was not regarded highly enough to cause a lot of good people to want to succeed me."

The six politicians thought by nearly everyone to be the strongest candidates each side could offer all declined to run. Two were Republicans and four Democrats, of whom only three actually gave the race serious consideration. Neither party had a primary, although the Republicans did have a closely contested convention. In an age when progressive ideology and political reform had opened up party processes and brought effective participation and elective office within the reach of ever more citizens, most of the men and women who could have run for Conable's seat in 1984 chose not to. These were people who had unmistakable political ambition and were dedicated to public life, but who nevertheless turned their backs on a rare opportunity to seek a seat in the House of Representatives.

Two years later, however, the battle everyone had been expecting in 1984 finally took place. A primary on the Democratic side was followed by a bruising campaign bearing all the trappings of a modern congressional race—big budgets, extensive media coverage, and an unprecedented grass-roots mobilization effort. The challenger ended up with 51 percent of the vote in a photo finish that kept the pollsters and analysts guessing about the outcome until late on election night. It was one of only six races across the country in which an incumbent went down to defeat.

Even more surprising was the shift in political representation that marked the changing of the guard from Conable to the constituency's newest member of Congress. Over the span of two elections, the district first selected a hard-line conservative known for his abrasive, issue-oriented style, then did an about-face and sent to Washington a feisty Democratic populist with a reputation for accessibility and constituent service. Neither of these politicians who eventually represented the people of upstate New York bore the slightest resemblance to the cerebral tactician Barber Conable. In the space of a few years, a district that had espoused moderate Republicanism for a century lurched first toward the right of the political spectrum, then toward the left.[12]

How could conventional wisdom have been so wrong in predicting the scale and timing of electoral competition in New York's 30th district? How could such large ideological swings have taken place in back-to-back elections? To solve these puzzles we begin our story with Conable's announcement of his retirement in the winter of 1984 and follow a convoluted—but we believe unbroken—chain of events through the congressional election of 1986.

The thread binding together these events is political ambition: the drive to secure a seat in Congress against all comers. In 1984 Fred Eckert was the only local politician to seize quickly and vigorously the opportunity presented by Conable's retirement, and in doing so he forestalled much of the opposition that might have blocked his way to Washington. Yet his compelling desire to serve in the House diminished under the unrelenting pressures of legislative life, and a rival who had backed away from a fight with Eckert two years earlier saw in his flagging enthusiasm for the job a new political opportunity. Thus to understand how and why politicians decide to get into a House race, we need to appreciate how they develop in the first place their aspirations for a seat in Congress. In Eckert's case this meant going back to when he was a student in the sixth grade, but for his challenger it meant watching a political career evolve.

12. Generally it is the competitive congressional districts that show policy shifts when one representative replaces another. See Morris P. Fiorina, *Representatives, Roll Calls, and Constituencies* (Lexington, Mass.: Lexington Books, 1974), pp. 108–111.

A Head Start

At the time Conable announced his retirement, Fred Eckert was serving as the American ambassador to the Fiji Islands, ten thousand miles away in the warm waters of the South Pacific. While for the first three months of the struggle to succeed Conable other would-be candidates tested the political waters in frigid upstate New York, Eckert was neither present in the district nor able to work openly for the office he sought. Indeed he did not return to the 30th Congressional District to wage his campaign in person until just three weeks before the Republican nominating convention.

That Eckert won from such a great distance was an exceptional feat of political skill and a stroke of good fortune, for, as we shall see, at the outset of the election of 1984 there was nothing inevitable about his selection. But his eventual success was extraordinary for another reason: the substantial differences in political philosophy and style between him and Conable. One was a moderate with a subtle political touch, the other a right-wing ideologue with a heavy hand. These differences were apparent to nearly everyone to whom we spoke. One party leader summed up the prevailing view: "Eckert tries to paint himself as another Conable. But he's no Conable. He may be the best we've got, but he's very different. We're just going to have to forget Conable and start all over with this guy."

In some respects Eckert and Conable were not that different. Both emphasized the policy side of the legislator's job and left constituent service to their staffs. Both were fiscally conservative and favored a hawkish stance on matters of national security.[13] And both seemed uncomfortable with the glad-handing and backslapping that are a part of building support in a constituency. Eckert, a genuinely shy man who does not enjoy or have much skill at the small talk of politics, made it quite clear that he considered the public-relations side of politics a burden. "I really don't like to campaign," he said, "which may surprise a lot of people, since campaigns are my business. But I don't enjoy it. Some people do. That's what it's all about to them, and when they get to the legislature, they don't care what they do there. That's not me."

It was the differences between Conable and Eckert, not the similarities, that commanded most people's attention and raised the hackles of many Republicans when they discussed Eckert's candidacy. In their eyes, the two men approached the legislative craft with radically dissimilar objectives and espoused opposing views on social issues, such as abortion and women's rights.

In contrast to Conable, who enjoyed a reputation as the consummate insider and whose mastery of the legislative process earned him the accolades of his House colleagues, Eckert compiled a very different record during his years in

13. *Congressional Quarterly*, December 31, 1983, p. 2787; October 27, 1984, p. 2807.

office. As a member of New York's legislature, Eckert was a loner who bridled at the discipline that party leaders tried to impose. One close observer of those days in Albany told us: "In party caucuses, Fred would be the lone holdout in votes. He drove the leadership up the wall." Fiercely independent, he achieved victories in the state Senate through dogged persistence and a sure instinct for publicity, rather than skill at compromise or parliamentary procedure. Although Eckert won some battles and lost others, like every lawmaker in Albany, he almost always antagonized his colleagues, whether winning or losing. And when he left Albany to take up the ambassadorship in the Fiji Islands in 1982, few were sorry to see him go. Unlike Conable, who left Washington as a widely respected figure, on his departure from Albany, Eckert was the winner of no popularity poll.

Eckert's approach to issues further differentiated him from the man he hoped to succeed on Capitol Hill. Whereas Conable was a staunch supporter of Ronald Reagan's economic program, he was middle-of-the-road, sometimes liberal, on social and civil rights issues. In party politics, he was noted for wanting Republicans to forgo ideological litmus tests and reach out to a broad spectrum of political opinion. At an annual fund-raising dinner of Monroe County's Republicans shortly after he announced his decision not to seek reelection, he told the organization's faithful, "The Republican Party is the representative of what Americans have in common. It represents middle-class interests, not issues."

Eckert, on the other hand, prided himself as being a true conservative, and he regularly received the support of New York's Conservative party and Right-to-Life party—two endorsements that Conable never sought. At the Republican presidential convention in 1976, Eckert was one of the two holdouts from New York who supported Ronald Reagan, while the state chairman, who was from Rochester, and the rest of the Republican delegation backed President Gerald Ford. In a local party that retained its connections to the reformist, progressive tradition of Republicanism, Eckert stood out as an advocate of the views of the militant right wing.

The combined effect of Eckert's political style and substantive positions on the issues caused many political activists, both Republicans and Democrats, to view his candidacy with disfavor, and in some instances with hostility. Despite these liabilities, he was the undisputed front-runner for the Republican nomination and the general election, because he was the *only* politician who had known from the moment he heard of Conable's retirement exactly what he wanted to do and how he would go about doing it. Although the district had many other politically ambitious people in it, no one else in 1984 had Eckert's well-focused, unflagging, lifelong ambition to serve in the U.S. House of Representatives.

Eckert could proceed without hesitation or careful calculation in part because he had been thinking and dreaming for years about running for Congress. Nearly everyone to whom we spoke mentioned this. A prominent Republican who attended grade school with Eckert recalled his fascination with political history and the fact that he often argued about current events with his teachers. This absorption in public affairs continued into college and embroiled the eager young conservative in heated debates with his professors. Eckert himself could not remember when he first set his sights on Capitol Hill. "It's always been what I wanted to do," he told us. In his speech to the Republican nominating convention in May, Eckert recounted that shortly after he and his wife had been married he had taken her to Washington to show her the Capitol and confided to her that someday he would return there as an elected representative.

Eckert had prepared himself all along for his future congressional career by serving in the state legislature before accepting President Reagan's ambassadorial appointment. He made it quite plain to us that even if he had remained a state senator, he would have given up this position readily to run for Conable's seat, unlike other officeholders in Albany. When asked how long it had taken him to decide to run for Congress after local friends had informed him of Conable's impending retirement, he said quietly, "Less than a second. But the decision was not made on the spur of the moment. I was going to Congress from the state Senate just as surely as I was going from Fiji."

So while all the other local politicians spent the first month or two after Conable's announcement hesitating and calculating the personal and political costs of running, Eckert, still in Fiji and unable to announce his candidacy formally while he was still ambassador, seized the opportunity Conable had handed him. Soon, he even had his conservative friends in the capital looking for a suitable home for his family. He also launched a highly visible public-relations campaign in which a small group of associates from Monroe County, called the Draft Ambassador Eckert for Congress Committee, released the names of important political supporters within hours of Conable's announcement. While news of these endorsements was given to the press by his friends, Eckert himself was working furiously behind the scenes by long-distance telephone to court additional supporters.

In the first twenty-four hours after Conable's announcement Eckert made one call after another to his political allies in Rochester. One was to Rich Stowe, a former member of his state Senate staff and one of his closest political advisers. Their conversation summarized perfectly Eckert's reaction to the opportunity that had been handed to him.

"What do you think?" he asked Stowe.

"There's nothin' to think," Stowe replied.

"Yeah," said Eckert, "That's what I think too."

2

Context: The Political
Facts of Life

*You cannot know what you want to know about [a politician] until you
have knowledge of . . . context. By knowledge, I mean to include what
you learn by looking at the context yourself and what you learn by
seeing the context through the eyes of the individual politician."*
—Richard F. Fenno, Jr.

Every opportunity to run for Congress comes wrapped in a context—those few
undeniable realities of time and place that provide a modicum of order to an
otherwise topsy-turvy political world. Within this context would-be candidates
first assess the risks of a congressional campaign.

They begin with the campaign's context not only because of the concrete
structure it lends their decision making but also because the context of a
campaign naturally works to the advantage of some politicians and to the
disadvantage of others. For instance, the artificial boundaries that determine a
congressional district may capriciously improve the chances of one House
hopeful while hindering another's. Distant events in Washington or even over-
seas may play into the hands of one candidate and cause embarrassment to
another. Politicians know they cannot control the circumstances that make up a
campaign's context, but they do try to calculate carefully the effects these
givens have on their chances of electoral success.

Knowledgeable local observers generally agree about what constitutes the
political context in any given congressional district. They agree because they
construct the context by viewing the same publicly available data, by absorbing
the same campaign experiences, and by using the same rules and regulations to
fight elections. Context is thus fairly objective; it is the product of a district's
party registration figures, election results, political geography, and media markets. Also part of the political context are the laws and standard practices that
govern campaign finance and party nominations. Finally there is the national
backdrop: the view of network television pundits and local political insiders
about whether a year is going to be good or bad for a particular party.

The prospective candidates' initial thinking about running for Congress also begins with these givens because everything else about a congressional campaign is so uncertain. These generally agreed on facts give them an inexpensive, easy means of measuring how they stack up against the demands and uncertainties of a modern campaign. To make this initial assessment they compare their own political strengths and weaknesses with what is known about the district in question. The result gives would-be candidates their first reliable evidence about the advisability of entering a race. "The first thing I did when I heard about Conable's retirement was to sit down and look at the numbers," one prospective candidate told us, referring to party registration figures and the results of past elections. She was not alone: in the first few days after Conable's announcement, nearly every other would-be candidate in the 30th district did the same thing.

The hard realities of political life in upstate New York proved too discouraging for some: their candidacies appeared hopeless and they quickly turned away from the opportunity presented by Conable's retirement. Others saw the political environment giving them a clear advantage and continued.

One politician for whom the context ultimately was too discouraging was Paul Haney, a ten-year member of the Rochester City Council who had been a big winner in every one of his previous elections and was a key figure in the council's large Democratic majority. While working hard locally on such projects as Rochester's downtown revitalization, Haney quietly harbored an ambition to go to Congress. He had even set a timetable for himself. "I saw my run for Congress down the road, four or five years from now," he told us. "Conable's retirement comes too soon for me."

Haney, a hulk of a man whose shiny, bald head gave him a passing resemblance to the former Speaker of the House Sam Rayburn, had for several years believed he could present himself to local voters as the logical heir to Conable's mantle. Like Conable, Haney was known as a fiscal conservative who understood the intricacies of budgeting and taxation and whose background as an accountant made this image all the more believable. Like Conable he was seen as a thoughtful, informed, moderate politician with strong convictions and the courage and intelligence to heed them. And like Conable he saw himself as possessing superior legislative skills and believed these skills could best be put to use in the U.S. Congress.

When Conable announced his retirement Haney naturally thought about entering the race to replace him. Frequent calls from constituents and community leaders imploring him to run initially reinforced his inclination to seek the Democratic nomination. "My issues—fiscal responsibility, balancing the budget—don't inspire the cadres of people to go out and work the streets the way social issues do, but I have been really gratified by all the calls I have been getting from people urging me to run because they think I would be a good congressman," he told us. "When I see the numbers on the deficit, for example, I think I could sit down with people and make them understand how serious things are." But in less than six weeks Haney took himself out of the race. Not the voice of ambition within him, nor the pleas from people around him, nor the issues that mattered most to him proved strong enough to erase his impression that he had no hope of winning.

Two years later Haney said no to another campaign, this one for his own reelection to the city council. His ambition to serve in the U.S. Congress having been weakened by the expectation that Fred Eckert would have a long tenure, Haney decided to retire from politics altogether. Local politicians and pundits were shocked when he said that he would not seek reelection, but their praise and suggestions that he reconsider were to no avail. The lost opportunity to sit in Congress seemed to have drained Haney of some of the passion that is critical to an American politician's career.

Party Competition

Like every politician contemplating a run for Congress, Haney looked first at the 30th district's partisan balance. Could a Democrat win in this district, or was it a safe seat marked For Republicans Only?

A seat in Congress may be safe for a particular party or a particular incumbent.[1] Safe party seats develop when lopsided voter registration for one party denies the opposition a credible political base. Safe incumbent seats are produced by the personal reputations of sitting representatives and their skills in using the perquisites of public office.

As long as Barber Conable was the incumbent, New York's 30th district was a safe seat on both grounds. Registration figures for 1984 showed Republicans with the allegiance of 46 percent of the voters, compared with only 29 percent for the Democrats. The Republicans' plurality received a boost from Conable's extraordinary personal popularity. A telephone poll conducted in early 1984 revealed that 75 to 80 percent of the voters viewed him favorably.[2] Taken

1. Some analysts suggest that the high reelection rates of House members have more to do with long-term social and political trends than with the individual performance of incumbents. See Melissa P. Collie, "Incumbency, Electoral Safety and Turnover in the House of Representative, 1952–1976," *American Political Science Review* 75 (March 1981): 119–131; James C. Garand and Donald A. Gross, "Changes in the Vote Margins for Congressional Candidates: A Specification of Historical Trends," *American Political Science Review* 78 (March 1984): 17–30. Other evidence suggests that the incumbency effect is the result of deliberate actions. See Keith Krehbiel and John R. Wright, "The Incumbency Effect in Congressional Elections: A Test of Two Explanations," *American Journal of Political Science* 27 (February 1983): 140–157; Richard Born, "Generational Replacement and the Growth of Incumbent Reelection Margins in the U.S. House," *American Political Science Review* 73 (September 1979): 811–817.

2. "Benchmark Survey of New York 30th District, May 1984" (Prepared by Public Response Associates for the American Medical Political Action Committee, Washington, D.C.).

together these conditions easily explain why after his initial, narrow victory in 1964 Conable never again experienced a close election. Only once was he reelected with less than 60 percent of the vote. His reelection in 1982 illustrates the unassailable position he had established: while Democratic challengers elsewhere in the county were winning electoral bonuses because of the severe economic recession being blamed on Ronald Reagan's economic policies, Conable's opponent mustered just 28 percent of the vote.

Once Conable was not going to be the Republican candidate, knowledgeable insiders in both parties considered the district much more competitive. The absence of his extraordinary personality drastically altered the context. The Republican County chairman, Ron Starkweather, told us: "The Democrats could give us problems with the right candidate. We have the advantage, but without Conable it's no guarantee." His assessment was shared by the Democratic elections commissioner and party vice-chairwoman, Marguerite Toole: "The numbers are a little misleading. The right Democrat can win in that district." Nor was this view of a more competitive district confined to local political observers. Party officials in Washington agreed that with Conable out of the picture New York's 30th district had many more possibilities for a Democrat than its past voting history indicated. Even Conable was uncertain of how safe the district was for the GOP: "The district is supposed to be a little more Republican now, but I'm not sure it's as safe as it was for me," he said.

What could lead one to believe that the district, which had been held by the Republicans since the Civil War, could be won by a Democrat? The answer lay in the recent contests which took place in the district and nearby. In isolation the district appeared safe for the Republicans, but in the context of other local voting trends the pictured looked different. Paul Haney was familiar with this larger picture and felt confident that he could win in November.

Haney knew that a Democrat could count on the growing number of ticket-splitters and independents in upstate New York to produce a winning coalition. The registration figures for 1984 showed that fully a quarter of the district's registered voters did not align themselves with either major party: 22 percent were independents, 2 percent Conservatives, and 1 percent Liberals. In addition the growing tendency of the area's voters to split their tickets was apparent in elections of all sorts, from the presidential race of 1980 to a host of obscure town contests.

Since the early 1970s Democratic candidates in Monroe County had made steady inroads into previously Republican areas. Endowed with talented, vigorous party leaders and candidates, Democrats began their assault by taking control of the City of Rochester; Haney was among those who took part in this effort. In 1973 the party won a majority on the city council for the first time since the Great Depression, and gradually the Democrats increased their margin until by 1979 they held eight of nine seats. From 1973 the Watergate scandal further damaged the Republican party, and the Democrats benefited in the rest of Monroe County, capturing two seats in the state legislature in 1974 and increasing their representation on town boards, the county legislature, and the local judiciary. By 1980 the Democratic party took brief control of the county legislature and won countywide races for sheriff and judge. Then came the surprising outcome of the presidential contest that year, when voters in Monroe County, and in the entire 34th Congressional District as well, gave a slight plurality to Jimmy Carter in what was otherwise a sweep by Reagan of every corner of New York State outside New York City.

The gradual decline in the number of offices held by Republicans in Monroe County continued into the 1980s and spread to other parts of the 30th Congressional District. In Monroe County, the district attorney's office, the county clerkship, and several more state legislative positions slipped one-by-one into the grasp of the Democrats. And in Genesee County, a neighboring county with even more of a Republican tradition than Monroe and Barber Conable's home base, the voters elected in 1980 and reelected in 1983 a Democratic sheriff named Doug Call. Thus it was clear that many Republicans and independents in New York's 30th Congressional District, were, in the privacy of the voting booth, pulling the Democratic lever with dependable and increasing frequency.

Survey data point to a reason for the GOP's weakening grip. In a poll conducted in 1984, 49 percent of the voters in the 30th district said they were Republicans, but only 25 percent said they were strong Republicans the rest said they only "leaned" toward the GOP. Therefore, although the Republican party appeared to command the allegiance of half the registered voters in the 30th district, it could count on no more than a quarter. To be sure the poll showed Democrats with a smaller proportion of the electorate: 31 percent of the voters identified themselves as Democrats, of which only 16 percent were strong Democrats.[3] Nevertheless the survey made clear that the area's voters, 26 percent of whom identified themselves as independents, gave much room to candidates to maneuver outside the confines of party attachments.

For politicians in both parties these well-known facts had two important consequences. The steady erosion of Republican strength gave Democrats confidence that they had a chance of winning Conable's House seat. Indeed several contenders for the Democratic nomination, Paul Haney among them, had already demonstrated their capacity to hold what had once been Republican seats.

The district's precarious partisan balance also figured in the calculations of Republicans. They believed the most important consequence of their edge in voter registration was that the party could easily hold on to Conable's seat in later elections if it did not lose it in 1984. To Republicans the Democrats were strong enough to contest an open seat, but not yet strong enough to challenge a

3. Ibid.

Republican incumbent. Based on this thinking, the Republicans quickly decided to do nothing that might divide the party and weaken its chances. They were particularly intent on avoiding a bruising primary, which Republican insiders believed might cripple the organization and alienate enough weak Republicans and independents to allow a Democrat to win a narrow victory in November. One Republican party leader noted: "We Republicans don't seem to be as good at primaries as the Democrats. . . . We can't seem to patch up our differences afterwards. Whenever we have a primary we always end up losing the election." Thus the partisan balance in the district posed a real dilemma for the GOP: the potential long-term safety of the seat increased the probability that many Republicans would want the job and be willing to wage a primary to get it, but the candidate who won might be so battered that he or she could not achieve the larger victory in November.

For a Democrat like Paul Haney, the prospect of a primary in the Republican party was one more reason why he initially believed he had a reasonable chance of winning Conable's seat. If the other facts had not been so unfavorable he surely would have run. But after seeing some cause for optimism in the district's competitiveness, Haney found other factors that caused only despair.

Political Geography

In 1984 the boundaries of New York's 30th Congressional District clearly favored a politician from Monroe County. Although this geographical bias was a break with tradition, it was acknowledged by everyone. Local politicians agreed that the reapportionment of 1982 had diminished the longstanding electoral importance of the rural communities and rich farmlands to the west of Monroe County and heightened the influence of the suburbs around Rochester. This change in the balance of power caused comment because the rural areas had dominated elections in the 30th district for roughly three-quarters of a century, or as long as Monroe County had been divided into more than one congressional district.

Although the reapportionment of 1982 made this shift in power appear massive and abrupt, rural influence in the district had been lessening gradually for some time. By the 1960s district boundaries gave citizens in metropolitan Rochester a nominal advantage within the district, but the residents in the agricultural communities to the west still constituted a dependable majority of Republican voters because of their staunch partisanship and high rates of turnout.

Barber Conable's first election in 1964 illustrates the precarious balance that existed before 1982 between the rural and suburban parts of the district. At the time of Conable's first campaign in 1964, when he lived in Alexander in

Genesee County, only 39 percent of the district's residents lived outside Monroe County, but these rural residents' fierce loyalty to one of their own and their high rates of political participation gave them probable control of any Republican primary. This worked to Conable's advantage: his only opposition, two hopefuls from Monroe County, knew they could not possibly beat Conable in a primary and quietly dropped from sight, leaving the nomination to Conable uncontested.

As the circumstances of Conable's nomination faded from memory, and as long as he held on to his seat, the tradition of rural dominance appeared to live on. With Conable's retirement, however, the critical change brought about by the reapportionment of 1982 suddenly became apparent: 80 percent of the constituency now resided in Monroe County, shifting the district's demographic balance to the suburbs of Rochester. At last politics had caught up with demography, and the area's burgeoning suburbs were now the center of gravity in New York's 30th Congressional District.

The most important consequence of these new boundaries (and the concomitant shift of power that resulted from them) was the way in which the new lines altered the size of the political bases on which prospective successors to Conable could count in their campaigns. In at least two very important cases, those of Paul Haney and the Republican state Assemblyman Steve Hawley, the new boundaries were important in their decisions not to run. Faced with the facts of political geography, they concluded that they had too few certain supporters.

Hawley, a respected and experienced state legislator, had for several years seemed certain to benefit from the district's tradition of sending a rural politician to Congress. But within days of Conable's announcement, Hawley announced that he was out of the race. He explained to us wistfully his decision not to run: "I've had my eye on that seat for quite some time. I've always wanted to end up in Congress, and when Conable announced his retirement, I immediately began to assess my chances. A lot of people wanted me to run, but in the new district I've got less than 10 percent of the vote."

No longer a young man, Hawley had decided not to enter the race even though he was convinced he would never have another chance at Congress. "I can't beat Eckert in a primary unless several others from Monroe County also enter and divide the vote," he said. "And I just don't think that will happen."

It was a bitter realization for Hawley that only two years earlier in the Assembly he had voted for the very reapportionment that now blocked him. But he was a seasoned politician who recognized the political facts of life: his objectives had to change with the political context in which he found himself, and so he turned to the task of securing his legislative seat and retaining his position in the assembly as minority whip. "I made up my mind quickly," he said, "because I knew I had to get out there and campaign if I were going to do it. And also I didn't want to give the younger guys around here too much time to think about running for my assembly seat, if I didn't go for the House. I'm disappointed, but you can't pick your time in politics."

Political geography was nearly as critical to Paul Haney's thinking as it was to Steve Hawley's. Although reapportionment had changed the balance of power within the 30th district from the surrounding rural counties to Monroe County, Haney gained none of the advantage that Hawley lost: the new boundaries had made the constituency not urban but suburban, and when Haney looked at his political base he saw even less than Hawley's 10 percent. But because Haney had never contemplated running for Congress with a large, natural base of support he was not immediately discouraged. To him a small political base meant simply that other factors would assume a larger importance. For example, he would need more money and organizational support to reach out effectively to the district's voters who had never had any direct connection with him.

It gave Haney little comfort that his glaringly weak starting position was shared by every other city politician from Rochester. In drawing the lines in 1982 for New York's 30th Congressional District, lawmakers in Albany had carefully carved up the city and placed bits and pieces of it in three different congressional districts. Consequently not one city politician from Rochester was well-placed to run for Conable's seat. The way the district's boundaries were drawn benefited exclusively the politicians who represented the suburbs in Monroe County, and Haney and Hawley were not among them.

While this shift in the electoral balance of power was thought by local politicians to be the most obvious change in congressional politics caused by the reapportionment of 1982, they also saw three other significant consequences. First, the new boundaries circumscribed an unusually compact congressional district. Second, they formed a constituency that had an unusually high congruity with a single media market. Finally, by creating what was essentially a single-county district, the boundaries enhanced party control over who would be Conable's successor. For politicians considering a run for Conable's seat, these three consequences were important.

The district's compactness meant that all the pieces of a winning coalition were in close proximity. By car one could travel from one end of New York's 30th Congressional District to the other in less than two hours, and the district's most populous sections were only minutes apart by expressway. To an underdog this compactness was particularly important because the weaker candidate has to work harder to build a winning coalition. Conable himself commented on the advantages of the 30th district for an unknown candidate when he ruefully told us: "Frank Horton has been teasing me about the district because it is so easy to campaign in. No one can touch him in his district, the way it is laid out, because his district stretches all the way to Oswego. But he says I'm a sitting duck, and maybe he's right."

In addition to its physical accessibility, the district could even more easily be reached through the mass media. The local newspapers and major broadcasting facilities were all based in the City of Rochester, and they saturated the surrounding area. Even the outlying villages to the west belonged to Rochester's communications network. Prominent politicians in the metropolitan area could therefore count on high name recognition among the voters before a campaign ever began, and those who needed to increase their visibility in the district could do so relatively easily. An intensive media campaign could also be carried out efficiently: advertisements in local newspapers or on local radio and television would reach citizens who would actually be voting in November; relatively little of a candidate's message and money would be wasted on voters in some other congressional district.[4]

By contrast contenders for House seats outside large urban areas normally have to penetrate the markets of more than one city to reach all the voters; Horton's district, for example, is a sprawling territory comprising five media markets. And although congressional candidates in large communities such as Manhattan or Buffalo avoid Horton's problem, they must pay high advertising rates, even though only a small proportion of those who receive the campaign messages actually vote in the election districts at which the advertising is aimed.

Monroe County's dominance of the 30th district had a final consequence for potential candidates for Conable's seat: the county's party leaders had an unusually prominent role in the selection of candidates.

Usually congressional boundaries cut across many local ones. In these cases the presence of party organizations of fairly equal influence from more than one county tends to fragment the authority of party leaders over recruitment, which has already been eroded by decades of party reform.[5] As a result party leaders sometimes feel less responsible for congressional candidates and concentrate on countywide elections that have high visibility and are more directly under their control. In the laissez-faire atmosphere that develops from such a lack of party interest and control, potential congressional contestants are generally free to pursue their own objectives and work out their own political alliances.

But in the newly defined 30th district, Monroe County's party leaders felt a particularly strong responsibility for the selection of the congressional candidates. They sought candidates from within their own organizations and worked

4. James E. Campbell, John R. Alford, and Keith Henry, "Television Markets and Congressional Elections," *Legislative Studies Quarterly* 9 (November 1984): 665–678. The authors devised an index of congruity between congressional districts and media markets that revealed New York's 30th to be the most efficient media market in the country in 1970. Our recalculations found the district's congruity to be only slightly lower in 1980.

5. Robert J. Huckshorn and Robert C. Spencer, *The Politics of Defeat* (Amherst: University of Massachusetts, 1971).

hard to maintain control of the nomination process. In addition, their views on prospective candidates were sought by the press and their fellow party members. Because critical decisions on recruitment were being made within a single jurisdiction, leaders of Monroe County's major parties were able to direct the flow of information and act as brokers among all the potential competitors. Particularly in the early days, when no one was quite sure what was happening, this was a strong position in which to be.

When all these lessons of political geography were fully understood, Hawley saw no hope for his congressional candidacy. Although in the general election the district's compactness and the ease with which its voters could be reached through the mass media might have helped him overcome his narrow political base, it was clear that a rural candidate could obtain the nomination only if politicians from Monroe County failed to press their natural advantage effectively, and Hawley saw no sign of this happening. In fact, soon after Conable made his announcement, potential candidates from Monroe County expressed the sentiment that it was their turn to take the seat, and they moved aggressively to stake their claim. Monroe County's party leaders acted similarly: they made clear that they had no intention of supporting the candidacy of someone from outside the county as long as one of their own wanted to run. For rural candidates such as Hawley a primary against a native son from metropolitan Rochester who had the backing of Monroe County's party seemed unwinnable.

At first glance the political geography seemed less damaging to Haney. Unlike Hawley he had the advantage of being from Monroe County, and although the district included only a few voters from Rochester, its overlap with Rochester's media market left Haney a glimmer of hope. A strong organizational effort and an intense advertising campaign could produce an unexpected victory.

Such a campaign would require a dependable political organization and plenty of money for televised advertising, however, and Haney had neither. A man of modest means, he was poorly prepared to take on the financial commitments of a wide-open congressional race. In addition to having no ready cash of his own he had limited experience raising money from others, because his previous campaigns for the city council never required any large-scale fund raising. Nor had these campaigns, which were basically conducted door-to-door, required much of an organizational effort. To run for Congress Haney would need to build a cadre of campaign workers almost from scratch, and for Haney this seemed particularly difficult. Neither charismatic nor gregarious, he was far more comfortable away from the crowd, indulging his intellectual interest in governance and public policy, than in the streets, building the personal political machine he needed.

Money

When Haney contemplated how much of other people's money it would take for him to run for Congress he was confronted with the skyrocketing cost of campaigns. Expenditures for House races across the country, which equaled $44 million in 1974, rose to $175 million by 1982.[6] Inflation accounted only for half of this growth: while the Consumer Price Index doubled during the period, campaign spending quadrupled.[7] The average spending per candidate in 1982 amounted to $265,000 for incumbents, $152,000 for challengers, and $284,000 for contestants for open seats.[8]

Voters and politicians in New York's 30th Congressional District had no firsthand knowledge of these mounting campaign costs. Campaigns in their district had typically been low-key, low-cost affairs, because Conable did not need much money to win and his opponents could not raise much for a hopeless cause.[9] Conable had spent only $64,600 in his last race, and throughout his career had made a point of refusing contributions from PACs and all donations larger than fifty dollars from individuals.[10] His Democratic challengers raised even less money, and yet they faithfully followed his example of relying entirely on local sources and small contributors for what little money they did raise.

In 1984 many in upstate New York believed Conable's district would lose its innocence about campaign costs. Each contender would have to spend liberally to improve his or her name recognition, and most would be eager to exploit the area's favorable position with respect to media markets by investing heavily in television and radio. Such a media strategy could make a primary alone cost $100,000, and the general election another $150,000 to $300,000.

This estimate was actually quite low compared with what was finally spent by newcomers to the House in 1984 (an average of $459,000).[11] But in early 1984 even the relatively modest sum of $300,000 posed a challenge to Monroe County's politicians because it was unprecedented, and most of them were unsure of how it could be raised. The absence of serious competition in the past had meant that experience in raising large amounts for a congressional race was

---

6. Ornstein et al., p. 65.

7. Ibid., p. 60.

8. Ibid., pp. 65–66.

9. Gary C. Jacobson's work on congressional campaign spending shows a clear relationship between how much candidates are able to raise and how well they are expected to do at the polls. *Money in Congressional Elections* (New Haven and London: Yale University Press, 1980), chap. 3.

10. Michael Barone and Grant Ujifusa, *The Almanac of American Politics, 1986* (Washington, D.C.: National Journal, 1985), p. 977.

11. Steven V. Roberts, "The Rich Get Richer and Elected," *New York Times*, September 24, 1985, sec. A, p. 26.

limited. Traditionally political funds in Monroe County had been raised by a relatively small group of local people, and most potential successors to Conable therefore lacked the broad-based network of contributors necessary to fund a modern congressional campaign. One longtime campaign financier in the Republican Party told us: "Monroe County is not used to coming up with the big dollars for a campaign. A five-hundred dollar contribution seems huge to the givers here, and so outside money will be critical in this one."

Outside money indeed figured prominently in the 30th district in 1984. In general PACs fund more than 30 percent of the cost of House campaigns, the national parties about 6 percent.[12] In campaigns for open seats, the greater competitiveness attracts national givers, and this outside money is one reason candidates in such races typically spend more than twice as much as challengers to incumbents.[13] In 1984 the likelihood that outside money would play a role in the 30th district was heightened by the relatively small number of open seats in the nation. The retirement rate from the House in 1984 was the lowest it had been in eighteen years,[14] only twenty-two members having decided not to seek reelection, and only five more seats were opened when incumbents lost primaries. Thus if local candidates were ever to raise the money needed to win Conable's seat in the House, 1984 seemed a good year in which to do it.

The PACs and national parties would not be equally eager to contribute to every candidate who sought a donation. Those who fit the conventional profile of a successful congressional candidate, such as state legislators, would be more credible and find more money than others with less impressive credentials. National organizations with money and resources apply fairly standard criteria when screening the hundreds of politicians who approach them for contributions, and what interests them most are previous experience in public office and money already in the bank. "We want to know where they're getting the rest of their money before we talk seriously," noted one national staff member. "If they don't have a plan for contributions, then we don't want to waste our time. Because even if we maxed out with them, it is still a small percentage of what they need." (To "max out" is to contribute the maximum allowed by law.) Money from Washington flows to those who can raise a lot on their own, and for this reason the rich in politics get richer and the poor stay poor.

In addition, the national parties and PACs look first and most favorably at those with connections to Washington's establishment. A sure sign of legitimacy is the presence of a well-connected backer who sets up appointments

12. Ornstein et al., pp. 80–81.
13. Ibid., pp. 80–81.
14. Ibid., p. 52.

between the prospective office-seeker and the contributors in Washington. A spokeswoman for the American Medical Political Action Committee (AMPAC), a highly respected and influential organization, described to us her reaction to a state legislator whom AMPAC eventually tried to recruit into the race in the 30th district: "Here was someone whose appointments around town were being made by———[a well-known Democrat], and who had a long-time association with Governor Cuomo. Clearly, this was someone we had to take seriously with connections like that."

Perhaps this statement simply illustrates what a small town Washington remains despite the cosmopolitan character it would be expected to have. But it also indicates the importance of national ties in obtaining access to the increasingly large sums of money needed for congressional campaigns. In practical terms this means that local politicians who have had experience and contacts outside their districts—in a federal agency, on a congressional staff, in state and national election campaigns, or in nationwide interest groups—have an immediate advantage in establishing themselves as candidates.

City Councilman Paul Haney found this out the hard way when he traveled to Washington in March to explore the possibilities of running and see what resources he could obtain from his party and its allied interest groups. He had raised no cash for his campaign and wanted some assurances about money. But the Democratic Congressional Campaign Committee gave him a chilly reception and no money. "All they did," he recalled with indignation, "was show me a list of PACs and then tell me that the PACs wouldn't talk to me until I was the designated candidate. They promised me nothing. I could count on no help from them at all."

Arriving at the national headquarters unheralded and with no connection to a prominent politician, Haney was just one of hundreds of office-seekers who visited the Democratic Congressional Campaign Committee during the spring of 1984, when prospective House candidates were looking for support and national and local party leaders were looking for candidates. Some months later, after the election, the committee's staff had difficulty remembering anything about Haney's appearance in Washington. Haney was by no means one of the stronger Democratic contenders in Monroe County, but it was rather his unfamiliarity with Washington, and his inability to gain access to national money and his party's organizational resources, that guaranteed his candidacy's failure. The need for money and organizational help from political groups outside the district is increasingly significant in modern congressional elections. Politicians like Haney who have not established the necessary relationship with the "Washington crowd" or who lack a local or state mentor influential with national power brokers soon find themselves stymied in their quest for a seat in Congress.

The National Climate

Although the need for resources from Washington clearly emerged as one of the most significant contextual factors in Haney's decision not to run for Congress, no other aspects of national politics—the president's popularity, the economy, and the relative strength of the major parties on Capitol Hill—ever seemed important. Context for Haney, and for every other politician we interviewed, was overwhelmingly local.

Although congressional races have traditionally been seen as local events decided primarily on the basis of the candidates' personal qualifications and the voters' longstanding party orientation, there exists much evidence that national concerns do somehow intrude on the local character of House elections. In subtle, often mysterious, ways, the strength of a party's presidential contenders and the performance of the national economy can be related to how the party fares in congressional districts all across the United States; this evidence bolsters the old political maxims that in congressional elections presidential candidates have coattails and that citizens vote their pocketbooks.[15]

Some observers of American politics see the national political climate playing an even more pervasive role in congressional elections than only affecting the voters' actions in November.[16] They contend that the national political climate not only influences voting behavior in November but also affects the recruitment decisions of would-be candidates in January and February. First, they argue that if it looks like a particularly good year for one of the two major

15. Aggregate studies of congressional elections reveal the presence of economic voting in response to changes in real disposable income and to the electorate's view of the parties' presidential contenders. See Gerald H. Kramer, "Short-Term Fluctuations in U.S. Voting Behavior, 1896–1964," *American Political Science Review* 65 (March 1971): 131–143; Edward R. Tufte, "Determinants of the Outcomes of Midterm Congressional Elections," *American Political Science Review* 69 (September 1975): 812–826; Gerald H. Kramer, "The Ecological Fallacy Revisited: Aggregate Versus Individual-Level Findings on Economics and Elections and Sociotropic Voting," *American Political Science Review* 77 (March 1983): 92–111. Some research on individual voting behavior raises doubts about whether voters reward and punish congressional candidates as a reflection of their national concerns; some scholars report no effects at the individual level. See Morris P. Fiorina, *Retrospective Voting in American National Elections* (New Haven and London: Yale University Press, 1981). Others report mixed effects. See James H. Kuklinski and Darrell M. West, "Economic Expectations and Voting Behavior in United States House and Senate Elections," *American Political Science Review* 75 (June 1981): 436–447; John R. Hibbing and John K. Alford, "The Electoral Impact of Economic Conditions: Who is Held Responsible?" *American Journal of Political Science* 25 (August 1981): 423–439; Morris P. Fiorina, "Who is Held Responsible? Further Evidence on the Hibbing-Alford Thesis," *American Journal of Political Science* 27 (February 1983): 158–164.

16. Gary C. Jacobson and Samuel Kernell, *Strategy and Choice in Congressional Elections* (New Haven and London: Yale University Press, 1981); William T. Bianco, "Strategic Decisions on Candidacy in U.S. Congressional Districts," *Legislative Studies Quarterly* 9 (May 1984): 351–364; Alan I. Abramowitz, "National Issues, Strategic Politicians, and Voting Behavior in the 1980 and 1982 Congressional Elections," *American Journal of Political Science* 28 (November 1984): 710–721.

parties, the party will be able to entice a stronger group of candidates to run for Congress because of the increased probability of success. Conversely, the party placed at a disadvantage by the national political climate will field weaker candidates because its chances of winning seem low. Thus even if voters on Election Day ignore the big issues and cast their ballots solely on the basis of the personal characteristics of the local candidates, the party helped by the national political climate will have the more attractive candidates on the ballot and will reap an electoral bonus. At the same time politically active citizens and interest groups will be more inclined to contribute money and effort to the candidates whose party is favored by the national climate, which gives these already superior candidates an even greater campaign advantage. Finally, as national party organizations and PACs become more involved in recruiting candidates to run in House elections, national concerns penetrate more deeply the local milieu. For these reasons the perception of an advantage for one party at the beginning of an election year helps promote electoral success at the end of the year; national political tides bias the recruitment of candidates early in the process and in the remaining months influence the campaign itself.

In the spring of 1984 in upstate New York these national factors were hardly discernible in the initial decisions of Barber Conable's prospective successors. The mood of the electorate and its consequences for the political fortunes of individual candidates were never mentioned spontaneously in our interviews, and when we ourselves introduced the subject of national tides it was generally brushed aside. From late February until early June, the business of recruiting Barber Conable's successor progressed in nearly complete isolation from events in Washington and from the political climate of the nation. Paul Haney was therefore not alone in concentrating on the local aspects of the 30th district's congressional race; everyone else did, too.

Why did the unprecedented growth in the American economy have so little impact on the decisions in winter and spring of potential House candidates? How could the popularity of an incumbent president who would win reelection by a landslide eight to ten months later fail to influence local politicians' strategic calculations about running and winning? Answering these puzzling questions requires distinguishing between the national climate in early 1984 and that later in the year, as well as understanding how the climate of early 1984 had different effects in Washington and upstate New York.

In the months immediately following Barber Conable's announcement, candidates who were thinking about replacing him had no clear sense of the direction in which the country was moving. Not until late spring, when most would-be candidates had already made their decisions to run or not to run, was the strength evident of Ronald Reagan and the Republican party. The unexpected depth of the recession of 1982 and the nation's slow recovery left doubts as late as early in 1984 about how voters would react in the forthcoming national election to economic conditions. And although the economic indicators were all favorable by January 1984, massive federal deficits still created uncertainty about whether the growth predicted by the administration would be sustained or falter under the weight of a mounting public debt. In addition, in the early months of 1984 doubt still surrounded the question of how competitive the presidential race would be. The Republicans had a popular incumbent, but in December 1983 he had fallen briefly behind Walter Mondale and Gary Hart in the opinion polls. Mondale was thought to be in command of a resurgent New Deal coalition and Hart of a potentially powerful, younger one. The glaring political weaknesses of both men did not become evident until halfway through the primaries, which continued until midyear. To Democratic congressional candidates first thinking about running, Mondale's presence on the ballot did not seem the liability it so clearly became later. These political signals from Washington in early 1984 were too inconsistent to weigh heavily in the initial deliberations of prospective contestants for a vacant House seat in distant upstate New York.

Even if the evidence pointing toward a nationwide Republican advantage had been clearer, it would still have had to be filtered through the unique and unsettled local situation of Monroe County. Although it was true that compared with many other parts of the country the recession of 1982 had been relatively mild in the 30th Congressional District, it was also true that the subsequent recovery never became as robust there as it did elsewhere. As a result, in early 1984 economic concerns still loomed large to many of the district's voters. In an opinion survey conducted in mid-May unemployment was cited by 27 percent of all respondents as the most pressing local problem (this was the highest figure reported for any category), and the economy in general was cited by 10 percent.[17] These specific concerns of the voters coincided with a more general pessimism, or uncertainty, that still characterized the local public mood. Although 43 percent of respondents agreed with the statement that "generally things are going in the right direction," fully a third agreed that "things are pretty seriously off on the wrong track." When this third of the constituency was combined with the 24 percent of the residents who expressed uncertainty about the nation's direction, no clear sentiment emerged in the 30th district that could have foreshadowed the GOP's success in November.

The caution evident in the responses to these questions was paralleled in feelings toward the president and his policies. On the one hand 62 percent of respondents approved of Reagan's performance, and 64 percent approved of his tax cuts. But there was a great deal of negative sentiment toward the president's record on the federal deficit, his defense spending, and his handling of many international issues. In addition, local voters expressed concern about issues

17. "Benchmark Survey of New York 30th District, May 1984."

ranging from Social Security and Medicare to toxic-waste disposal. Given this ambivalence on the part of the district's voters, and their having voted against Reagan in 1980, their level of support for him in 1984 seemed uncertain.

In explaining his decision not to become a candidate for Conable's House seat, a local Democrat acknowledged this confusing aspect of congressional politics in Monroe County and observed that the national tides would have no impact on the selection of the 30th district's new congressman. In response to our question about whether 1984 would be a bad year for a Democratic campaign, he was quick to emphasize that his reasons for bowing out of the race had been personal and had little to do with the national scene. "All throughout the spring," he noted, "the polls made it clear that people liked Reagan, but not what he stood for. The biggest effect of the presidential election will probably be on turnout, but in this county everyone votes anyway. I don't think much will change here, because of what's happening nationally."

Although the direction of the national tides and the local reaction to them were unclear to politicians in the 30th district, the recruitment of local candidates for Congress by national political organizations could still have provided a link between the district's election and broader national trends. By increasing their efforts to find good candidates when they think the national tides are running in their favor, national organizations can make their presence felt in local congressional races, as can national issues.[18] In many House districts this pattern has become one of the facts of political life that prospective candidates must consider in weighing their decision to contest a seat.

In New York's 30th Congressional District in 1984, however, national organizations initially were uninvolved in the decision making of local politicians. For only one potential candidate, Louise Slaughter, a Democratic assemblywoman of whom we shall say more in Chapter 5, were these groups important in the deliberations of spring 1984. Despite the increasing trend toward the nationalization of congressional recruitment in other districts and in other years, prospective candidates in Monroe County in 1984 were relatively free from such outside pressure, and this left them inclined to focus almost entirely on the local aspects of the race.

There are several reasons why the national parties and the high-powered PACs were relatively inconspicuous in the 30th district in 1984. On the Republican side, neither the staff of the congressional campaign committee nor the groups who typically fund Republican candidates saw any reason after Conable announced his retirement to launch a recruiting drive. Given the party registration in the district, they expected vigorous competition for the Republican nomination and therefore considered intervention in local politics not only unnecessary but potentially risky: a good candidate would probably emerge and

18. Jacobson and Kernell, passim.

nothing but grief could come from mistakenly backing an opponent of the eventual winner. "With a Republican seat like that," observed a staff member at Republican headquarters, "you usually get a good candidate . . . a state legislator or someone like that . . . who can win, and so we don't have to do much. We usually recruit in Democratic districts that have an incumbent: that's where we can do the most good in helping find people who will run."

As the Republican staff in Washington read the 30th district, Monroe County's party already had a candidate. "We made some calls, and we heard from Eckert and Conable and talked to the local leaders. It seemed like Eckert would be the candidate and the party supported him, and so there was nothing to do. We're not in the business of going into a district and telling the locals what to do," he told us. Although the national party was involved in local decisions in several other contests around the country for open seats, Republicans in Washington chose to remain apart from this one. And Republican PACs, expecting a competitive race, waited for candidates to approach them.

Thus whatever recruiting on the part of Washington that would take place in Monroe County in 1984 would come from Democratic organizations. Although the open seat gave the Democrats an unprecedented opportunity to capture a stronghold of the opposition, the Republican complexion of the constituency suggested that local Democratic candidates might need additional encouragement to make what would surely be a tough race. The people in Washington who might provide that kind of encouragement had other concerns, however, than the contest in New York's 30th district.

Strategists at the Democratic Congressional Campaign Committee had largely laid their plans for the forthcoming election by the time Conable announced his retirement in February 1984, and these plans did not include going after Republican seats. The Democrats had to protect twenty-six freshman congressmen, many of whom had won in 1982 by scant margins in normally Republican areas. In 1984 the party was committed to defending these seats before trying to capture any open ones. "We have to keep our folks in office, not go after new seats," noted one Democratic spokesperson. "Very early in the game we decided that 'incumbent protection' had to come first."

Next in importance were seats that had been opened by the retirement of Democrats. The party had a good chance of retaining these and was prepared to commit resources to contest them if a strong candidate asked for help. Given that these priorities were set and that the funds available to Democratic congressional campaigns were limited to $3 million, there was little money left over for other races. "We just don't have 'take-a-chance money' for districts like the 30th, and when we do give money, we are not going to be able to give very much. This year will be the first time we even 'max out' to some of our incumbents," observed a staff member at the committee.

Nonetheless, the staff of the Democratic Congressional Campaign Committee would be as receptive as it could to prospective candidates from the 30th district, and it did roll out the red carpet for at least two state legislators who made the pilgrimage to Washington. But only under extraordinary circumstances could the committee justify altering the campaign plans that political necessity had already dictated.

This left the field to the PACs that support Democratic candidates. Generally funds from PACs go to incumbents, whose high reelection rates produce the biggest political payoff. In 1982, for example, 68 percent of the $79 million contributed by PACs was received by incumbents, whereas only 14 percent went to campaigns for open seats.[19] But in 1984 the relatively small number of open seats competing for attention from Washington gave PACs an incentive to consider the 30th district carefully. After all, this race was potentially more competitive than several others for vacant seats. Labor groups in particular ought to have welcomed a chance to capture a seat held for years by one of their staunchest adversaries, whom they had worked vigorously once before to depose. But without a signal from the national party committee, Democratic PACs were no more willing than Republican PACs to enter the race.

There remained one small incentive for a few PACs to get involved in the race: many PACs try to maintain an appearance of nonpartisanship—though in practice they tend to favor one party over the other—and by participating in a race for an open seat like that to find Conable's successor they could satisfy this goal without antagonizing an incumbent.[20] "Look, a lot of the business PACs want to put in their annual reports that they give to both parties," said one well-placed official from a PAC. "An easy way for them to do that without hurting their Republican friends is to back a Democrat in an open race. This year they're all looking for a Democrat they can live with, especially with so few open seats." This concern with public relations could have gained the right local Democrat a sympathetic hearing from a few PACs that traditionally leaned toward Republicans, but we saw only one instance of this in the race to succeed Conable.

In sum, the varied factors that typically link congressional electoral politics at the local level to partisan trends on the national level were operating very weakly in New York's 30th district during the spring of 1984. The strength of the economic recovery and the extent of the incumbent president's popularity were uncertain all across the nation in the early months of 1984, and this national uncertainty was heightened by the mood and past voting behavior of the local electorate. Democrats did not think the national tides were running in their favor, but neither did they expect their hopes for a seat in the House of Representatives to be drowned in a tidal wave of Republican sentiment.

19. Larry Sabato, *PAC Power: Inside the World of Political Action Committees* (New York: W. W. Norton, 1984), p. 75.
20. Ibid., pp. 88–90.

What seems clear to us from the events in upstate New York in 1984 is that for national tides to have a telling, uniform impact on congressional recruitment they must begin running, and running clearly, far in advance of the November elections, and they must have enough force to sweep aside contrary local conditions. In 1984, at least in New York's 30th district, these forces failed to develop.

Party Nominations

The race to replace Barber Conable, more firmly rooted in local politics than national politics, was circumscribed by one last set of fairly clear-cut conditions: the state laws, party rules, and local political memories that imposed legal and practical limits on the candidates seeking to get their names on the ballot. These procedural and cultural facts of life are important, because politicians can win election to Congress in the fall only if they get themselves on the ballot in the summer. And in American politics, getting on the ballot with a realistic chance of winning almost always means gaining the nomination of one of the two major political parties, in conformity with legal and technical requirements that vary considerably from one state to the next, and even from one county to the next.

If congressional elections are looked at solely from a national perspective this significant local variable in the nomination process may get lost. Getting on the ballot in an American general election increasingly means winning a primary and little else, because a century of reform has left many local political parties in a weakened condition, and politicians who want badly enough to run in November can do so only if they are willing to enter a primary. These ambitious politicians need not be party loyalists or team players to enter the fray; they need not even hold the same political views as their fellow partisans. All they need is initiative and a loyal political base that can be counted on in a primary election, because turnout in primaries is extremely low.[21] Not surprisingly the men and women who win election to Congress in these modern circumstances tend to describe themselves as "self-starters" and to see their victories as testimony to their individual political skill.[22]

This picture of weak party control over congressional nominations and of primaries filled by ambitious political loners conforms with a modest trend in recent House elections, which shows a small but steady growth in the number of

21. For example, in 1984 the average turnout per district in New York State's primary was 33,000. See Barone and Ujifusa, pp. 901–988.

22. Fishel, p. 58; John W. Kingdon, *Candidates for Office: Beliefs and Strategies* (New York: Random House, 1968), pp. 68–73.

primaries held during each congressional election cycle.[23] Although the number of incumbents who lose these increasingly frequent primaries is small—usually no more than eight or nine nationwide—these races are gradually becoming more competitive, especially in the Democratic party.[24] In contests for open seats, primaries are overwhelmingly prevalent in both major parties. In such races in recent years, 90 percent of the Democratic congressional nominees and 72 percent of the Republican nominees have gone through a primary.[25]

The frequency and competitiveness of these primaries vary from one district to another, depending on the cohesiveness of the local party organization. In some communities in the United States, and in most in New York State, party officials retain a considerable degree of control over the recruitment of candidates and party nominations.[26] These organizations are sufficiently visible and active locally that they remain a significant factor in the selection of congressional nominees, if not always a controlling one. Thus the national trend toward candidates who recruit themselves and weakened party control over congressional nominations must be viewed in the specific, local context of the rules and histories of particular party organizations.

In New York's 30th Congressional District, for example, the local party organizations are found to have retained a good deal of political influence. Nevertheless, in the first few days after Conable announced his retirement, most observers of politics in upstate New York expected the 30th Congressional District to follow the national pattern and foresaw a primary to determine the nominees of the two major parties. A primary was seen as a particularly strong possibility in the Republican party because many of its members had waited so long for the opportunity to run for Congress, and because the party's majority status made its nomination particularly attractive. Also, despite the party leaders' control over the flow of information in Monroe County during the first few days after Conable's announcement, the state laws and local party rules governing the selection of congressional nominees appeared to invite a challenge to organizational authority by means of a primary.

New York State designates the second Tuesday in September for primary elections, and this late date is advantageous for two reasons to politicians seeking to enter a primary. First, it gives candidates ample time to collect signatures and file petitions with the county election boards. This certification

23. Richard Born, "Changes in the Competitiveness of House Primary Elections, 1956–1976," *American Politics Quarterly* 8 (October 1980): 495–505.

24. Ornstein et al., p. 50; Born, pp. 503–504.

25. Born, pp. 503–504; Jacobson and Kernell, p. 33.

26. Snowiss, pp. 637–639; Linda L. Fowler, "The Electoral Lottery: Decisions to Run for Congress," *Public Choice* 34 (December 1979): 399–419; James L. Gibson et al., "Whither the Local Parties? A Cross-sectional and Longitudinal Analysis of the Strength of Party Organizations," *American Journal of Political Science* 29 (February 1985): 139–160.

process can be a barrier to candidates lacking access to the party's grass roots, but because the filing deadline is in mid-June, outsiders can mobilize their own volunteers. For instance, because Conable announced his retirement in mid-February, the four and a half months before the filing deadline guaranteed that any candidate who wanted to enter the race would not be closed out. Not only does a primary in September give candidates the entire summer to organize a campaign, but a victory so late in the season gives the winner momentum for the general election. Many observers of politics in New York State consider this momentum an important political asset that more than compensates for the potential divisiveness of a late primary.[27]

The nominating procedures within the local party organizations gave further leeway to candidates interested in seeking the nomination. Republicans were required by their party's rules to select their nominee at a party convention at which all local committeemen and committeewomen would cast secret ballots. Some fourteen hundred delegates—of which about 60 percent were men and 40 percent women—would be eligible to select the congressional candidate, and if the Republicans from the outlying counties participated in the nominating convention, as they eventually agreed to do, the number of potential delegates would increase by another 20 percent. The Republican party adopted this unwieldy system for choosing its candidates after the Watergate scandal as part of a widespread effort to freshen its image. While such democratic decision making may have been good public relations, it undermined the ability of party leaders to control easily and directly the recruitment of candidates.

Because of the large number of delegates, a great deal would depend on the turnout at the convention. Party rules prohibited proxy voting, used by party chiefs in many county organizations around the state to deliver the support of delegates at conventions to hand-picked candidates. As a result of this prohibition rival party factions in the 30th district were free to mobilize their own supporters. But even if the leaders of these rival factions were successful in getting their people to the convention, they would have to control them carefully to keep them from defecting to other candidates—a difficult task given the system of secret balloting. In this volatile environment party discipline was difficult to enforce and rival candidates could bargain and cajole their way to the party's nomination.

The nominating system of the Democrats contrasted sharply with the wide open practices of the Republicans. The Democrats' executive committee, made up of its high officials and the leaders of the town and city committees, was allowed to pick the party's nominee in a closed meeting. The party's rank and

27. Donald Bruce Johnson and James R. Gibson, "The Divisive Primary Revisited: Party Activists in Iowa," *American Political Science Review* 68 (March 1974): 67–77; Walter J. Stone, "Prenomination Candidate Choice and General Election Behavior: Iowa Presidential Activists in 1980," *American Journal of Political Science* 28 (May 1984): 361–378.

file would be consulted informally, but the broad base of the party would have no direct voice in the final selection of a candidate unless the executive group's decision was challenged in a primary. Outwardly the Democratic leadership appeared able to exercise total control over the selection of the party's nominee, and the party's vice-chairwoman stated emphatically at the beginning of the recruitment season: "There will be no primary on the Democratic side. We'll sit down with the main candidates and decide who has the best chance of winning among them."

Despite this firm talk, the party's history suggested that it would have trouble preventing primaries if determined challengers were bent on seeking the nomination. There had never been an election year in recent memory when the party was free of such a battle for at least one office, and in 1984 the party's leaders were in a particularly disadvantageous position to control internal competition for a congressional seat if any developed. First, the leadership was in transition: the longtime party chairman, Larry Kirwan, who had rejuvenated the organization in the 1970s, had resigned in fall 1983, although he retained a strong presence through his position as vice-chairman of the state Democratic committee. His successor, the prominent local attorney Nathan Robfogel, underwent major surgery shortly after assuming his new responsibilities. While the day-to-day operations of the party were carried on by a seasoned politician, Vice-Chairwoman Marguerite Toole, who was also the party's commissioner on the county elections board, the future of the party was unclear in the weeks immediately following Conable's retirement. Kirwan participated in early deliberations about potential candidates and carried on his own recruitment efforts; Toole had operational responsibility for dealing with would-be contenders and the press; and Robfogel had the formal authority to formulate a party strategy, which he was not able to exercise until his recovery in April. These circumstances invited challengers to make their own plans and fashion their own alliances within the party.

In addition, the Democrats in the 30th Congressional District were preoccupied with presidential politics. New York's primary was scheduled for mid-April, and it promised to be a crucial test for Walter Mondale's floundering campaign. As a result, the reputation of the local party establishment and its labor allies, who had backed Mondale, was on the line in New York State, as was that of Governor Mario Cuomo. If they could not deliver a victory in the primary for Mondale, it would be a major blow to the party hierarchy and to Mondale's campaign. For this reason, the search for Conable's successor was peripheral until the presidential question was decided, and this created a favorable climate for the congressional aspirations of mavericks.

The vulnerability of both party organizations to free-lance candidates was compounded by the presence of two small but active parties, the Conservatives and Liberals, in Monroe County and throughout New York State. In November

1984 both would endorse congressional candidates in the 30th district and occupy separate lines on the ballot. It was probable that the Liberals would endorse the Democratic candidate and that the Conservatives would endorse the Republican; in this case the endorsements would have little practical effect. On occasion, however, the minor parties endorsed candidates defeated in the primaries of the major parties, thus allowing dissident Republicans and Democrats a place on the ballot in November. In the U.S. Senate election of 1980, for example, Senator Jacob Javits ran as a Liberal after having lost the Republican primary to Alfonse D'Amato, and Javits's presence on the ballot in November may have cost the Democratic candidate the election. Similarly, a state Senate election in Monroe County in 1974 was won in an upset by the Democrat Jack Perry after a losing contender in the Republican primary split his party's vote by running as a Conservative. The memory of these defeats made local party leaders extremely sensitive to the claims of candidates with support from the edges of the ideological spectrum, who could play the role of spoiler in November. This gave additional leverage within the major parties to these candidates.

The state laws, party rules, and local political memory caused Republican and Democratic leaders in Monroe County to move cautiously in the first few days after Conable announced his retirement. They remained officially neutral, allowing every politician in the area to come forward, and they used their visibility as party spokesmen to praise a wide range of potential candidates. A few well-known Republicans made early endorsements, but with one notable exception these meant little in the struggle for the party nomination. This early caution protected party leaders from making commitments that could prove impossible to enforce later, and it allowed them to present to the public an image of the parties as open, accessible organizations.

This picture of openness was misleading, because it was only a partial picture. Prospective candidates in both parties recognized that the leadership commanded substantial resources, which would prove invaluable in the fall campaign: the party designation would provide access to local contributors and considerable resources to mobilize voters. Indeed the local party apparatus in New York State is among the strongest and most effective in the nation.[28] This meant that prospective candidates had to work within the party if they could, and this was especially true for Republicans, who showed a pronounced tendency to avoid primaries at almost any cost. More than one Democrat noted that the Republicans know better how to keep their people "in line." And while many Democrats hoped internecine warfare would divide the opposition, they recognized that a party culture restrained many Republican office-seekers from airing their differences.

Once this complex and sometimes contradictory picture was fully appreci-

28. Gibson et al., p. 155.

ated, prospective candidates for the open seat in New York's 30th district knew that their legal environment invited them to enter the September primary. At the same time they knew that challenging the local party hierarchy would be a costly proposition, and could well be a losing one. Clearly any congressional aspirant could wage a primary fight, but only if he or she had the stomach for it. It was equally clear that if local party leaders became divided over a candidate, almost nothing would prevent a headstrong, free-lance candidate from capturing the nomination in a wide-open primary.

Paul Haney and Steve Hawley, who understood all of this, wanted no part in such a primary and never considered it a suitable option. Perhaps they harbored too little ambition to go through a bruising, expensive primary. Or perhaps they were simply realists about their chances of success, given all the other, less hopeful facts of political life of which they were already aware. Whatever the reasons, neither of these experienced politicians took long to end his candidacy and leave the field to other candidates.

Although the political context was crucial in so quickly eliminating Haney, Hawley, and others like them from the race to replace Conable, it also served another important function in allowing insiders to gauge the relative strengths of other prospective candidates. The partisan balance of the district, the realities of political geography, the crucial role of outside money, the inconclusive impact of national tides, and the disruptive potential of a determined primary contestant all signaled that certain kinds of politician would have an advantage over others. For example, any Republican with a large suburban constituency in the district, a knowledge of media campaigning, access to national PACs, and the backing of Monroe County's Republican leadership had automatically to be considered a formidable contender.

It was the political context that almost immediately caused Fred Eckert to be recognized by local observers as the strongest candidate in the race. Despite his absence from the district, his reputation for ideological extremism, and his penchant for making political enemies, the campaign environment fortuitously favored his candidacy. That he had enjoyed success in bitter party primaries and made clear that he was prepared to fight another all-out battle for the nomination simply reinforced his favored position.

No one whom we interviewed disputed that Eckert had all the contextual factors on his side and that he was the only likely candidate for whom this was true. He immediately became the man everyone else had to beat, and the standard against which all other would-be candidates measured their own chances of success. People might disagree with him on the issues, or dislike him personally, but they could not argue with the political facts of life, which in spring 1984 made Fred Eckert the odds-on favorite to replace Barber Conable in the U.S. House of Representatives.

3

Uncertainty: The District Nobody Knew

House members see electoral uncertainty where outsiders would fail to unearth a single objective indicator of it.

—*Richard F. Fenno, Jr.*

By focusing exclusively on numbers in disregard of the area and shape of a congressional district as well as party affiliation within the district, the Court deals in abstractions which will be recognized even by the politically unsophisticated to have little relevance to the realities of political life.

—*Justice Harlan, in the dissent to* Wesberry v. Sanders

Despite the clarity of many factors surrounding the race to replace Barber Conable, politicians in upstate New York could not escape a pervasive feeling of uncertainty about the congressional district in which they were thinking of competing. New York's 30th Congressional District, newly created by the state's sweeping reapportionment of 1982, contained a constituency few really understood. Radically different in design from the districts that preceded it earlier in the century, it was a district mired in political confusion, a state of affairs that caused many would-be candidates to misread the possibilities presented by Conable's retirement.

As long as Conable was the incumbent, uncertainty about the district's political center of gravity or its potential for supporting various ad hoc personal coalitions was of little significance. Because local politicians were no more inclined to challenge Conable in his new district than they had been in his old one, no one felt any need to understand the new constituency's political character. Everyone simply called the new district "Conable's district" and left it at that.

This limited understanding of the area's politics meant that when Conable removed himself from the congressional landscape he also took the sense of the district with him. New York's 30th district was a mystery without him. It was not rural, and it was not urban. Much of it was suburban, but the suburbs were of many varieties. It was often called conservative, but few could agree on precisely what this meant, because, for one thing, it had failed in 1980 to vote for Ronald Reagan. Without Conable some political observers were not even confident the district was safely Republican, because the one House election conducted inside its boundaries had pitted Conable against an unusually weak challenger. The ensuing rout told local political observers nothing they did not already know: at best the election of 1982 established a floor for the Democrats—the 30 percent of the vote that presumably was the least they could get.

This abbreviated history contained so few clues to the future that no one with whom we spoke professed a clear understanding of the district's essential character. "It's a crazy district, the product of a legislative-court conspiracy to wipe out compact, coherent districts," a local lawyer told us. Equally puzzled was an experienced elected official who had given some thought to running herself. "It's a crazy district," she told us. "It's so dispersed. There are no centers to it. That's why I think it will be such an expensive race, because it will have to be a media campaign." A prominent Republican insider could offer no insight into the district either. "The district has changed with the new reapportionment," he said, "and I guess I'm uncertain about how to easily characterize it."

Only one person of the scores we interviewed painted any kind of graphic picture of the new district, and the picture he drew was more interesting to fishermen than to politicians: "Geographically, the district doesn't make any sense at all. It does look like a creature with a fish hook in its mouth, though."

Even Conable experienced some uncertainty and confusion. Although at the time of his retirement he had come to regard the district's puzzling character as an advantage (because of the obstacles it posed to would-be challengers) he objected strenuously to the new boundaries when they were first proposed. "The district doesn't make sense in political terms at all," he noted, "but I like it that way now. It's so diffuse that there is no one issue that can defeat me. There are no dominant interests, and that gives me room to balance things."

All this uncertainty about the district's political personality was important, because it made unclear to potential candidates the probability of their winning and keeping the seat. In some instances the ambiguities merely raised the costs of finally deciding not to run by compelling people to search for hidden clues to the district's underlying character. In other cases the failure to understand the district instinctively and immediately led to serious miscalculation. For Assemblywoman Audre "Pinny" Cooke, for instance, it meant losing the only chance to go to Congress she was ever likely to have.

The "Redheaded Social Worker"

To an outsider in the early months of 1984, Audre "Pinny" Cooke surely appeared to be a strong contender for the Republican congressional nomination in New York's 30th district. She had six years of experience in the state

Assembly, a proven record as a vote-getter, and exceptional name recognition in Monroe County. She was so highly thought of as a politician that in 1982 she had been mentioned as a possible candidate for lieutenant governor. Yet she did not seek her party's designation and was never mentioned publicly as a potential candidate for Conable's seat. The most visible female politician in the area, she was nonetheless out of the running before the race began.

A social worker by training, Pinny Cooke is a redhead with a warm, ready smile. She comes from an upper-middle-class Jewish family. Before her entry into politics she was for many years the director of a facility for the handicapped, and even after her election to the legislature in Albany, her abiding social concerns kept her intimately involved with many of Rochester's charitable and cultural organizations. It was not surprising therefore that she took a progressive stance on most social and economic issues and was identified in 1984 by the American Civil Liberties Union as the most liberal Republican in the New York State Assembly.

Cooke's trademark, however, is her political style, not her liberal leanings. She emphasizes her accessibility, her empathy, and her desire to help constituents. Although Cooke strongly supports such women's causes as the Equal Rights Amendment and abortion rights, her image is not that of an ideologue. Rather, her approach is always nonpartisan and nonideological, a pragmatic mix of common sense and chicken soup that has attracted support across the Republican spectrum, as well as among moderate Democrats and independents. In her race for the Assembly in 1984 this all-embracing style even won her the endorsement of the Conservative party.

The chance for such an unlikely Republican to go to Albany arose when the Democratic incumbent in the 132nd Assembly District resigned in 1977 in the middle of his two-year term. The unexpected vacancy occurred as the local Republican party was still reeling from a string of stunning losses suffered in the aftermath of Watergate. Party leaders were unusually receptive to Cooke because they felt they needed a candidate who was different, would freshen the party's image, and was willing to buck the prevailing Democratic tides.

Although Cooke had experience running campaigns for other Republicans, she had never run for office herself and was virtually unknown to the general public. But her background and style were newsworthy and served her well against a bland Democratic opponent who was no more a household name than she was. "The press just couldn't get over the fact that the Republicans were running a redheaded social worker and the Democrats had a banker in pinstripes," Cooke recalled. The GOP's unconventional strategy paid off, and the party ended its five-year losing streak with a narrow victory in the special election. After this first test Cooke quickly made the district her own, and her subsequent election performances left no doubt she could keep her seat in the Assembly as long as she liked.

Despite her impressive history as a vote-getter and party soldier, Cooke's name did not appear on the long list of Republican hopefuls that circulated in the press after Conable announced his retirement. Nor did she immediately take herself seriously as a potential candidate: just hours after Conable's announcement, when pressed by a reporter in her office in Albany about her intentions, she recalled telling him, "I haven't even thought about it."

Cooke had in fact not thought about entering the race to succeed Conable because she had given very little thought to running for Congress in any circumstances (to the extent that she had, she had always assumed she would run in the 29th district, represented by Frank Horton). She was in fact so unaware of her own chance to go to Congress that within forty-eight hours of hearing of Conable's retirement she agreed to endorse Fred Eckert's bid to succeed him. Eckert and his campaign committee then quickly released news of her endorsement to the local media. They wanted her out of the picture before she had time to appreciate the opportunity she was ignoring.

At the time of Cooke's endorsement of Eckert she was under intense pressure from Monroe County's Republican chairman, Ron Starkweather, and the party's senate leadership in Albany to challenge a Democratic state senator, Jack Perry. For ten years the Republicans had tried vainly to defeat Perry, ever since he had rankled them by achieving the first local political upset attributable to the Watergate scandal. The state party was eager to unseat Perry because it was threatened by unexpected Democratic inroads in the State Senate, for decades a stronghold of the GOP.

To encourage Cooke to run, the Senate leadership commissioned a poll at its own expense, the results of which showed her to be a strong candidate. "I have rarely seen the kind of positive ratings she has," Starkweather said. The pollster who conducted the survey had another way of describing the results: "She could run for Congress with those numbers," he said. But Cooke's impressive personal ratings never elevated her to the status of a congressional candidate; if anything the debate over whether to run for the Senate seat, which she saw as little more than a lateral move, seems to have distracted her from the larger opportunity present in the 30th Congressional District.

By April, Cooke was having second thoughts. Surprised at the negative reaction Eckert provoked among many Republicans, stung by criticism from other women politicians for backing a man whose positions on major women's issues were so at odds with her own, and increasingly convinced that Eckert was a weaker candidate than she had initially assumed, Cooke began to consider running for Conable's seat herself. Not only was she flattered by appeals from her female colleagues to send a message to Eckert, but she also felt some responsibility as the county's most visible female officeholder to provide an alternative to him. She called him in Fiji to remind him of the conditions she had set for her initial support and told him he had not kept his promise to soften his stance on feminist issues. The matter came to a head at the press conference launching Eckert's campaign, at which a reporter asked the candidate about Cooke's wavering commitment. "The endorsement still stands," he declared, and in the next few days Cooke did nothing to contradict him.

For Cooke to rescind her endorsement would have made her look inconsistent at best and downright foolish at worst. More important, having held herself out of the race for so long, she had squandered valuable time during which she could have organized. Eckert's return from Fiji had stepped up the pressure on undeclared delegates to the convention to make a decision, and the convention itself was now less than a month away. In these circumstances Cooke would need a far more vigorous organizational effort against a two-fisted competitor like Eckert than she could possibly put together on four weeks' notice. One of the most popular politicians in the area was, as she put it, "boxed in," and as Cooke reviewed the events of the preceding few months for us she commented ruefully, "I'll probably feel bad about this for the rest of my life."

How did a six-year veteran of political wars land in such a predicament? Why did she allow herself to get "boxed in"? In large part Cooke failed to appreciate the nature of the constituency in the 30th district and comprehend how changes brought about by the reapportionment of 1982 opened the door to Washington for her and many other upstate politicians. Confused about the new district's true identity, she made her decision to back Eckert and forgo her own candidacy based on an understanding of the district that, although accurate in earlier times, had become obsolete in the 1980s.

The Old Tradition

Until New York's redistricting of 1982 destroyed several decades of tradition, Monroe County's two congressional districts manifested well-defined political profiles that were widely understood by citizen and politician alike. From the beginning of World War I, Monroe County was split north-to-south to create an eastern congressional district and a western one (see map 1). The dividing line was the Genesee River, which bisects the City of Rochester. To each half of Monroe County created by this division the state legislature traditionally added a small complement of rural counties to give each district the required population and ensure a Republican majority.

This was the configuration of Monroe County's districts for eighteen of Conable's twenty years in the House of Representatives. Until 1982 he represented the district to the west, the 35th, and from 1962 his colleague Frank Horton represented the district to the east, the 34th.

By using the river as the dividing line, the state legislature formed two politically and culturally distinct congressional districts that unambiguously conformed to the traditional habits of the area. Since the turn of the century the

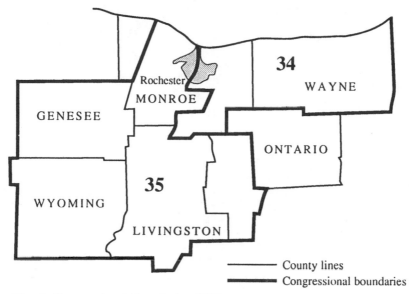

Map 1. Congressional Boundaries, 1980

east side of the river has been inhabited by the established, wealthy elements of Monroe County, the progressive political reformers and mainstream, establishment Republicans who have dominated political life in the county since the Civil War. On the west side of the river have lived the ethnic, working-class, culturally more conservative Republicans, who have provided the labor force for Rochester's basic industries.

The longstanding cultural and ideological differences between these two House districts is not immediately revealed by the data presented in table 3.1, which are of the kind normally used to analyze congressional constituencies. Registration figures, for instance, show both districts to have been solidly Republican in 1980. The registration of the old 35th district was 49 percent Republican and 31 percent Democratic, the 34th district 45 percent Republican and 32 percent Democratic. In the congressional elections of 1980 both Republican incumbents were reelected with more than 70 percent of the vote. Even the outcome of the presidential election of 1980 was similar in both districts: Jimmy Carter carried each by a slight plurality.

Despite this picture of apparent similarity, the disparity in political temperament between voters on one side of the Genesee River and those on the other was understood and called to our attention by nearly every local political leader we interviewed. Repeatedly they described the old districts in terms such as these:

"Sure, the east side is more liberal than the west side, and it's always been

Table 3.1   Party Registration and Election Returns, 1980 (in percent)

	34TH CONGRESSIONAL DISTRICT	35TH CONGRESSIONAL DISTRICT
Registration		
Democratic	33	31
Republican	45	49
Independent	21	17
Other	2	3
Vote for Congress		
Democratic	22	25
Republican	78	72[a]
Vote for president		
Carter	46	46
Reagan	44	45
Anderson	10	8

SOURCE: Monroe County Board of Elections.
[a]Includes votes on Conservative line.

that way. And the east has always been represented by a liberal, too. Even Democrats have occasionally captured Horton's old seat," we were told by a longtime observer of politics in Monroe County.

No one better understood the different politics of Monroe County's two districts than the congressmen who served in them for the twenty years before the lines were redrawn. During that time Horton established one of the most liberal records among Republicans in the House of Representatives and was regularly endorsed by organized labor in Monroe County. In 1982 the AFL-CIO's Committee on Political Education (COPE) judged him to have voted in agreement with their positions 66 percent of the time, whereas the U.S. Chamber of Commerce (CCUS) gave him a rating of 35 percent; the American Civil Liberties Union (ACLU) gave him a rating of 58. By every measure shown in table 3.2, Horton reflected the moderate, progressive tradition of his constituency east of the Genesee River.

These same measures tell a different story about Conable. In 1982 Conable supported the positions of the Chamber of Commerce more than four times as often as those of organized labor. That same year the *National Journal* gave Conable a conservative rating of 61 percent on economic issues, while it gave Horton a liberal rating of 55 percent. His voting record resembled Horton's only with respect to what the *National Journal* categorized as cultural issues, such as the Equal Rights Amendment and abortion, on which Conable's strong commitment to individual liberties was evident.

The predilections of east and west for lawmakers of decidedly different

Table 3.2   Monroe County's Two Traditions of Representation (Ratings by Interest Groups, in Percent, 1982)

	HORTON 34TH CONGRESSIONAL DISTRICT	CONABLE 35TH CONGRESSIONAL DISTRICT
Americans for Democratic Action	50	25
American Civil Liberties Union	58	25
Committee on Political Education, AFL-CIO	66	16
Chamber of Commerce of the United States	35	70
National Journal		
Economic rating		
Liberal	55	38
Conservative	45	61
Cultural rating		
Liberal	58	61
Conscrvative	42	39

SOURCE: Michael J. Barone and Grant Ujifusa, *Almanac of American Politics, 1984* (Washington, D.C.: National Journal, 1983), pp. 852–855.

views showed up most vividly in the election of 1980 for the U.S. Senate. A divisive Republican primary pitted the liberal incumbent, Jacob Javits, who at the age of seventy-six was seeking a fifth term, against a staunchly conservative challenger, Alfonse D'Amato, who gained a decisive, upset victory and went on to win the general election. The clear ideological differences between Javits and D'Amato made the results of the primary revealing. This may be seen from the results from Monroe County shown in table 3.3: in the eastern congressional district, which is liberal, D'Amato won by 6 percent, whereas in the more conservative, working-class, western district he won by 22 percent.

Although defeated in the primary, Javits ran in the general election as the nominee of the Liberal party. Thus D'Amato was pitted against two quintessential liberals, the aging incumbent senator and the Democratic nominee, Congresswoman Elizabeth Holtzman. This three-way contest showed the voters' ideological proclivities as clearly as had the primary. In the 35th district D'Amato won a clear majority of the vote, but in the 34th he won only by a plurality, as the liberal candidates together claimed 54 percent of the vote.

For roughly three-quarters of a century these two very different political cultures had given Monroe County's congressional districts a well-understood electoral tradition. For just as long, upstate politicians like Pinny Cooke had used these traditional identities to gauge how well they fit the local political profile and estimate their chances of success in a congressional campaign. But after the reapportionment of 1982 these old reliable political cues were suddenly gone.

Table 3.3   Two Political Cultures in Monroe County: U.S. Senate Election, 1980

	34TH CONGRESSIONAL DISTRICT		35TH CONGRESSIONAL DISTRICT	
	Number	Percentage	Number	Percentage
Republican primary				
D'Amato	7,084	53	4,420	61
Javits	6,403	47	2,811	39
General election				
D'Amato	74,372	46	64,191	52
Holtzman	65,686	41	47,509	38
Javits	20,963	13	12,792	10

SOURCE: Monroe County Board of Elections.

Confusion Out of Certainty

Instead of continuing the two congressional cultures of which upstate politicians had such a solid intuitive understanding, the reapportionment of 1982 caused muddle and widespread confusion. Perhaps state lawmakers had no choice other than to break so completely with their past districting practices: partisan politics, federal law, and the census of 1980 combined to undermine the established upstate tradition. Whatever the reasons, when the reapportionment was completed Monroe County's congressional tradition, which had lasted for decades, was ended.

The break with the past began with the census of 1980, which cost New York five seats, reducing the number in its delegation to thirty-four. As a result the state legislature in Albany, which is charged with drawing the boundaries of congressional districts, sought to mollify the most powerful political interests: the federal courts and the senior House members of both parties. Because the Democrats controlled the state Assembly and the Republicans the state Senate, neither party could draw the new district lines solely at the expense of the other. A compromise was required, the outcome of which was quite predictable: the seats to be eliminated would be those of the junior congressmen. Senior members—Conable, Horton, Jack Kemp, LaFalce—would be protected.

Accomplishing this would shatter the traditional arrangement in upstate New York, however. Conable would have to cede to Kemp much of the outlying rural area to the west of the Genesee River in which he considered himself most at home politically, while scavenging Republicans from Horton to the east. At the same time, for the benefit of LaFalce he shed some Democrats from the city and a neighboring blue-collar suburb. Other considerations that once entered the process of designing districts—accepted local traditions and existing politi-

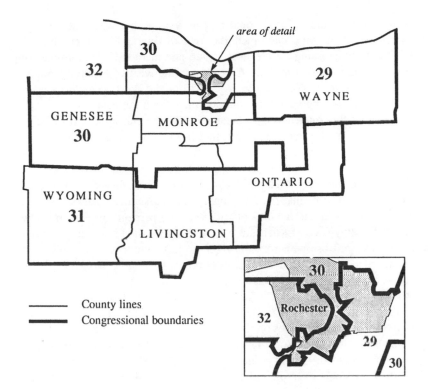

Map 2. Broken Tradition: New Congressional Boundaries, 1982

cal jurisdictions—were pushed aside to create three new constituencies in Monroe County: the 29th, the 30th, and the 32nd, each safely secured for its incumbent and each dutifully drawn to the Supreme Court's specification of "one man, one vote" (see map 2).

In this new configuration at least one part of the old tradition remained: Republicans continued to parcel out Rochester's Democrats so that they were not the core constituency of any one of the three new districts. Once again the City of Rochester, with a population of nearly 250,000, was deprived of clear-cut representation in Congress, just as the Democratic party was denied a safe seat.

In every other way the new districts were marked by radical change. The most apparent for the 30th district was that the rural counties that had always been a major part of the constituency were now a minor one. As noted in chapter 2 the outlying areas made up less than 20 percent of Conable's new district, and only Genesee County remained intact. But the lines of the new

30th district violated the old traditional map in yet another way, one perhaps even more important: they combined the two distinct political cultures of Monroe County by crossing the Genesee River, and included large numbers of residents (though not all) from both the east and the west of Monroe County. The more conventional, conservative voters from the west were thrown together with the more liberal, reform-minded ones from the east.

As a result of this maneuvering Conable's 30th district appeared to be as safely Republican as the traditional 35th had been; some thought it was even more so. Registration figures in the new district showed 46 percent of the voters to be Republicans—nearly the same proportion as in the old district. And by excluding most of the central city's blacks from the 30th district and placing them in the 32nd district that bordered on it, the legislature ensured that the proportion of Democrats in the new district was two percent lower than in the old district. The tiny slice of Rochester's core that remained in the new district was just a makeshift bridge across the river to tie together the two halves. It came as no surprise that after the reapportionment Conable won handily in 1982, by about the same margin as in 1980.

Nevertheless local politicians were usually at a loss to explain the political complexion of the new district. Some said the new district was better for Democrats because progressives on the east side were more hospitable to Democrats than were the more socially conservative rural Republicans that had formerly been included. Others pointed to the decline in Democratic registration and the east side's overwhelming support for Horton and his Republican predecessors, and concluded that the 30th was more solidly Republican than the old 35th. These two descriptions were typical of the opposite points of view we so frequently heard:

"The new district is more Republican. The old west-side voters now in the 32nd District were registered as Republicans, but they voted Democratic."

"The east-side Republicans are potential Democratic voters. Having voted for a liberal Republican for so long, it will make it easier for them to vote Democratic."

Even Conable felt some uncertainty about how to deal with his new district, at least with respect to the part east of the river. Talking to us one afternoon after he had announced his retirement, he commented that he was to give a speech that evening to an east-side Republican town committee. "I don't know what to say to these people," he said. "I've never represented upper-middle-class people before." Obviously there was a bit of hyperbole in his remark, and reports on the speech he delivered that evening were unanimous in their praise. But Conable did evidence some uneasiness about representing the other side of the river. He was not at home there, this was not his natural territory, and his remark to us expressed real doubt about how to present himself to an unfamiliar constituency.[1] To some extent this highly experienced congressman was just as confused about how to approach his new district as were his less experienced local colleagues.

It is now much easier to understand why Pinny Cooke misjudged her opportunity to run for Congress: she based her calculations about the race on the old district's tradition, not the new, reapportioned reality. She saw herself as an east-side politician who had no convincing claim to Conable's west-side seat, as a liberal who would be out of step with the natural conservatism in Conable's rural district. Further, she was a resident of the Town of Brighton, one of only four of Monroe County's communities excluded from the 30th Congressional District, and she therefore thought herself ineligible to run. When all these misperceptions were combined Cooke simply saw no hope for a serious congressional candidacy in 1984. As she told us in early May, "I didn't think about running, because I didn't know I could."

The Suburban Shuffle

Not all the uncertainty that bedeviled politicians from upstate New York contemplating a run for Conable's seat can be attributed to the redrawing of the district boundaries and the consequent loss of an established tradition. Another force created political uncertainty: the extraordinary mobility of the American people. After all it was massive population shifts that provoked the reapportionment in the first place.

Like the rest of the United States, Monroe County and its environs underwent substantial changes in population between the census of 1960, which affected Conable's arrival in Congress, and the census of 1980, which affected Eckert's. During these two decades the population of Monroe County increased by more than 100,000, or roughly 20 percent. As was the case elsewhere in the country, the growth was in the suburbs; the city's population declined markedly, as shown in table 3.4.

Clearly these demographic changes obscured Monroe County's political identity and made it difficult for a politician to interpret the new electoral environment by using old political facts. No doubt these changes contributed to the decline of the local Republican party, the increasing strength of the Democrats, and the growing ranks of the politically unaffiliated. These in turn created the volatility among voters that for more than a decade had affected the rules governing politics in Monroe County.

1. This sense of "at homeness" is dealt with in Richard F. Fenno, Jr., *Home Style: House Members in their Districts* (Boston: Little, Brown, 1978), pp. 21–24.

Table 3.4   Demographic Change in Monroe County

	1960	1970		1980	
		Number	Percent change	Number	Percent change
City of Rochester	318,611	296,233	−7.6	241,741	−18.4
Suburbs	267,776	415,684	+55.2	460,497	+10.8
Total, Monroe County	586,387	711,917	+21.4	702,238	−1.4

SOURCE: Monroe County Board of Elections.

No politician needed the census data to see that the area was changing. As an established party leader told us, "When we campaigned in the county legislative race, we went door-to-door to every house in the town. The campaigns were every two years, and I think about half of the people were new to the district each election." State Senator Perry made a similar point about the changes in his legislative constituency. Noting that his state Senate district had once included the Town of Perinton, now in the 30th Congressional District, Perry observed, "I carried that area with 52 percent of the vote in 1980, but you know there are so many condominiums there I wonder if any of my old constituents are even left." Like the rest of the United States, Monroe County was constantly on the move, and increasingly the only trait that its residents shared was that they had come from somewhere else.

Statistics compiled by the Monroe County Board of Elections make this point with startling clarity (see table 3.5). Nearly one-third of the county's voters in the election of 1984 had first registered at their current address after 1980, and only 13.7 percent had lived at the same address since before 1960. Not all these new registrations were coming from voters who had previously resided in other parts of the nation or in entirely different political environments: much of the migration occurred within Rochester's metropolitan area. But a considerable proportion of the turnover in Monroe County could be attributed to professionals employed in such high-technology firms as Xerox, Eastman Kodak, and Bausch & Lomb, who were highly mobile. In any event the figures make clear the unsettled quality of the local electorate.

Such turmoil does not lend itself to the clear definition of a political identity. This and the disarray brought about by reapportionment make it easy to see why some politicians might be deceived about the true nature of the 30th district. It is just as easy to see that where such uncertainty does reign many politicians will not be prepared for the daunting task of figuring out a workable campaign strategy.

Had Assemblywoman Cooke done so, she would have concluded that despite what she had at first thought, the mobility of the local citizens, the loss of

Table 3.5   Length of Residence at Current Voting Address, Monroe County, 1984

YEARS AT CURRENT ADDRESS	PERCENTAGE
24 or more	13.7
20–23	4.7
16–19	6.8
12–15	7.0
8–11	10.8
4–7	25.2
3 or less	31.8
	100.0

SOURCE: Monroe County Board of Elections.

political tradition in Monroe County, and the residency requirement for members of Congress were not genuine barriers to a serious bid for Conable's seat. None of these factors made her ineligible to run, and some created more opportunities than problems.

In the first place, the Constitution has never required House members to live in the district they represent, although this has usually been their custom; they are required only to maintain residence in the state they serve. But as Americans have become more mobile and congressional boundaries more arbitrary, even the convention of living in the district has lost its force, especially in circumstances similar to those of the 30th district. Of course a genuine outsider or someone who has long been absent from the district may not be acceptable as a candidate, and at least one potential contender for Conable's seat was ruled out by party leaders for just this reason, but finer distinctions about residency have regularly been ignored in the suburbanized environment of the 30th Congressional District. "Everyone knows that what district you live in is an accident," noted one Democrat. "There's no rhyme or reason to it, so what difference does a few blocks make, one way or the other?" Surely this was the case with Cooke. Her home was but a mile from the new line separating the 30th district from the 29th, and she had represented the 30th district's second largest town in the Assembly for six years. Also, her many years of community service gave her contacts far beyond the borders of Brighton. Clearly, Pinny Cooke was no carpetbagger.

Furthermore, the mobility of the area and the political uncertainty hanging over it gave Cooke a real opportunity to redefine the district's political personality to her own liking, using the east side of the river as her base. But the power of old traditions blinded her to the possibilities created by changing conditions.

Having missed her chance to contest the vacant seat in the 30th Congressional District, Cooke will not have a similar opportunity in the neighboring 29th, where she initially thought her political future lay. By the time the present incumbent, Frank Horton, retires, Cooke will be too old to claim his seat. Nearing her sixtieth birthday in the spring of 1984, she could not expect to match Horton's service of more than twenty years. And local Republicans, who are well aware of the importance of seniority in Congress and stressed repeatedly in our interviews that a representative should make a long-term investment in a congressional career, would find it difficult to back Cooke, because of her age. Equally important, the same reapportionment that made the 30th district accessible to a progressive Republican like Cooke also changed the philosophical complexion of the 29th district by adding to it many rural and small-town voters from several very sparsely populated outlying counties. In the primary of 1984, the magnitude of this change was visible for the first time as a little-known, quite conservative Republican challenger received 38 percent of the vote running against Horton. Clearly Cooke would have a far more difficult time getting elected in Horton's new district than she would have had in Conable's new one.

This is not to say that Cooke would have won either the party's designation for Conable's seat at the convention or its primary in September, because she had many political liabilities as a candidate that offset her strong personal appeal. The party's leaders in Monroe County thought Eckert the stronger candidate and did not encourage Cooke at any time to aim higher than the state Senate. In addition her reputation among business interests was shaky enough to raise doubts about her ability to raise money from the usual Republican contributors. (The eventual endorsement by the Chamber of Commerce of Cooke's Democratic opponent in her race for the Assembly in 1984 was viewed as a sign of displeasure by businesses over her handling of an economic development measure before the assembly.) Finally, as a congressional contender Cooke would have to confront the doubts voiced among party activists that she was a political lightweight—superb at constituent relations, but not strong enough on the substance of issues. To some extent this was an inevitable consequence of her political style and part of her appeal as an alternative to Eckert's abrasiveness, but Cooke herself sometimes contributed to the perception that she was not tough-minded enough for the rough-and-tumble of politics in Washington. Doubts such as these were reinforced when she addressed twelve hundred Republican delegates on the first night of the party's county convention in 1984 to second the nomination of the woman the leadership had chosen to run against Jack Perry after Cooke had rejected the offer. After enumerating the qualities of the party's choice she reflected on how "marvelous" it would be to have another Republican woman as a companion in the state legislature. Then, before her astonished, embarrassed colleagues, she burst into tears.

The point of Pinny Cooke's story is not that she was the most likely successor to Barber Conable but that she misunderstood her only chance to go to Congress, if indeed she wanted to go. By underestimating her own pivotal position in the new politics of the area, she failed to exert any real political leverage on Fred Eckert, and this failure also altered the political possibilities for other politicians in Monroe County.

Calculations from Experience

A congressional district with new boundaries, an uncertain tradition, and a transient population left those aspiring to succeed Conable with one last means of understanding the local political picture: they could use the knowledge they had gained from representing parts of the 30th district while they held other offices. If their political base inside the district was large enough, their own experience with the voters could overcome the uncertainty surrounding the new district's political predispositions and at the same time give them a strong electoral foundation from which to mount campaigns in the primary and general elections.

In most cases, however, the political base known from personal experience was too small to be of much help. Of all those who seriously considered running to succeed Conable not one had first-hand knowledge of even half the district. Fred Eckert's old state Senate district, which included about 35 percent of the new congressional district, was the largest base from which to wage a campaign, and even that was considerably larger than those of his most serious opponents. Most of them had political bases that ranged from 10 to 20 percent of the 30th district.

Table 3.6 shows the overlap between the 30th district and other districts, and thus the size of the political bases on which various officeholders could presumably rely. The data reveal how little personal exposure local politicians had and how much of the congressional district was unknown territory. For instance, if they held a countywide office in one of the rural counties, they probably knew less than 10 percent of the 30th district first-hand. If they served on the Rochester City Council or in the Monroe County Legislature and their districts shared at least some real estate with the 30th district, the overlap was probably considerably less than 10 percent. State Assembly incumbents fared a bit better, with a little more than 10 percent of the 30th district in their political base. State senators were in the best position: they had direct experience of almost 20 percent of the 30th district.

In the twenty years since Barber Conable had left the state Senate and gone to Congress, reapportionment and demographic trends had weakened the link between state lawmakers and congressional districts. New York's declining

Table 3.6 Overlap between 30th Congressional District and Other Districts

	OVERLAP WITH 30TH CONGRESSIONAL DISTRICT (IN PERCENT)	
	Average	Range
Monroe County offices (16)	80	80
Offices in 3 rural counties (28)	7	3–10
State Senate seats (3)	17	.5–35
State Assembly seats (9)	11	3–23
Rochester City Council seats (9)	10	1–16
Monroe County Legislature seats (21)	4	.7–6
Town supervisor offices and mayoralties in Monroe County towns (15)	5	.7–17

SOURCE: Boards of elections of Monroe, Genesee, Ontario, and Livingston counties.

population had cost the state seven seats in Congress, and the average congressional district had grown in size from 432,000 to 515,000. At the same time the number of seats in the state legislature remained constant. The mathematics of these divergent patterns were simple: in 1964, a state Senator in New York might represent as much as 71 percent of a congressional district (although none did), but in 1984 this figure fell to 56 percent. The portion of a congressional district that could lie within a state Assembly district fell during the same period from 27 percent to 23 percent.

Only one group of elected officials had a broad, secure political base within the 30th Congressional District: the sixteen persons elected to county positions in Monroe County, which contained 80 percent of the congressional district.

For reasons peculiar to Monroe County and to the individuals involved, not one of these sixteen made any effort to seek Conable's seat. In the first place, twelve of the sixteen were judges in state courts, and in New York judges do not usually run for Congress. Not one member of the state's current congressional delegation has judicial experience, and our inquiries about why this was so brought looks of incredulity: with salaries of more than $90,000 in 1984 and lengthy terms between elections, judges are thought to be a very different breed of political animal.

The other four—the county executive, the county clerk, the district attorney, and the sheriff—might all have been expected to be serious contenders. All but the sheriff were mentioned as possible successors to Conable, and many observers believed that the county executive, Lou Morin, would have been the most formidable Republican candidate. Besides Conable, he was the only person widely thought to be a sure winner in the 30th district. None of the four showed any real interest in the race, however. In fact, within forty-eight hours of Conable's announcement, Morin had called a press conference to endorse Eckert.

At the age of sixty-three, Morin was at the end of his political career and had no desire to go to Washington. Before his bid in 1983 for county executive he had in fact announced his retirement. At the time he was already serving as Monroe's county manager, an appointive post he had held for more than a decade. During this period it was a weak office filled by a vote of the county legislature and defined by the progressive council-manager system of reform government, which has deep roots in local politics. In 1983, however, the office was reconstituted: its authority was expanded and made more independent of the county legislature. As part of the change, the county executive was to be chosen by countywide election. Only after party leaders made a highly publicized pilgrimage to Florida to urge Morin to run did he do so. He won the election in a landslide and in 1984 remained an extraordinarily popular political figure. But he had no further political ambitions.

The county clerk, Pat Adduci, a Democrat, had no interest in the post either. Up for reelection in 1984, she hoped to win an impressive victory that would put her in a commanding position to run for county executive in 1987, when Morin was sure to retire. Unlike Morin, whose political ambition was waning, hers was growing, but her outlet for it was not a seat in Congress.[2] (Not long after her solid reelection as county clerk Governor Cuomo appointed her commissioner of motor vehicles, a job that paid $75,000 a year.)

The district attorney, Howard Relin, had no previous experience in office before his successful campaign in 1983. As a Democrat he had waged one of the most expensive political campaigns ever conducted in Monroe County and staged a major upset in capturing the district attorney's office. He was firmly wedded to the law, however, and showed little inclination to go to Washington and sit in Congress.

Once the potential challengers who had substantial political bases were out of the picture, almost anyone could have made a rational decision to run for Congress in New York's 30th district. But because the district's image was clouded it would take time and careful reflection to appreciate the wide-open electoral possibilities.

Why Polls Don't Help

Modern social science would appear to hold the perfect remedy for decision making in a district nobody understands: the public opinion poll. A small sample of voters interviewed with modern survey techniques could profile the attitudes and habits of the unknown voters and give quick, scientific definition to any district where tradition and experience were not good guides. But in no

2. In the election of November 1984 Adduci won a smashing victory in a hard-fought campaign with more than 62 percent of the votes cast and defeated her nearest rival by a margin of 60,000.

case did public opinion surveys influence the decisions of either the unseen candidates or the declared ones as they weighed running in New York's 30th Congressional District. Local politicians instead relied on their instincts, their personal advisers, and the flow of rumor and intelligence that circulated among local activists in both parties.

Nevertheless, opinion polls are a staple of contemporary congressional campaigns (especially those for open seats, where 80 percent of the candidates report using them), and the contest in the 30th district was no exception.[3] Both party nominees eventually employed professional polls during the campaign proper, and the data they obtained about voters' concerns were a necessary, legitimate part of their election effort, particularly when it came to raising money, as we shall see in a later chapter.

The value of polling in the period of decision making that preceded the campaign was, however, negligible. Most of the politicians we interviewed stated flatly in response to our inquiries that a poll would not be at all necessary to their deliberations, because they were focusing on the personal aspects of making the race. Did they have the stomach for a tough election? Did they have the external resources, both financial and organizational? Should they impose on their families the costs of being a House member? Would government decision making be more rewarding in Washington than in Rochester and Albany? Did they want the increased visibility and pressure of life in Washington? Answers to these questions did not depend on surveys.

Moreover, for all but the few prospective candidates who held countywide offices or very visible positions in the state legislature, the most glaring finding of any opinion poll would be a fact they already knew: they were not well-known to voters in the 30th district. Given the jumbled pattern of jurisdictions in the district, it was clear that few local politicians considering the race would be well-known to large numbers of constituents; at the same time the district's advantageous position with respect to the media markets meant that a candidate could overcome his or her lack of recognition through advertising. Knowing precisely how well-known they were was therefore far less important to prospective candidates than whether they could put together the resources to become better-known. In other constituencies across the country that lack Monroe County's accessible media outlets, the need for accurate estimates of name recognition might create greater demand for opinion polls in the early stages of recruitment, but in Conable's district these concerns were not important enough to justify the expense.

It is the high cost of professional polls that rules out their use by most potential candidates. A telephone survey of four hundred respondents costs

3. Edie N. Goldenberg and Michael W. Traugott, *Campaigning for Congress* (Washington, D.C.: C Q Press, 1984), p. 55.

about $7,500 to $10,000 to design, implement, and analyze. The funds for such an investment generally come from the national parties, PACs, or the prospective candidates themselves, and anyone who can attract this much money from outside sources or is willing to spend it is already well along the road to becoming a declared candidate.

The same uncertainty about the 30th Congressional District that prevented politicians like Pinny Cooke from seeing themselves as potential candidates to begin with also prevented them from commissioning polls to help them reach a decision; without a clear sense of the constituency initially they never progressed to the strategic stage at which a poll might prove useful. Even if Pinny Cooke had commissioned a poll the numbers would not have spoken for themselves; they would have required interpretation, and Cooke's uncertain, even inaccurate, view of the district would have left her with an equally uncertain, inaccurate view of the poll's findings.

Ultimately a poll is more a statement of intent by a politician, a sign that he or she is already planning a campaign and raising the necessary money, than a tool to help the politician decide whether to run in the first place. Of the two polls of which we are aware that were conducted in Monroe County in the spring, one was commissioned by Town Supervisor Don Riley of Greece, who eventually became a declared candidate at the Republican convention, the other for Louise Slaughter, a state assemblywoman who was the most likely Democratic nominee until she pulled out of the race in mid-June. We shall have more to say about both these politicians in later chapters. For now suffice it to say that neither relied on a costly poll to decide whether or not to run. Slaughter withdrew before she had even seen the results of the poll, and Riley depended on personal contacts within his party for his most trusted political intelligence. In each case the decision ultimately depended on calculations about what other prospective candidates were doing and how much support the candidate could muster among political elites—public officials, party activists, financial contributors, and various interest groups. Mass attitudes and mass appeal played a very small role.

Uncertainty's Impact

If one were to judge New York's 30th Congressional District solely on the basis of its demographic data, one would have difficulty finding a constituency that seemed more predictable. Having Rochester at its hub, 80 percent of its population in a single county, a largely white, middle-class population, and decidedly Republican propensities, could there be any doubts about the political complexion of this upstate area? Nevertheless the politicians who observed the 30th Congressional District day-to-day and even the veteran House member who represented it in Congress found its character puzzling. The district had lost its identity when the state legislature cast aside its traditional boundaries and cultural dividing lines, and no new identity had emerged because the mobility of local residents and the confusing pattern of political jurisdictions inside the district's borders inhibited any quick redefinition of its personality. When the 30th district ceased to be "Mr. Conable's district," it simply became no one's, or everyone's, and local people were not sure which.

This uncertainty about the district's character led to confusion over who had rightful claims to be the area's next member of Congress, which caused many local politicians to miss a genuine opportunity to go to Washington. Pinny Cooke, for example, initially assumed that the old distinction between east and west still mattered in the district, learned too late that it did not, and ultimately lost her chance to challenge the front-runner, Fred Eckert. Cooke was not alone in failing to understand how things had changed in the new district. Another state legislator, Jim Nagle, was slow to recognize that his southeastern constituency was now a solid base from which to fight for the Republican nomination. Because Nagle, like Cooke, was on the wrong side of the river according to the old tradition, he did not think seriously about running, as we shall see in the next chapter, until he had spoken to Conable, who told him: "You know, Jim, if you look at the map you have as much claim to this district as anyone else."

Eventually the interesting possibilities created by the reapportionment of 1982 became reasonably clear to activists in both parties as they talked and speculated. As they deliberated, some local politicians eventually saw themselves fitting the district's ambiguous profile. But all this sorting and thinking took time, and soon the filing deadline in mid-June for candidates, which had been fourteen weeks off at the time of Conable's announcement in February, seemed imminent. Valuable time had passed, and Eckert, who had known what he wanted from the outset of the campaign in February, had been working while others engaged in speculation and soul-searching.

Eckert used to his benefit the uncertainty that worked to everyone else's disadvantage. His highly focused ambition to serve in Congress meant that he could turn his attention immediately to the strategic aspects of the race—setting up a campaign organization, reserving advertising time for the primary, and rounding up endorsements—without puzzling over whether he should run. He could begin to assess the risks of the election itself because he had already grappled with the district's new identity and come to grips with its unknown quantities. In 1982 he had even used money left over from his last State Senate campaign to poll what would later be his constituency. "Fred has a good sense of where the people he has represented before are, and on the east side, he doesn't seem worried," commented a former aide in the state Senate. "We did a general, countywide poll two years previously, and it confirmed what we already thought, so doing one at this stage would be a waste of money." When it was also taken into account that Eckert had represented a larger portion than any of his potential rivals of Conable's district, it was little wonder that he felt relatively secure about his sense of the district.

One elected official who might have approached the 30th district with the same confidence as Eckert was his successor in the state Senate, William Steinfeldt. But Steinfeldt was no threat. If he had been as ambitious, as smart, and as competitive as the man he replaced, an ambassador trying to run for Congress from Fiji would have been seriously handicapped by the very boundaries that actually proved so beneficial. But by good fortune, which he seemed to have in abundance, Eckert's old state legislative seat had been put in the hands of an aging curmudgeon, who antagonized so many voters during his brief tenure in Albany that he lost his solidly Republican sinecure in the election of 1984.

The general confusion about the nature of the 30th district also presented several tactical advantages to Eckert. First, he profited from the old preconception about the district: that it belonged to a conservative from the west side of the Genesee River. Eckert was both of these, and therefore fit the image that still lingered in most people's minds.

In addition, the confusion created by the district's new boundaries strengthened the publicity campaign launched by Eckert after Conable's announcement. By projecting himself so strongly into the race from the very start, he hoped to create an atmosphere of invincibility that few would be inclined to challenge, and he was extraordinarily successful with this ploy. In the first few weeks of March we noticed a widespread consensus in both political parties that Eckert was a sure winner. Only later did people begin to appreciate that few of his endorsements were from politicians in the district, and that a sizable group had begun to form within the party hoping to deny Eckert the nomination. As one experienced campaign organizer put it in April, "There's a coalition of the disaffected all waiting for someone to give them a foxhole to jump into . . . but whoever does it has to get out there early and take advantage of access to the delegates before Eckert gets home." But no one did; uncertainty about the district and the strength of Eckert's opening charge paralyzed the opposition.

Pinny Cooke illustrates this well. She could have been the spoiler in Eckert's carefully orchestrated long-distance campaign had she not taken herself out of the race so early. Women in the party felt they had a genuine grievance against Republican leaders for their early alignment with Eckert. They were angry that they had not been consulted about a man so many found so unacceptable, and affronted that no woman had even been included on the lists of prospective Republican candidates that Starkweather had circulated in the press after Conable's announcement. This kind of intense feeling among a small number of political activists can prove exceedingly potent in a primary election with a low turnout, and could have served well a candidacy by Cooke. Also, the most likely immediate result of her candidacy would have been to bring other candidates into the race. As noted earlier, Assemblyman Steve Hawley needed a primary to split Monroe County's vote and overcome the disadvantage of his small base in Genesee County. Other Republican politicians were hoping for a primary as well: none wanted to compete one-on-one against Eckert. But in a race involving three or four candidates, Assemblyman Jim Nagle, Town Supervisor Don Riley of Greece, and one or two others might have taken the plunge. Thus Cooke's misunderstanding about the district's true identity had effects far beyond her own career and greatly advanced that of Fred Eckert by altering the calculations of some of his most formidable opponents.

In the muddled political circumstances of the 30th Congressional District, Eckert was helped in one last way. The whole of Eckert's public career had been dedicated to the conservative political cause. As the undisputed champion of the right wing in Monroe County, Eckert had two added strengths in an uncertain political environment. First, he had a clear image and high name recognition; he was known, and most of his potential challengers were not. Second, Eckert had a small but dedicated group of activists on whom he could call for support, and in a district with no clearly defined political center, a candidate with an intense coalition, albeit a minority one, has an advantage.

The kind of confusion that prevailed in New York's 30th district and helped Fred Eckert succeed Barber Conable also has implications for the recruitment of candidates in congressional districts in other parts of the country. In similarly muddled constituencies it appears that potential contestants have a good deal of leeway to pursue a congressional seat, because it is up to them to redefine the district on the retirement of an incumbent. When a district lacks a clear identity, any number of new "owners" can fill the void suddenly created, and such a district is therefore potentially quite competitive—even more than its demographic profile may suggest. A district known only by the name of its current occupant can just as easily bear anyone else's name: there is no other easy way to describe it, and little else to hold it together.

The confusing political amalgamations that pass for congressional districts in the 1980s can throw an additional obstacle in the path of aspiring House members by adding one more dimension of risk to the already uncertain business of running for office. In such a setting one type of politician seems more likely than others to profit. Those whose ambition is intensely focused on a House career are clearly favored because, undeterred by uncertainty, they can act swiftly to create momentum for their candidacies. In addition it appears that more ideological politicians, ones with a mission and a message, can more easily impose their stamp on politically ambiguous territories. Where all is muddle and murkiness, they can count on the support of a hard core of enthusiasts to contest a primary successfully and quickly define the district's political center of gravity.

Finally, in a district where traditions have vanished, there is no substitute for direct electoral experience with the voters in estimating the nature of the unknown. Having held office is of course invaluable in any district because of the name recognition and campaign organization that an officeholder obtains. But in an uncertain district a direct link with voters is even more vital, because other types of political indicator are open to question. It is not the experience per se that increases the confidence of a candidate thinking about a congressional run, although it is clearly important; rather it is the overlap of past and present electorates that is a reliable, comforting predictor of voters' preferences in the larger district. Yet we have seen that as political jurisdictions among the different levels of government grow more disparate, this indicator becomes less available in the early stages of recruitment. In the end, uncertainty about a district presents as many barriers to competition as it does opportunities.

4

State Lawmakers:
A Tale of Two Cities

The representatives of each state . . . will probably in all cases have been members, and may even at the very time be members, of the state legislature.

—The Federalist, *no. 56*

The State legislator must be made more happy in his career. . . . The key to rehabilitation of the [state] legislative branch is in the legislator's job and his attitude toward it.

—*Charles S. Hyneman*

Many members of Congress prepare for their careers in the House of Representatives with an apprenticeship in their state legislature. This was the path to Washington taken by Barber Conable in 1964, by his Democratic colleague in the 31st district in 1974, by nearly a majority of Conable's fellow New Yorkers serving in the House at the time he retired, and by roughly half of the House's total membership.[1] But in 1984 not one sitting member of New York State's legislature entered the race to replace Conable. The reason for this unexpected turn of events lies in a modern tale of two cities—a story of the changing distribution of power and perquisites between a highly professionalized state legislature in Albany and an increasingly fragmented, overburdened Congress in Washington.

State legislative experience is valuable to those who aspire to national office, because lawmakers in the state capital learn to deal with complex issues, bargain, and tend a constituency.[2] They also hone their campaign techniques and build their local name recognition.[3] This experience provides a valuable

1. Michael J. Barone and Grant Ujifusa, *Almanac of American Politics, 1984* (Washington, D.C.: National Journal, 1983).
2. The idea of the legislature as a school in which lawmakers learn a craft is explored by William K. Muir in *Legislature: California's School for Politics* (Chicago: University of Chicago Press, 1982).
3. For discussion of how campaigns enable politicians to become skilled at communicating and organizing see Marjorie Random Hershey, *Running for Office: The Practical Education of Campaigners* (Chatham, N.J.: Chatham House, 1984).

head start in a congressional race, which is why observers of House elections often classify as competitive races those in which a state legislator runs.[4] In the view of one national party official, "A state legislator is, by definition, a good candidate."

This is particularly true in a complex political environment such as New York, where the state Assembly and Senate are model preparatory schools for prospective members of the House of Representatives. "My friends in the Assembly all read the *Congressional Record*," noted one freshman Republican from a rural, upstate county. "They think of themselves as congressmen-in-training." A state senator voiced similar sentiments: "It's a logical sequence. I started out thirteen years ago in the county legislature, and after five terms in the Senate, it is the obvious next step." Another member of the legislature said: "Everyone knows I have had my eye on that seat." Eckert too shared the view of the state legislature as a place to serve an apprenticeship for a congressional career. "Even while I was leaving the [state] Senate," he recalled, "I knew that eventually I would go on to Congress."

These perceptions about the appropriate path to Congress pervaded our early interviews with party leaders and other insiders, and they dominated the local media as well. Before the news of Barber Conable's vacant seat was an hour old, members of the press had descended upon the state delegation in Albany hunting for candidates. One member, Pinny Cooke, learned of Conable's announcement when a reporter burst into her office demanding to know if she would run. Another Democratic lawmaker recalled with some exasperation, "I kept saying no, but the reporters never stopped asking. They just couldn't believe I meant it."

On everybody's early lists of possible Republican candidates from the state legislature were the assemblymen Steve Hawley and Jim Nagle, and Assemblywoman Cooke. Hawley and Cooke, as we have seen, were not active candidates for very long, but Nagle gave serious consideration to making the race until early May. The potential Democratic contestants included state Senator Jack Perry, Assemblyman Roger Robach, and Assemblywoman Louise Slaughter. Of these, Robach refused even to consider the idea of running, while both Perry and Slaughter engaged in serious deliberations about seeking their party's nomination before dropping out during the spring recruiting season. The four remaining state lawmakers who represented parts of Monroe County were not a factor in the preliminary discussions: one was too old, another lived outside the district in a neighboring county and had been connected with local politics only since the reapportionment of 1982, and the remaining two represented constituencies in the inner city.

4. William R. Bianco, "Strategic Decisions on Candidacy in U.S. Congressional Districts," *Legislative Studies Quarterly* 9 (May 1984): 351–364; Bruce W. Robeck, "State Legislator Candidacies for the U.S. House," *Legislative Studies Quarterly* 7 (November 1982): 507–514.

Almost any of these state legislators would have been a strong candidate, but none stepped forward to contest the nomination. Some considered a candidacy only briefly; others deliberated for months. Yet whether the decision not to run was easy or difficult—and for some it was even painful—it centered on one fundamental calculation: a seat in the state legislature was too desirable to risk for the uncertain benefits of a career in Washington. The incentives that in the past had drawn so many lawmakers to Washington were no longer as compelling as the reasons for staying home. Intrigued by the idea of replacing Conable, these seasoned politicians recognized that a career in the House held out the promise of greater influence and prestige over the long run, but were not willing to risk their present posts in the short run. As one lawmaker commented early in March, "None of us wants to give up what we have."

Their decisions to remain in Albany meant that Eckert's strongest potential rivals in both parties voluntarily took themselves out of the running. This was the chief reason why the race in the 30th district never heated up as anticipated. But their failure to seek Conable's seat in the House did more than dampen electoral competition; it also raised an interesting question about the traditional course of political ambition. Why did lawmakers who could see themselves in Congress and had the means to get there choose to stay in Albany? What was so valuable about their careers in the state legislature that they did not want to give them up?

What happened in New York was the professionalization of the Assembly and Senate along lines similar to the U.S. House of Representatives.[5] Over the past two decades, New York's state legislature had become a career-oriented institution that offered its senior members high salaries and enough electoral security, staff, and personal influence to make service in Albany increasingly competitive with service in Washington. As the members of the Assembly and Senate reaped more rewards and developed more resources to meet their increased responsibilities, the expected gains of a race for Congress no longer appeared to outweigh the very real advantages of remaining behind. Moreover, this gradual transformation occurred while the job of a member of the House came to be regarded as increasingly difficult.[6]

5. H. Douglas Price, "Congress and the Evolution of Legislative 'Professionalism,'" in Norman J. Ornstein, ed., *Congress in Change: Evolution and Reform* (New York: Praeger, 1975), p. 4; Lawrence C. Dodd, "Congress and the Quest for Power," in Lawrence C. Dodd and Bruce I. Oppenheimer, eds., *Congress Reconsidered* (New York: Praeger, 1977), pp. 269–307; Morris P. Fiorina, David W. Rohde, and Peter Wissel, "Historical Change in House Turnover," in Ornstein, pp. 24–27.

6. In the last decade retirement among House members has increased noticeably. See Stephen E. Frantzich, "Opting Out: Retirement From the House of Representatives, 1966–1974," *American Politics Quarterly* 6 (July 1978): 251–273; Joseph Cooper and William West, "The Congressional Career in the 1970s," in Lawrence C. Dodd and Bruce I. Oppenheimer, *Congress Reconsidered*, 2nd ed. (Washington, D.C.: CQ Press, 1981): pp. 86–91; John R. Hibbing, "Voluntary Retirement from the U.S. House: The Costs of Congressional Service," *Legislative Studies Quarterly* 7 (February 1982): 57–74.

The stories of these state lawmakers from Monroe County who might have gone to Congress reveal much about the changes in New York's Senate and Assembly and the way in which professional legislators who serve in the state capitals across the United States view the rewards of political life in Washington. We treat three of them in this chapter and the fourth in the following chapter. The decisions of all four provide a valuable perspective on the traditional pattern of recruitment of congressional candidates and the conventional view of the House as the ultimate objective for ambitious lawmakers.

A Bite of the Big Apple

Assemblyman Roger Robach was the Democrat who worried Republicans most when they considered their chances of capturing the 30th Congressional District. Robach had gained his seat in the state legislature by upsetting an incumbent in the aftermath of Watergate. During ten years of service in Albany he had survived vigorous challenges by the Republicans and built up extraordinary electoral margins. His safe seat in an otherwise Republican area was situated west of the Genesee River and included the district's largest town, Greece, as well as several other western suburbs and the only Republican part of the City of Rochester.

Robach's base in Greece was what worried the Republicans, because this was also the home constituency for two of their party's strongest contenders, Town Supervisor Don Riley and Ambassador Fred Eckert. Robach had already beaten Riley in a race for the Assembly and could make considerable inroads into Eckert's support. While Eckert had been in Fiji, Robach had been tending the voters back home and built a reputation for close personal contact with his constituency. Like Eckert, Robach embraced the conservative beliefs so prevalent in the western portion of the district. He regularly received the endorsement of the Right-to-Life party and the Conservative party, and had a voting record in the Assembly not much different from that of Eckert in the Senate. Finally, Robach was the chairman of the Commerce Committee in the Assembly, and six years in this position had given him standing in the community as well as access to business people and organized groups in the district. More than any other Democrat, Robach could raise money locally for a congressional race.

The Democratic party's leaders had asked Robach to run for Congress before and considered him a strong possibility now that Conable's seat was vacant. He was not interested, however, and refused even to discuss the matter. "I said no, because I didn't want to go to Congress," he recalled. "I am happy in the Assembly and enjoy what I am doing there." Some of his reasons were personal—such as having made a commitment to stay close to his family in

Rochester—but his desire to remain in the Assembly appeared to be motivated as well by a strong preference for legislative life in Albany.

Robach had not intended to be a career legislator and in many respects had not completely become one. He retained a salaried position at Eastman Kodak and when the legislature was not in session spent considerable time on company business. In addition, Robach believed he was past the point in his life when he could transform himself into the type of politician who is successful on Capitol Hill. "I am just fifty years old," he noted in 1984, "and I don't want to wait ten years to be able to get something done. If you're going to make that change, you should be forty so that you'll have ten years afterwards to make use of your clout. As near as I can tell, junior congressmen do three things: they collect money from PACs to scare off an opponent for the next three elections; they try to get the press to talk to them; and they try to make an impression on the Speaker. I would just be too frustrated spending my time reading things into the *Congressional Record*."

Robach was unwilling to pay the personal costs of changing political careers, because he wanted to remain involved in the private sector and was satisfied with the opportunities he enjoyed in Albany. Named chairman of the Commerce Committee after only two terms, Robach had prospered in the system of disciplined parties that characterized New York's state legislature. "The seniority rule is not as rigid as it is in Congress, and the party can move you up pretty quickly if they like what you do," he commented. "In the Assembly, [Speaker] Fink gives the chairmen a great deal of scope to negotiate on bills and make decisions. If you do the job, Fink will back you. From what my friends in Congress tell me, it isn't like that for the newer members of Congress."

This preference for the Assembly was reinforced by a strong sense of identification with the system of party government that is practiced in Albany. Robach valued the collegiality he had found among his fellow Democrats and had made many close friends—a relationship made possible by the relatively small size of the legislature. Most important, Robach believed that individual lawmakers could get more done with a strong party to back them. He likened the Speaker to a circus ringmaster who knew how to get people into line while at the same time allowing them to perform. Because of this control, Robach concluded, "the party allows the members to make things happen."

Robach had made a niche for himself in Albany, and he was satisfied with it. "If this had come up a few years ago," he said, referring to the vacant congressional seat, "I might have been interested." But at this point in his life he was content.

In contrast to Robach, the Democratic state Senator Jack Perry was most interested in the possibilities created by Conable's retirement. Perry viewed himself as a "legislative type" whose obvious next steps was the House of

Representatives. He made it plain to local leaders and the press that he was interested, and quickly began to explore the various aspects of a congressional candidacy. It was Perry's name that the staff of the Democratic Congressional Campaign Committee heard most frequently when they made inquiries in the district about likely contenders. His credentials as a candidate were so impressive that when Perry traveled to Washington in mid-March to hold exploratory discussions with the national party and PACs, Congressman Tony Coehlo, the head of the campaign committee, "ran out the red carpet for him," as one staff member described it. By early April, however, Perry had withdrawn and announced his intention to seek another term in the state Senate.

Perry's withdrawal caused considerable surprise. Some of his fellow Democrats thought he would run because he was bored being in the minority party of the state Senate, and others remarked that his margins of victory had been declining slightly over the years. If he was going to lose eventually, they reasoned, why not go down trying for the big one? Moreover, Perry was known in the community as a tough, tenacious politician who did not shrink from a fight—a reputation he earned after years of defending the seat he had taken from the Republicans in a three-way race in 1974, when a primary split the Republican party and the loser of the fight for the nomination had run as a Conservative. His image as an aggressive campaigner was exceeded in Monroe County only by the battling campaign style of his former colleague in the Senate, Fred Eckert. In addition, Perry's constituency on the east side contained a sizable portion of the 30th district, and he had represented other portions until the reapportionment of 1982. His previous successes against heavy odds and his substantial base in the 30th would have made him a solid candidate had he decided to run.

Although Perry's experience in the state Senate marked him as an obvious contender for Conable's seat, there was among local Democrats a noticeable lack of enthusiasm for his candidacy, which seemed puzzling at first. His reputation for coldness and egotism was partly responsible, for as one elected official in the party noted, "If Perry runs against Eckert, it will be a dog-fight. . . . They're so much alike, the voters will end up depressed." But the local reservations about Perry had a more pragmatic foundation: in 1982 he had backed the wrong Democrat, Mayor Edward Koch of New York City, in the gubernatorial primary. The majority of Monroe County's Democrats favored Lieutenant Governor Mario Cuomo, so that when Cuomo upset Koch in the primary—in large part because of his strong showing upstate—Perry's position on the losing side left him somewhat isolated politically.

This minor breach would not have prevented Perry from pursuing the Democratic nomination, if he had wanted it. But it did pose some short-term logistical problems in putting together the initial pieces of a campaign. In Washington, the Democrats told Perry what they told every other non-incumbent: the party's scarce resources would be used primarily to protect existing Democratic seats and Perry could count on no more than $15,000 to $20,000 from head-quarters. The message from the national PACs must have been equally daunting, for PACs typically demand that a candidate demonstrate the ability to raise money locally before committing their resources to a campaign; at least one group he had asked to fund a poll turned him down. These national organizations forced Perry to find state and county funds to launch his bid for Congress, and without the enthusiastic support of Governor Cuomo and local party leaders, it was not at all clear how this might be done.

Perry denied that money troubles were responsible for keeping him out of the race: "Money was a factor, but not a real obstacle. I figured I could put together $125,000, and the rest would come, though it would have been very tedious to raise it." Perry's confidence notwithstanding, both the press and the Republicans thought otherwise.

In assessing his reasons for staying out of the race, Perry stressed the relative merits of remaining in Albany. The press release announcing his decision not to run emphasized his seniority (sixth among his fellow Democrats) and quoted him: "After nine years as a state senator, I do not want to leave Albany at a time when my seniority puts me in a position to be of the greatest value to my community." Later, Perry elaborated on this theme: "In the short run, it just wasn't a promotion," he concluded. "In the longer run, it would be, because nothing at the state level can rival the scope of the federal government. But immediately, it turned out not to be as attractive as I thought, once I started looking into it." He came to this conclusion after weighing the investment he had made in the state Senate.

Perry had made effective use of his years in the Senate to attain a position of influence. He served on the most important committees and looked forward to becoming the chairman of either Finance or Education—the two most prestigious ones—in the event the Democrats gained control of the Senate. In the meantime, he held the third highest-ranking position in his party as chairman of the Democratic Conference. This post, which he had occupied since 1978, gave him a large staff and the opportunity to shape his party's legislative strategy in the state Senate. Perry's district office was, in fact, far larger and had more aides than most congressional offices in upstate New York. Perry also served on the state's Job Training Partnership Council, which promoted economic development.

It was the prospect of future influence in Albany that proved most compelling. Perry believed that the Democrats were in a strong position to gain control of the state Senate in 1986, which would have brought him a major chairmanship. "If I thought the Democrats would remain in the minority forever, I would have been more favorable toward running for Congress," he observed. "But I don't think that's the case."

The promise of a committee chairmanship contrasted strongly in his mind with the long wait he would have if elected to Congress. "It's partly the size," he said. "You have to wait too long and compete with too many people before you can accomplish anything." In addition, the striving for status bred an atmosphere in the House that Perry found repellent. "There's no romance, as I thought there would be. When you look closely at the Congress, the politicking has gotten too intense, with everyone trying to prove he's the better legislator. It's all personal prestige and one-upmanship. . . . Even the people I know who have safe seats worry all the time, because their prestige is constantly on the line in D.C."

Perry's misgivings about life in the House of Representatives were compounded by policy concerns. Ideologically, he was a liberal Democrat who felt at ease with the relatively homogeneous party caucus in the state Senate. "I feel comfortable philosophically with my colleagues," he noted, "and I don't think it will be much fun to be a Democrat in Washington during the next two years. It will be like 1981, when the party was split between the liberals and conservatives." Moreover, Perry's policy interests lay in education, an area in which the state plays a large role in financing and setting standards for the public schools and managing an extensive university system. New York's expenditures on education were nearly half the total of all federal spending for the entire country in 1984,[7] and Perry recognized this. "In a state like New York," he said, "education is as important as at the federal level . . . probably more so in the next couple of years. It will never be a high priority item in Congress, the way it is in Albany." Given his background as a high school and college teacher, his work as an educational consultant, and his nine years of seniority on the Education Committee, Perry had a long-term investment in education that he could not easily exploit in the House.

For Perry the real drawback to service in Washington was the difficulty of defending a congressional seat if he won it. "I would have had to fight five elections against a stable of Republicans," he said. "They have plenty of people to throw at me, and they just would have kept on coming." Perry had already fought five close elections and had finally obtained a little breathing room after the reapportionment of 1982, when his district gained a few more Democratic voters. He was a master at using incumbency to build goodwill and recognition among the voters, and would certainly have made good use of the

7. In fiscal year 1984 New York State spent $5.843 billion to support local school districts, the state university system, operations for the state Education Department and Higher Education Services Corporation, and contributions to the teachers' retirement fund. See *New York Statistical Yearbook*, 11th ed. (Albany: Nelson A. Rockefeller Institute, 1985), pp. 345–347, 403. The estimated federal education budget for fiscal 1984 was $13.520 billion. See U.S. Office of Management and Budget, *Budget of the U.S. Government, FY 1984* (Washington, D.C.: U.S. Government Printing Office, 1984).

perquisites of a congressional seat. But having struggled to establish his position in a Republican constituency, he not only understood the tremendous effort involved in securing a House seat, but recognized that the demands of reelection would hinder his pursuit of influence in Washington. At the age of forty-eight he feared becoming a congressional errand boy, shuttling home at every opportunity from the Capitol to stave off an ever-present Republican threat.

Even though Perry's status as a member of the Senate's minority party invited a change, the advantages of a House career would represent only a marginal improvement over the short run if his prediction about a Democratic majority in the state Senate were to come true in the next two years. Poised as he was on the verge of real influence in state government, he found the short-term costs of starting over as a marginal freshman in the House unacceptably high. "There is a time in your life when you want to prove that you can win elections," he concluded. "I felt that way once, and I went out and did it against overwhelming odds in a Republican district. I have nothing to prove in this community now."

Assemblyman Jim Nagle had more reason to be dissatisfied with a career in the state legislature than did his Democratic colleagues. As a member of the Republican minority who lacked an important party or committee post, Nagle had few expectations of advancement if he remained in the Assembly. Unlike his neighbor, Assemblyman Steve Hawley, he did not obtain the rewards of party leadership, and he had no illusions about becoming a committee chairman in some future Republican majority. Nagle was frustrated: "The New York legislature is the most partisan place in the world," he said emphatically, "and if you are in the minority, it is like going up against a brick wall. . . . The freshmen Democrats have better offices and staffs than some of the senior Republicans." Nagle viewed Congress as more egalitarian and as a place where individual members could more easily exercise influence regardless of their party affiliation. "In Congress," he observed, "everyone has the tools to do the job."

Nagle's interest in going to Congress was limited initially, because like many politicians from Monroe County he saw the 30th district as a west-side seat. But he received many calls from local party people urging him to run, and when Conable observed to him one day, "You have as strong a claim on the seat as any one," Nagle began to think seriously about making the race. His interest grew when the bandwagon effect Eckert was trying to create from Fiji began to lose momentum. "If you knew how many people had been called and declined to endorse Fred," he observed in March, "you would be surprised." By May he was convinced he could win his party's nomination at the convention, and many local Republicans agreed.

As noted in chapter 3, redistricting had given Nagle a claim on the 30th district, because his Assembly district included the southeastern, suburban portion of the 30th and wound north and west to encompass some of its west-side towns. Before the reapportionment of 1982 Nagle had represented other portions of Conable's territory as well. Therefore he was well-known in the district and his name recognition was endowed by an image as a "nice guy." Virtually everyone called Nagle likable and popular with his constituents. He appealed to Republicans who disliked Eckert's abrasive style and believed that to be effective a legislator needed to cooperate with fellow lawmakers in Washington, which they feared Eckert could not or would not do.

Despite his personal interest in leaving the partisan world of Albany and his strong political claims to Conable's seat, Nagle withdrew from the contest just a few weeks before the convention, throwing his support to Eckert. Although he had misgivings about the personal costs of moving to Washington, he would gladly have gone to Congress if he could have done so without fighting a primary. But Eckert was in the race to stay and made plain that if he had to he would challenge the party's choice in a primary.

The certainty of a primary drove Nagle out of the race for two reasons. First, like most Republican state legislators, he had never entered one before and had no experience with the primary electorate; nor did he have the temperament to adapt to the more confrontational political style characteristic of primaries. A gentle, almost diffident, man, Nagle became visibly upset when his Democratic opponents attacked him during previous election campaigns, and few of his fellow Republicans imagined him standing up to the hardball tactics of Eckert. Leading the secure, well-regulated life of an assemblyman in a safe seat, Nagle had never acquired the protective shell that could shield a politician during the short, intense primary season. Further, Nagle's ill-defined stance on public issues gave some party members the impression that he would not wear well in a primary. However much they might like him personally, the Republican activists who turn out in primaries might find Nagle too indecisive to win the nomination. Insiders continually called him a political lightweight. "With all the years he's spent in politics, I still don't know where he stands on the issues," one party leader noted with some exasperation.

Nagle was also dissuaded from entering a primary because he depended on his legislative salary. As a full-time lawmaker, Nagle faced the prospect of starting a new career if he lost the Republican nomination for Congress. Now in his early fifties, he received a generous salary and state pension that would not be easy to replace. He noted that he and his wife were finally comfortable after educating their children, and the risks of giving up this security were considerable. He also doubted that a congressional salary would go as far, given the high cost of living in Washington. Throughout the spring, as Nagle contemplated his candidacy, his fellow Republicans told us: "Jim just can't afford to run for Congress."

The thinking of Robach, Perry, and Nagle revealed the subtle effect of the professionalism of New York's legislature on the desire for higher political office. Each man saw a career in the House as a step up the ladder—but not a big step, and not one that would be realized immediately. Each man recognized that the greater challenge of Congress came at a very high price and that his political ambitions could be satisfied to a considerable degree by remaining in the state Assembly or Senate. Were these stories just rationalizations? Or did they represent a realistic assessment of the relative worth of careers in the two institutions? Eckert's supporters suggested that Robach, Perry, and Nagle lacked the courage to stand up to Eckert, but a closer look at career patterns in New York's legislature suggests that the trade-offs each man perceived between legislative life in Washington and legislative life in Albany were very real indeed. Cold calculation, not a failure of nerve, prompted their decision to stay in Albany.

The Money in Albany

Generous salaries make it possible for legislators to become full-time lawmakers by allowing them to be absent from their communities for long periods and permitting them the freedom to devote their energies at home to constituent service. But salaries remained poor in state legislatures during most of the twentieth century, and they guaranteed that most of the legislatures would have little prestige and status compared with Congress. The quality of lawmakers at the state level suffered, prompting many observers of state politics to advocate higher salaries,[8] and from the 1960s reformers of state government had some success in raising lawmakers' pay. By the end of the 1970s most states had begun to address the question of salaries, and several made serious efforts to raise them, including New York, which by 1984 had the fourth highest in the country.[9] In the twenty years between Barber Conable's departure from the state Senate and his retirement from the House of Representatives, the base salary for New York's state legislators increased by nearly 250 percent, in the last six years alone 100 percent. In 1984 legislators enacted an increase of another 33 percent when they returned to Albany after the November election, which put the base salary for members of each chamber at $43,000.

This alone did not keep in Albany legislators who might otherwise have gone to Washington. Yet virtually everyone we interviewed both in and outside the legislature thought that a career in Washington for which lawmakers would be paid $75,100 would effectively result in a reduced income, and no one viewed the higher salary accorded a member of the House in 1984 as an

8. Citizens Conference on State Legislatures, *State Legislatures: An Evaluation of Their Effectiveness* (New York: Praeger, 1971), chaps. 2, 5.

9. Council of State Government, *Book of the States, 1984–85*, vol. 25 (Lexington, Ky., 1984), pp. 92–93.

inducement to run for Congress. In real terms the traditional gap between the salaries of members of Congress and those of state legislators had all but disappeared.

There were three reasons for this surprising development: the payment of living expenses during the legislative session (the smallest but most common of the three types of payment), the compensation of members who assume leadership responsibilities, and the great opportunities for earning outside income available to many legislators.

All of New York's state representatives are reimbursed for their living expenses while the legislature is in session, and because the typical session lasts about eighty days (from early January to late June, in addition to a brief period in the fall), their minimum living allowances amounted to $4,400 in 1984 and to $6,000 in 1985 when an increased per diem rate went into effect. Such compensation has the effect of raising the real disposable income of state lawmakers in comparison with their counterparts in Washington: not only do they avoid the cost of two residences borne by most members of Congress, they also receive money for living expenses that federal lawmakers must take from their own pockets. With these payments taken into account the real salary for legislative service in Albany was $37,330 in 1984 and $49,000 in the next legislative session. And it was common knowledge in the spring that these substantial raises would be forthcoming for candidates victorious in the fall election.

These estimates of real income are probably conservative, because they do not include reimbursements for travel or take into account the leeway legislators have in figuring their per diem expenses. Although travel costs are regulated on the basis of receipts for automobile mileage and rail and airline tickets, there is considerable latitude in the submission of claims for per diem. As long as legislators are on legislative business they are eligible for daily reimbursement, regardless of whether or not the legislature is in session. A review of the disbursements to legislators for the years 1984 and 1985 suggests that most lawmakers submit claims for more than the number of days in the session, by arriving a day before legislative business commences, leaving the day after they have completed their week's business, or traveling throughout the state for hearings when there is no scheduled meeting in Albany. In the two years examined, the average member of the Assembly received additional compensation for per diem and travel expenses of $16,188, the average state senator $15,270. Legislators from Monroe County of course obtained compensation far greater than the average because of their distance from Albany. Their average for the two years was $19,265, ranging from $15,438 to $27,171.[10]

10. Compensation data compiled by Jay Gallagher, Gannett News Service, and made available to the authors.

The most significant additions to legislative salaries in New York are made for leadership responsibilities. Leaders of the majority and minority parties, and the chairmen and ranking members of all standing committees, some subcommittees, and special task forces are given payments in lieu of reimbursement for specific expenses. (These payments are commonly known as "lulus.") The in lieu of payments have become an institutionalized part of the legislative reward system amounting to several million dollars a year.

It is by virtue of these generous lulus that some of New York's legislators earn as much as most lawmakers in Congress. For instance, the speaker of the Assembly and majority leader of the Senate receive a base salary, the per diem and travel payments awarded to all members, plus $30,000 as party leaders. When all these payments are added together, their earnings for 1984 were close to $70,000. In the legislative session of 1985 their total real compensation would increase to nearly $80,000—approximately 5 percent more than members of the 99th Congress would earn. Extra payments in New York's legislature are not made only to the speaker of the Assembly and the Senate majority leader: when all lulus paid in both chambers are considered, a total of eight other party leaders and committee chairmen receive nearly $75,000 or more. The compensation of another five legislators is very close to that figure.

Income supplements from lulus are not as impressive for other members of the state legislature, but they are quite substantial. Nearly half of New York's senators earn $60,000 or more from their legislative positions. Because the Assembly is larger, a smaller proportion of its members are paid high salaries: about one-quarter earn more than $60,000, and another 43 percent average around $50,000 to $55,000. Table 4.1 reveals that fully two-thirds of the members receive some additional income.

Monroe County's state legislators garnered their share of lulus. Two-thirds of the area's lawmakers received supplements to their base salary, and although none of them was in the highest level of earnings, Senator Perry and Assemblyman Hawley earned more than $62,000. Of the three who did not receive a salary supplement, two were freshmen and another a junior member who was next in line for a chairmanship of either a major committee or a minor committee.

What is most striking about table 4.1 is the broad distribution of resources in both chambers. The divided control of the legislature—Republicans dominate the upper chamber and Democrats the lower—has forced the leaders to spread the wealth among the maximum number of members. Perquisites are not confined to a few powerful lawmakers but rather are extended to all but the most junior legislators. In the Senate, for example, everyone is entitled to a piece of the action; in fact there are more positions eligible for extra service payments than there are legislators. By law no such "double dipping" is allowed: each member may receive only one allowance, so those holding multiple responsibilities choose the highest-paying one.

Table 4.1 Compensation in the New York State Legislature

	PAYMENTS TO ALL MEMBERS	
	1983–84	1985–86
Base salary	$32,930	$43,000
Per diem payments[a]	4,400	6,000
Total	$37,330	$49,000

	IN LIEU OF PAYMENTS			
	1983–84		1985–86	
	Average	Number of Members Eligible[b]	Range	Average	Number of Members Eligible[b]
---	---	---	---	---	---
Assembly (150 seats)					
Party offices[c]	$13,900	27	$7,000–$30,000	$13,900	27
Positions on major committees[d]	$13,400	10	$11,000–$24,500	$13,400	10
Positions on minor committees[d]	$7,700	53	$6,500–$10,000	$7,800	65
Senate (61 seats)					
Party offices[c]	$12,600	14	$3,000–$30,000	$15,250	20
Positions on major committees[d]	$13,400	9	$11,000–$24,500	$13,600	9
Positions on minor committees[d]	$7,700	49	$6,500–$9,000	$7,800	53

[a]Assumes 80 working days in session.
[b]Some members hold more than one position.
[c]Includes offices of majority leader and minority leader.
[d]Includes positions of chairman and ranking member.
SOURCE: New York Assembly Public Information Office.

The bill to increase the compensation of New York's lawmakers for 1985 expanded the scope of the system of lulus, although it did not increase the size of the payments for the most influential posts. Instead, the amounts awarded to the lower-ranking jobs were raised—doubled in some instances—and the number of participants was increased. The lesser party positions received substantially greater rewards, and some chairmanships of task forces and legislative commissions became eligible for these payments for the first time. The chairman and ranking minority member of the Assembly task force on farm, food, and nutrition, for example, earned $9,000 and $6,500. (The task force should not be confused with the standing committee on agriculture, which has its own lulus.)

A further financial benefit to a career in the state legislature is the opportunity for unlimited outside income. Two-thirds of the state lawmakers take advantage of this by practicing law, managing real estate or insurance businesses, or running a family farm.[11] The importance of economic ties outside the legislature is illustrated vividly by the story of a Democrat from New York City who turned down his party's nomination in a safe congressional district because he did not want to give up his position as a college professor.

This financial flexibility enjoyed by New York's lawmakers ceases if they enter Congress, for two reasons. The first is the demand on one's time imposed by congressional sessions that run all year long. New York's legislature, by contrast, conducts most of its business from January to June, with a short two-week session in the fall. Moreover, when House members do get home, they have a much larger constituency, which leaves them less time for personal business. One politician from Monroe County contrasted his time spent at local functions with the demands placed on the area's Congressmen as follows: "After I was elected, I used to spend all my weekends going to party dinners and group affairs, and I would always see Congressman Horton there. And then one day it dawned on me that he had all those other people to take care of, too. I wonder when he did it, since I was fully committed with a much smaller area."

The second factor enhancing the financial status of state lawmakers is the absence of regulations governing outside income. New York's legislature imposes on its members no limits on outside income or reporting requirements. Congressional rules, on the other hand, limit what House members may receive from outside occupations or speaking engagements: in 1984 the limit was $30,000 a year. They also require detailed financial statements that must be filed with the House Ethics Committee, to disclose possible conflicts of interest. The difference in rules means that some practices that are acceptable in Albany are not in Washington, as the case of Assemblyman Robach clearly illustrates.

Robach continued to hold the administrative post at Kodak he secured before he ran for the Assembly. By his account he is careful to be paid by Kodak only during the six months or so that the legislature is not in session. Robach notes that he has not been eligible for promotion in the company because of the demands of legislative business, but he does have the benefit of continued contributions to his pension. Kodak is the area's largest employer, and many of Robach's constituents work in the company's facilities in his district. Voters in the area seem to value this connection to the source of the community's economic well-being, rather than find it a conflict of interest. Nor have Robach's fellow legislators in Albany raised questions about the propriety of an employee of one of the state's largest industries being the chairman of the Assembly's

11. Interview, Wesley P. Clark, staff member, Office of the Speaker, New York State Assembly.

Commerce Committee. If he were in the U.S. House of Representatives, his salary from Kodak would be subject to limits and public scrutiny, and his chairmanship would be forbidden by House rules.

The combination of high salaries and outside earnings means that New York's lawmakers risk a financially comfortable life if they take on a race for Congress. Because congressional and state legislative elections are both held in even-numbered years, state legislators must relinquish their seats to run for Congress, and this can be a disincentive to higher office to those who rely solely on a state legislative position for support. Lawmakers with no outside income were particularly aware when Conable's seat fell vacant of the costs of running: some had severed their ties to previous careers, and some were earning substantially more than they would if they reentered their old careers. Other options would certainly arise if a race for Congress were lost, but their appeal was limited from the vantage point of a secure seat in the state Senate or Assembly. For Democrats there were more options because of their party's control of the governorship and the access to appointed positions it provided. There were drawbacks, however, as one legislator noted: "I don't want the Governor to think he has to get me off the streets. Besides, Cuomo's administration has been in place for two years and there really isn't that much available now that would be of interest."

In sum, changes over the last twenty years designed to make the position of state legislator financially more attractive have had the unintended, yet very real, consequence of moderating competition for higher office. Although money did not appear to be an overriding factor in the decision of lawmakers from Monroe County to remain in the Assembly or Senate, the congressional salary provided no real incentive to make the race. As Assemblyman Robach noted, "I didn't try to find out about congressional salaries, because I wasn't interested in running, but I probably wouldn't do any better than I am doing now."

The Incumbency Effect in Albany

For politically ambitious men and women, a seat in the House of Representatives is as close to a secure job as one can find in the upper reaches of American public life. Although many incumbents have fought at least one tough battle during their congressional tenure, they typically can look forward to a succession of weak opponents and comfortable electoral margins once they get past their initial election. Such security has long been a powerful force in fostering careerism among members of Congress, and an even more compelling inducement to run for the House in the first place.[12] Because reelection rates in the

12. See H. Douglas Price, "The Congressional Career: Then and Now," in Nelson W. Polsby, ed., *Congressional Behavior* (New York: Random House, 1971), pp. 14–27; Nelson Polsby, "The

House average 90 percent, a politician could not expect a safer shelter from reelection worries—except for a seat in New York's state legislature.

In Albany, members of the Assembly and Senate regularly surpass the electoral performance of their counterparts on Capitol Hill. In 1984, for example, 10 percent of the members of Congress who ran for reelection were defeated, but only 7 percent of New York's state senators and 3.6 percent of the Assembly's members were beaten.[13] On average, the percentage of the total vote won by incumbents in each chamber was 70 percent—a figure comparable to that in the House. Even losses in primaries, which account for no more than 3 percent of the defeats in the House, are scarcer in New York. When New York's lawmakers think about running for Congress, they consider trading a nearly riskless electoral environment for one that is merely safe.

Lawmakers in New York State obtained their freedom from electoral insecurity by using many of the time-honored techniques of their counterparts on Capitol Hill. Constituent service and pork-barrel projects are staples of legislative life in Albany, and they allow members to claim credit with constituents much as House members have done so effectively in recent years. The average number of staff members per legislator in the state capital is only slightly lower than in the House (see table 4.2), and the district offices we observed among Monroe County's Albany delegation rivaled in size those of the local congressmen. Local legislators also maintained high visibility in the community through frequent newsletters and press releases; if anything they obtained more coverage from the local media during our period of observation than their counterparts in Washington.

The most intriguing aspect of the ability of New York's lawmakers to court the favor of voters lies in the efforts of the political parties on behalf of those holding marginal seats. During the election season and throughout the legislative year, the leaders of both parties in the Assembly and state Senate direct funds and projects to members they wish to protect. They excuse their more vulnerable members from the floor on close votes and encourage them to vote with the opposition on issues that can cost support at home. Democrats from the Republican areas of upstate New York, for example, have higher rates of absenteeism on close votes and a greater tendency to vote with the Republicans

Institutionalization of the U.S. House of Representatives," *American Political Science Review* 62 (March 1968), 144–168; Samuel Kernell, "Toward Understanding Nineteenth Century Congressional Career Patterns: Ambition, Competition and Rotation," *American Journal of Political Science* 21 (November 1977): 669–693; Robert G. Brookshire and Dean F. Duncan III, "Congressional Career Patterns and Party Systems," *Legislative Studies Quarterly* 8 (February 1983): 65–78; Donald R. Matthews, "Legislative Recruitment and Legislative Careers," in Gerhard Loewenberg et al., *Handbook of Legislative Research* (Cambridge: Harvard University Press, 1985), pp. 17–56.

13. Compiled from the annual editions of the *New York State Legislative Manual* (Albany: Department of State).

on certain issues.[14] The party could punish this behavior if it chose to, because the leaders control committee assignments, chairmanships, campaign funds, and staff and office allotments. Yet it is clear that they not only tolerate defection but actively encourage it when electoral survival is at stake. This is undoubtedly one reason why the liberal state senator Perry was perceived by a quarter of his constituents as being politically conservative in a poll conducted in his district in 1984.

The true force of a party's efforts to protect its most vulnerable members comes into play during the campaign season. Both parties provide polling services, technical advice, and considerable assistance with election mailings. They also maintain political staffs throughout the state to monitor the electoral climate and provide help when it is needed. There are no limits to what the party can contribute, and leaders are free to concentrate their resources where they believe it will do the most good. On average, the Democrats contributed 19 percent and the Republicans 17 percent of the funds spent by their candidates for the Assembly in 1984; each figure is more than twice the proportion typically contributed by national parties to congressional candidates.[15]

These figures do not tell the whole story. Much of the aid is unreported, or at least impossible to trace, as legislative employees are shifted about the state as electoral needs dictate. The parties employ their funds strategically, focusing on the competitive races and gearing their spending to outlays by the opposition. Freshmen, especially marginal Democrats, are the great beneficiaries in this partisan duel, as are candidates specifically recruited by legislative staff in Albany to run against vulnerable incumbents. As our colleague Jeff Stonecash has observed after extensive analysis of campaign finance data: "The senior incumbents in Albany fit the congressional model of fund raising. They are entrepreneurs who raise their own money, but the party behaves very differently towards its junior and marginal members. They both concentrate on the vulnerable candidates, although the Democrats have more money to work with." As a result, marginal legislators in New York State are better equipped than members of the House of Representatives to defend themselves in competitive races, and on average they enjoy higher rates of reelection.

In addition to campaign financing, state lawmakers gain assistance in their bids for reelection from obscure budgeting devices known as member items. These are inserted into the governor's budget after it has been submitted to the legislature, expressly to fund projects in specific constituencies. The grants, totaling $26 million in 1984 and $40 to $70 million in 1986, are divided evenly between the upper and lower chambers, within each of which roughly two-

14. Interview, Jeff Stonecash, associate professor, Department of Political Science, Syracuse University, January 1985.

15. Data compiled by Jeff Stonecash.

thirds go to the majority party (the Democrats in the Assembly, the Republicans in the Senate).[16] Members submit requests for special grants to the party leaders, who approve the distribution of funds with relatively little public discussion or accountability. Not surprisingly, a disproportionate share of the grants ends up in the districts of marginal members whom the party wishes to defend. Extra items are included in the supplemental budget, which is usually passed at the end of the session to take care of any unmet needs. Although it is impossible to determine just what sums eventually find their way into the state budget as member items, for many are well hidden, what is significant for our purpose in understanding political recruitment is that the state budget is a strategic instrument for reelecting marginal members, and that it is used far more explicitly and directly than in the House of Representatives. Marginal lawmakers in both institutions generally lack the political influence and committee chairmanships to look out for their own electoral interests, but those serving in Albany at least benefit from the active intervention of party leaders in ways that House members could scarcely imagine.

The extraordinary electoral success of incumbents in New York's legislature holds some important lessons about the incentives that draw state lawmakers to Congress. First, it is clear that in New York politicians whose only goal is security need look no further than Albany. While legislators in many states may envy the high reelection rates enjoyed by members of Congress and the resources that make them possible,[17] New Yorkers have no reason to do so. By the same token, New York's lawmakers are so unaccustomed to electoral risk that they may require a greater degree of certainty about their prospects in House elections than legislators in other states.

A second lesson may be drawn from the success of New York's incumbents: their pervasive use of reelection strategies similar to those commonly employed by members of the House suggests that a lawmaker from New York who won a seat in Congress would be very difficult to dislodge. Indeed not one of the former state legislators who have served in Congress in recent memory has ever been beaten; the last was Bertram Podell in 1974, who had been indicted by a federal grand jury before the primary. Having learned the art of serving a constituency in Albany, these politicians arrive in Washington already knowing how to play the reelection game, and it is relatively easy for them to put familiar tactics to work in the larger setting of the House.

16. Frank Lynn, "Albany Finances Hometown Projects," *New York Times*, January 26, 1986, sec. 1, p. 27.

17. David Ray, "Membership Stability in Three State Legislatures: 1893–1969," *American Political Science Review* 68 (January 1974): 106–112, and "Voluntary Retirement and Electoral Defeat in Eight State Legislatures," *Journal of Politics* 38 (1976): 426–433; Charles M. Tidmarch, "Party Competition in State Legislative Elections, 1970–1978" (Paper prepared for delivery at the Annual Meeting of the American Political Science Association, September 2–5, 1982, p. 6.)

The most significant aspect of the electoral security enjoyed by New York's legislators is its effect on the ambitions of members who come from the minority party in their districts. These are politicians with no natural majority on which to build, who have survived in the Assembly or state Senate by building personal coalitions. Through constituent service, pork-barrel projects, and constant publicity they battle the adversity of party registration figures. Having demonstrated a mastery of the skills that keep so many House incumbents in office, state legislators with such a knack for surviving in hostile environments would seem perfectly adapted to the challenges of congressional politics. Why would the tactics that work so successfully in a state constituency not serve equally well at the federal level?

The experiences of Perry and Robach, who represented Republican constituencies in Monroe County, offer a few clues about the limits of applying the state legislators' reelection formula to Congress. State Senator Perry had never carried more than 55 percent of his district in any election, and Assemblyman Robach had won several of his elections by narrow margins, too. Yet neither seemed worried in the spring of 1984 about holding on to his seat, even in the face of a strong Republican at the top of the ticket. After the election the two legislators spoke of their victories in the language of incumbency. "I win," Robach mused, "because one of my trademarks is my visibility in the district. . . . I communicate with my constituency,"[18] Perry noted that in four heavily financed efforts to oust him, the Republicans had tried everything: "Finally, they came up with an opponent who agreed with me on so many issues, people couldn't tell us apart."[19] Each had been successful by creating a strong personal identification with the electorate that transcended party affiliation.

This stragegy depended heavily on campaign support from outside the district, assistance that came largely from the party leaders in Albany and their allies in state government. As members of the minority party locally, the Democrats in the legislature could not count on a substantial fund-raising base inside their districts, yet they obtained adequate resources to run because, as one local party leader put it, "[Assembly Speaker Stanley] Fink and [Senate Minority Leader Manfred] Ohrenstein take care of that." Once free of financial worries, these lawmakers had the time to devote to the kind of personal coalition building that was responsible for their previous successes.

The financially more secure world of state legislative campaigns in New York contrasted sharply with the Darwinian environment of congressional elections, where the national party organizations are limited by law in what they can contribute to House candidates, and their overall support for candidates

18. *Times Union* (Rochester), November 7, 1984, sec. B, p. 6.
19. Ibid.

averages no more than 6 to 10 percent of total campaign receipts.[20] The Democratic party's impoverished condition constrained its contributions even further,
especially where non-incumbents were concerned. State lawmakers would,
therefore, have no recourse other than the national PACs, which might be
expected to cast a cold glance on a Democratic bid in a congressional district
where Republicans predominated by a margin of two to one. They would also
have to persuade potential donors that they could attract voters from the opposition party in large tracts of the county where none of them had run before:
owing to the unusual makeup of the 30th Congressional District Perry had
represented only 25 percent of its voters, Robach 18 percent. It was a daunting
task after the relative ease of obtaining resources in state legislative districts,
made more difficult by the short fund-raising season remaining for candidates
who had not considered running for Congress until mid-February. Perhaps it
could be done, but as Perry noted: "I don't think raising money was a real
obstacle to the race. I just didn't want to do it."

Legislative Life in Albany

When Barber Conable left the New York State Senate in 1964, retirement from
the state legislature was common. In that year 19 percent of the senators left
their chamber, as did 17 percent of the Assembly. Although New York's legislature was more stable during Conable's era than most others around the country,[21] a relatively small proportion of its members made a career of service in
Albany. Twenty years later the pattern was quite different, the retirement rate in
the state legislature having declined to roughly 6 percent.[22] Throughout the last
decade, the rate of retirement from the state Assembly and Senate was consis-
tently lower than the 10 percent prevailing in the House of Representatives, and
without the sudden drop in House retirements in 1984 to their lowest point in
two decades, New York's legislature would have been demonstrably the more
"careerist" of the two institutions in its retention of members. The average
tenure in the House of Representatives is 4.6 terms, in the state Senate 6.4
terms, and in the Assembly 3.9 terms.

What about New York's legislature has been so attractive that it keeps
legislators in Albany for so long? One must realize first that legislative business
in New York is very demanding. Spending per capita is the fourth highest in the

20. Norman J. Ornstein et al., *Vital Statistics on Congress, 1984–1985 Edition* (Washington,
D.C.: American Enterprise Institute, 1984), p. 78.

21. Wayne L. Francis and John R. Baker, "Why Do U.S. State Legislators Vacate Their
Seats?" *Legislative Studies Quarterly* 11 (February 1986): 119–126.

22. Figures for the House are in Ornstein et al., p. 19. Those for the state legislature were
calculated from data in *The New York Red Book*, 87th ed., ed. George A. Mitchell (Albany:
Williams Press, 1983).

nation, and the legislature was responsible for a budget in 1984 of more than $35 billion. The legislature oversees a bureaucracy of twenty major departments, twenty-three executive agencies, and a host of miscellaneous offices and independent authorities; it regulates education from kindergarten to graduate school and supervises a public university system of 380,000 students.[23]

In meeting these heavy demands the legislative branch had become a very complex organization. The length of the legislature's session tripled from the time Barber Conable had served in it two decades earlier, the number of bills introduced had almost doubled, and the number of permanent committees had risen to thirty-one in the Senate and thirty-two in the Assembly. Along with this growing sophistication the legislature acquired a workload and structure similar to those of the House of Representatives. Table 4.2 shows that the amount of legislation passed in 1984 was actually greater in the Assembly and Senate than in the U.S. House. Legislators in Albany served on as many committees and had access to almost as much staff assistance per member as their counterparts in Washington. More important from the perspective of the individual member was the opportunity for personal influence through the chairmanship of committees.

More than one-third of the Assembly's members from the majority party led a standing committee, while in the state Senate every member had this opportunity. The task forces and special subcommittees in each chamber further expanded the involvement of members. The twenty-three special committees in the Senate and thirty-two in the Assembly gave every member of the majority in the Senate and two-thirds of the members of the majority in the Assembly at least one leadership responsibility; some lawmakers held more than one.

The widespread opportunities for chairmanships and service on task forces has meant that the party leaders can offer challenging positions to junior members and groom them for further responsibility. But the large number of influential positions has appealed particularly to the more senior members. As we saw earlier in this chapter, both Robach and Perry valued the opportunities for influence to which their seniority entitled them. Other legislators felt the same way and dreaded the prospect of starting over in the House. "I don't want to wait in line all over again," one lawmaker remarked. Another pointed out, "Look how long a man of Conable's talents had to spend before he became influential. He's been down there twenty years and it's only recently that he began to carry any weight."

The opportunity for influence in New York's legislature was heightened in the eyes of some by the scaling back of President Reagan's administration of federal involvement in domestic programs. As Perry noted, "The feds are dumping a lot of things on the states—complicated matters like toxic-waste

---

23. Mitchell, ed., pp. 693, 731.

Table 4.2   Legislative Activity in New York and the U.S. House

	NEW YORK (1984)		U.S. HOUSE (1983)
Number of bills passed	1,035		704[a]
Total legislative staff	3,957[b]		8,752[c]
Average number of staff members per legislator	18.8		20.1
Average number of committee and subcommittee assignments per member	5.7		5.8
	ASSEMBLY	SENATE	
Average number of committee assignments per member	4.3	6.5	1.7
Average number of subcommittee assignments per member	.8	2.3	4.1
Percentage of members of majority party holding chairmanship of committee or subcommittee	63.3	100.0	47.6

[a]1982–83 session.

[b]Excludes district staff.

[c]Excludes district staff and staff of special congressional agencies such as the Library of Congress, General Accounting Office, Congressional Budget Office, and Office of Technology Assessment.

SOURCES: Norman J. Ornstein et al., *Vital Statistics on Congress, 1984–1985 Edition* (Washington, D.C.: American Enterprise Institute, 1985), chaps. 4–6; New York State Assembly and New York State Senate documents on committee assignments.

control and development of a new infrastructure for industrial growth. The states will have to find solutions to problems the federal government has given up on." Judging from the frustrations voiced by junior members of the House in a recent survey and their expectation that they would have to wait six years for the chairmanship of a subcommittee, these judgments cannot be dismissed as mere rationalizations for staying in the state legislature.[24]

The most compelling aspect of legislative life in Albany was the environment of political decision making created by the party leadership. New York's legislative leaders have the power to reward and punish members through control of the legislative agenda, assignment of members to committees and appointment of the committee chairmen and ranking members, and the imposition of party discipline, which enables them to set legislative priorities and

24. Christopher J. Deering, "The New Apprenticeship: Strategies for Effectiveness for New Members of the House" (Paper presented at the annual meeting of the American Political Science Association, Washington, D.C., Washington Hilton, August 30–September 2, 1984.

mobilize votes on the floor.[25] It is a system that promotes institutional efficiency at the expense of individual antonomy, but it can make service in the legislature more satisfying for some. Both Robach and Perry, for example, believed that a cohesive party allowed members to be more effective, because they could see their ideas enacted into policy, not just claim credit for introducing them.

More importantly, the party leadership has offered protection to the membership on controversial issues. When the political heat is on, the Assembly speaker and Senate majority leader absorb much of its intensity by negotiating with the governor, mediating the demands of interest groups, and killing troublesome bills. They work out differences in party caucuses, so that members can present a united front that is less susceptible to assaults by interest groups and reprisals by constituents, while on the most controversial bills the leaders may turn everyone loose for the final tally. During the special session after the election of 1984, for example, the legislature met to consider the question of salaries. Assemblyman Robach recalled: "The speaker came down hard on the senior people to vote for it, but he wouldn't let the freshmen or marginal members vote for it even though some of them wanted to." Such maneuvering was made possible by the relatively low salience of events in Albany in the news media.

Some politicians find the imposition of party discipline a major drawback to service in the New York legislature, and they value the greater opportunity for individual accomplishment in the House. In recent years, legislators in Washington have enjoyed increasing freedom to pick their own issues, set their own agenda, and put their personal stamp on legislation. This greater autonomy comes at a price. Held accountable by the public for each controversial bill, House members have become vulnerable. As one seasoned observer of life on Capitol Hill observed: "Life in the House is life in a fishbowl, and members unwilling to operate in public are often uncomfortable."[26] In addition, the lack of discipline and high degree of conflict in the House are also responsible for much of the current dissatisfaction among members over the way the chamber conducts its business. These sentiments in turn shaped the thinking of prospective candidates, such as Assemblyman Nagle, who recalled a political dinner held in spring 1984 that affected his decision not to run: "There were several Washington legislators present and the talk was all about how much more difficult the job had become and how it was no fun anymore." A trip to Capitol Hill several weeks later reinforced this negative impression: "I got the same

25. John J. Pitney, Jr., "Leaders and Rules in the New York State Senate," *Legislative Studies Quarterly* 7 (November 1982): 491–506.

26. Alan Ehrenhalt, "House Politics: Reliving the Good Old Days," *Congressional Quarterly Weekly Report*, February 2, 1985, p. 211.

story from my friends down there. 'Don't do it. It's not worth it.' " Senator Perry heard similar advice: "My friends told me not to do it . . . that they have seen personality changes in many of the members once they get there. They all said to me, 'Jack, you don't want to get like that.' I don't know if it's always been that way, but it's a view of Congress I don't relish."

Given the contrasting styles of legislative life in Albany and Washington, we might reasonably ask whether those who leave the comparative ease of lawmaking in New York for the rigors of Washington share certain traits. In fact they do: short tenure, membership in the minority party, and excellent prospects for electoral success. From 1974 to 1984 seventeen state senators and members of the Assembly gave up their seats to run for Congress. They tended to be younger than candidates who followed other career paths to Washington, and they had a relatively small investment in the state legislature at the time they left (their average seniority was about two and a half terms). All but three served in the minority party at the time of their retirement. Finally, those who attempted to change careers made the decision to run when their chances of electoral success were exceptionally high. Only four of the seventeen contested close primaries to secure their party's nomination for a safe congressional seat, and only three challenged marginal incumbents. The other ten—60 percent of those who gave up their positions in the state legislature to run for Congress— did so with the expectation that they could not lose. Those who ran electoral risks tended to be those with a small investment in their career in Albany.

These patterns indicate that lawmakers are likely to leave legislative positions in Albany in fairly specific circumstances. But there is another, more subtle, aspect of legislative life in Albany that figures in the decision to stay or go. Its outlines are discernible in the decisions of the two Democratic assemblymen who resigned their seats in 1984 to run for Congress, as well as in that of Fred Eckert, who unquestionably would have given up his position in the Senate to compete for Barber Conable's vacant seat if he had not already abandoned it for the ambassadorial post in Fiji. All three politicians had considerable seniority, belonged to the majority party, and faced competitive races that made their decisions somewhat risky. But none occupied a position of real influence at the time he retired from the state legislature. And all three were sufficiently young (in their late thirties to mid-forties) to make service in the House pay off if they won, or redirect their ambitions if they lost. Most importantly, none of the three expected to become an influential insider in the partisan organization of the state legislature. Unlike Perry and Robach, they saw their futures in Albany as holding little promise; the only means available to them for enhancing their legislative careers was to seek election to the House of Representatives.

Thus, even though the legislature of New York State is a highly professional body that can offer its members considerable power, the number of posts available to satisfy the truly ambitious politician is still relatively small. The proliferation of subcommittees and task forces may satisfy the desire for recognition and influence in the short run, but are insufficient to inspire a long-term commitment on the part of all its members. Retaining the most ambitious lawmakers, in particular requires admitting them to the inner circles of party and committee leadership, and this neither party can do given the current low turnover. Paradoxically, as the New York legislature has become more attractive to professional politicians, it can accommodate fewer and fewer individuals who expect to make a career there, unless more room can be found at the top.

Recruitment of Professional Legislators

The promise of a generous salary, electoral security, and personal influence has lured politicians to careers in the House of Representatives for many years. But now, at least in New York State, these benefits are available closer to home and at a much lower personal price. Thus when Conable's seat became vacant not a single incumbent state lawmaker contested the nomination. The progression from state house to Capitol Hill that has been such a pronounced feature of politics in New York did not occur as expected, and as a result voters in Monroe County did not get a competitive race in the 30th district.

If the balance of incentives in other states shifts as their legislatures introduce similar rewards for careerism, will the events in Monroe County be repeated in other communities across the country? No systematic investigations of advancement to Congress from other state legislatures exist, but there is anecdotal evidence to suggest that we did not simply stumble on an isolated phenomenon. In Texas, for example, a race for the open seat in the 6th district in 1984 also was turned down by the area's two state senators, who between them represented nearly the entire congressional constituency. One of the major factors in their decisions was their reluctance to give up positions of influence in the Texas Senate.[27] Colleagues have reported similar stories in California. And other evidence suggests that the trade-offs between service in the state capital and in Washington may not always tip the scales in favor of the House. A recent study indicates that the number of state lawmakers who seek the nomination for congressional seats is quite small, and that those who make this choice are concentrated in states with amateur, part-time legislatures.[28] Finally, of the 38 percent of freshman legislators in the 99th Congress who had experi-

27. Bruce Robeck, "Sacrifices Great for Office-Seekers," *Eagle* (Bryan-College Station, Texas), April 22, 1984.
28. Robeck, p. 509.

ence in a state legislature, 70 percent came from legislatures with low pay and high turnover.

The decisions of state legislators in Monroe County to remain in Albany raise some larger questions about the meaning of professionalism in American politics. We commonly presume that one of the hallmarks of a professional politician is progressive ambition: the desire to climb ever higher up the ladder of elected office.[29] It is equally true that the professional's urge for status may be tempered with an equally strong propensity for caution.[30] Having invested so much in establishing a career at one level, he or she is understandably averse to hazarding the investment on any electoral venture that looks too risky. Thus the lawmaker who may have the strongest drive to run for Congress and the necessary skills and reputation to wage a successful campaign is likely to be the most reluctant candidate, unless the conditions for running are optimal. An incumbent opponent, an unfavorable national climate, an adverse partisan balance in the constituency—these are the political hurdles that an experienced state legislator would have a good chance of overcoming. They are precisely the kinds of obstacle, however, that make the costs of running for the House unacceptably high to the savvy professional.

In addition, what New York's lawmakers have to say about the relative worth of legislative careers in Albany and Washington bears close attention, for it tells us something about the incentives that draw ambitious people to the nation's capital. Conventional wisdom about the motivations of members of Congress holds that their chief objective is security—a cozy sinecure subsidized by the taxpayers and untroubled by electoral competition—and that everything within the institution is subordinate to this one goal. Yet we have seen in New York State that legislators run even fewer electoral risks for nearly comparable pay, and when they evaluate the advantages of moving from one level of lawmaking to another, it is influence—the realities of power today balanced against the prospects of power tomorrow—that tips the scales in one direction or another. For professional legislators, Congress is the pinnacle of one's career only in that it allows one to accomplish what cannot be achieved at home.

29. Joseph A. Schlesinger, *Ambition and Politics: Political Careers in the United States* (Chicago: Rand McNally, 1966); Gordon S. Black, "A Theory of Professionalization in Politics," *American Political Science Review* 64 (September 1970): 865–878.

30. See David W. Rohde, "Risk-bearing and Progressive Ambition: The Case of the United States House of Representatives," *American Journal of Political Science* 23 (February 1979): 1–26.

5

Women: Knowing
Their Place

The biggest asset for a woman candidate is being a woman, and the biggest liability is not being a man.
—*Barbara Curran, former assemblywoman from New Jersey*

Feminist bumper stickers boldly declare: "A woman's place is in the House . . . and in the Senate." Yet the demography of Capitol Hill contradicts this claim. In early 1984 women made up just 5 percent of the Congress, and after the election in November their numbers remained unchanged. Finding the tough female competitors who would make the bumper sticker's slogan a reality proved more difficult than many in the women's movement had anticipated, and so women occupied only six more seats in the 99th Congress than they had during Dwight Eisenhower's administration. Not only was the number of women holding the positions that could prepare them for a congressional career too small (a serious campaign could be waged in only a few House districts), but among experienced female politicians there was an understandable reluctance to run unless the race promised a strong likelihood of success. Like their male counterparts, experienced women in politics thought about the costs of losing a race and the value of other political options open to them. Together the scarcity of eligible women and their desire to hold on to gains they had already made meant that at a given time in any particular district the chances of finding a woman both ready and willing to undertake a battle for the House were relatively low. When it came to recruiting candidates, a good woman was hard to find.

In the spring of 1984, however, it was thought in New York's 30th Congressional District that the Democrats might nominate a woman. The speculation in Monroe County about a woman running for Congress reflected interest in the "gender gap," a term applied to the decided preference nationally among female voters for Democratic candidates in the elections of 1980 and 1982.[1] But local circumstances were at work as well.

---

1. For a detailed analysis of the differences in political attitudes between men and women see Keith T. Poole and L. Harmon Zeigler, *Women, Public Opinion and Politics* (New York: Longman, 1985).

Over the previous decade the Democratic party had nominated women in some difficult races with rewarding results, because the media attention and heightened name recognition from which women benefit when they seek public office, and their somewhat different styles as politicians, turned out to be effective aids for the Democrats in overcoming their minority status in Monroe County and attracting ticket-splitters among the voters.[2] Several dramatic upsets staged by women in state and county elections raised expectations that this strategy might work at the congressional level, particularly on the east side of the 30th district, where there was a progressive political tradition.

The Democratic party's vice chairwoman, Betsy Toole, remarked in early March: "Women—that's what went through my mind when I first heard Conable's seat was vacant. The right woman could win in this district, you know." In addition, a woman would offer voters a clear choice of political styles if Fred Eckert were the Republican nominee. As one female official sarcastically speculated: "If the race is one obnoxious man running against another obnoxious man, then Eckert will win. Republican women will vote for their obnoxious man, and the Democrats for theirs, and it's a Republican district. But if the Democrats run a woman. . . . "

The emergence of Eckert as the Republican front-runner sparked similar calculations in his party. Eckert's candidacy provoked a backlash among some Republican activists who objected to his antagonistic stance on women's issues. A Democratic country legislator, Nan Johnson, recalled that several highly placed Republican women spoke to her about their dissatisfaction with Eckert: "They wanted me to run, and if I didn't, they were hoping another Democratic woman would." But other women were even more strongly opposed to Eckert because of his disparaging style in dealing with them. Some Republican women spoke of a primary to send Eckert a message that he had to take their participation in party business more seriously. "It's not just the issues, said one female Republican official. "After all, people disagree about those things. No, it's his attitude; when we're in a room together, he looks right past me. He makes me feel like I'm the wallpaper."

As a result of these crosscurrents circulating in the district, some observers suspected that a Democrat who could tap the sentiments of disaffected women might be able to create a winning coalition. "Fred Eckert will be the next Congressman," predicted a close associate of Barber Conable who had raised campaign funds in the district for many years, "unless a bright, articulate woman comes along."

A bright, articulate woman almost did come along. Louise Slaughter, an assemblywoman in her first term, very nearly became the Democratic candi-

2. Women appear to have an advantage in gaining name recognition when they seek public office. See Alan Ehrenhalt, "The Advantages of the Woman Candidate," *CQ Weekly Reports*, March 6, 1982, p. 551.

date. She could have had her party's nomination without a primary if she had wanted it, because she had strong support within the local organization and high name recognition around the district. She also had enthusiastic backing from the Democratic Congressional Campaign Committee and from some prominent national PACs. Throughout the spring she was courted in Monroe County and wooed in Washington by a group of professionals who thought she had a good chance of winning. But eventually she turned them all down and joined the ranks of the unseen candidates, leaving the race a traditional, all-male contest.

Why did a woman who seemingly had all the ingredients for a successful congressional campaign reject an opportunity seemingly made-to-order? As a woman, she recognized that a seat in the House represented a level of achievement that few among her sex could reach, and she desired it intensely. But as a legislator in the New York Assembly, she was painfully aware of what she would forfeit if she ran and lost. As a woman she was not sure she would be taken seriously in a bid for Congress, and especially doubtful about raising the money she would need. But as a successful lawmaker who had captured a Republican seat from a well-entrenched incumbent, she knew herself to be a formidable campaigner who commanded respect for her political skills. This conflicting mix of perceptions—uncertainty about where her real interests lay and confusion about how high she should aspire in politics—kept Slaughter in a state of indecision until early June. In the end she opted for reelection to the Assembly; she was just not ready to accept the risks of trying to change places.

The local implications of Slaughter's decision were obvious: when she turned her attention to retaining her seat in the Assembly the Democrats lost one of their strongest candidates. Her withdrawal from the congressional contest also raised larger questions about the advancement on Capitol Hill of women in general. First, the open seat in the 30th district presented a genuine chance for women to increase their presence in the House, especially because in 1984 such promising vacancies were so scarce. Generally a high proportion of the women running for Congress must challenge strong incumbents; over the past decade, in fact, no more than 13 percent of the women competing in congressional elections ran for open seats, which are of course more desirable.[3] This percentage of female candidates seeking open seats was roughly equivalent to the proportion of male candidates with the same advantage, but women needed greater access to the more winnable races, not just the same access, to expand their meager representation in the House. By turning down the nomination in New York's 30th district, Slaughter passed up precisely the kind of contest that has the greatest potential for the advancement of women in Congress.

3. Jody Newman et al., *Perception and Reality: A Study of Women Candidates and Fundraising*, (Washington, D.C.: Women's Campaign Research Fund, 1984), p. 30.

The decision of an experienced female politician to forego the nomination in the 30th Congressional District challenges some preconceptions about the reasons why women are absent from the highest positions in American politics. We tend to assume that more women would serve in the House and Senate were they not denied access to them.[4] While the hurdles women have to overcome in attaining public office are very real and quite evident in the restricted number of strong female candidates, focusing exclusively on these obstacles obscures the similarities between successful women in politics and successful men. They run similar campaigns, they raise equivalent sums of money, and they appear comparable in the eyes of the voters.[5] As women climb the political ladder they come to think about their careers not in terms of gender but of the trade-offs that make political opportunities more or less attractive to them as individuals. Not surprisingly a good many women who consider moving to Washington find reasons to remain at home, just as men do.

The Kentucky Populist from Upstate New York

Although people in the 30th Congressional District spoke in general terms about the "right woman" taking the seat, they had only one woman in mind: Louise Slaughter. Only ten women held public office in the community above the level of town board: a judge on the State Supreme Court, two members of the state Assembly, the Monroe County Clerk, two county legislators, three members of the Rochester City Council, and the supervisor of the tiny town of Rush. A few well-known party activists completed the short list of possibilities. While speculation mounted about Conable's successor in the days following his announcement, none of the Republican women in this group was mentioned as a potential candidate, and of the Democratic prospects only Slaughter's name surfaced in the press.

4. This theme dominates the literature published during the past decade on women in politics. See for example Irene Diamond, *Sex Roles in the State House* (New Haven and London: Yale University Press, 1977); Jeane J. Kirkpatrick, *Political Woman* (New York: Basic Books, 1974); Wilma Rule, "Why Women Don't Run: The Critical Contextual Factors in Women's Legislative Recruitment," *Western Political Quarterly* 34 (March 1981): 60–77; Nikki R. Van Hightower, "The Recruitment of Women for Public Office," *American Politics Quarterly* 5 (July 1977): 301–314.

5. Janet L. Clark et al., "Women as Legislative Candidates in Six States," in Janet Flamang, ed., *Political Women: Current Roles in State and Local Government* (Berkeley Hills, Calif.: Sage Publications, 1984), p. 146; Barbara C. Burrell, "Women's and Men's Campaigns for the U.S. House of Representatives, 1972–1982: A Finance Gap?" *American Politics Quarterly* (July 1985): 251–272; Newman et al., pp. 25–27; Carol Jean Uhlaner and Kay Lehman Schlozman, "Candidate Gender and Congressional Campaign Receipts" (Paper presented at the Annual Meeting of the Midwest Political Science Association, Chicago, April 12–14, 1984, pp. 12–14); R. Darcy and Sarah Slavin Schramm, "When Women Run Against Men," *Public Opinion Quarterly* 41 (Spring 1977): 1–12; Ronald D. Hedlund et al., "The Electability of Women Candidates: The Effects of Sex Role Stereotypes," *Journal of Politics* 41 (May 1979): 513–524.

As a state legislator with a suburban base in the district, Slaughter was a natural candidate for Conable's seat. A seasoned politician with previous experience in the county legislature and a stint as the upstate coordinator for Mario Cuomo when he was lieutenant governor, Slaughter was a freshman Democrat who was well known, well connected, and well respected. That she was a woman simply added to her solid political credentials.

Slaughter attained much of her political success from a style rooted in the eastern hills of her native Kentucky. Although she had lived most of her adult life in upstate New York, she retained the "down home" manner and easy drawl of the Bluegrass State. She combined personal charm with a straightforward approach that many regarded as a reason she did so well in the rural, Republican portion of her constituency. "They like that Kentucky hill-country approach and her fierce independence," noted one Democratic leader. "That will help her over in the western portion of Conable's district." Another party leader summed up Slaughter's personal strengths this way: "She is strong on issues and good on her feet, but she's charming, too. If Eckert tries his usual stuff against her, he'll end up looking bad." In the eyes of party activists, Slaughter had mastered the difficult art for a woman politician of appearing both tough and feminine by presenting herself as a unique mix of feistiness and southern sociability.

Slaughter's personal appeal and reputation for independence were complemented by her stance as an atypical politician. She did not seem to fit the mold of the professional office seeker who methodically climbed from one position to the next, because her career had been a mixture of organizing citizen groups, holding public office, and helping to elect other candidates. "People are attracted to my type of candidacy," she noted, "because they recognize me as a woman who is hard-working and committed, not just out to advance my career." She described her advancement in politics as a series of unplanned opportunities rather than a set of carefully calculated steps, and she described her decision to run for the state Assembly in 1982 as spontaneous. "I was at the Democratic convention," she recalled, "and people suggested I run for the 130th, so I did."

Even though she had now joined the ranks of professional lawmakers in New York's legislature, Slaughter continued to differentiate herself from other officeholders. In response to our questions about the career ladders of elected officials, she told us repeatedly, "I just don't think about politics that way."

The ingenuous air of the antipolitician did not mask Slaughter's toughness and tenacity as a campaigner. She had run for the county legislature and lost twice before finally beating the Republican incumbent, and those who then worked with her recalled her drive for political advancement. "While we were together in the county legislature, Louise told me she would run for the Assembly any time she got the chance," one colleague recalled.

Slaughter had to pursue her political ambitions the hard way given her residence in the suburb of Fairport. She had had to run in Republican territory against senior incumbents, and it was this track record that gave credibility to her candidacy in the 30th Congressional District. She had first attracted attention in 1975 with an upset victory over an incumbent county legislator in the Republican strongholds of Fairport and Perinton. After two terms in the county legislature she reluctantly gave up her seat to work full-time as the upstate coordinator for Mario Cuomo, then lieutenant governor of New York. In 1982 she was back in the news with another upset, this time of an assemblyman who had served for ten years; this accomplishment was especially startling because it occurred in a district drawn to the incumbent's specifications where Republicans outnumbered Democrats by two to one. Slaughter further demonstrated her appeal to voters in 1984, in districtwide balloting for delegates to the Democratic National Convention. "Usually, the first few names are the ones picked for the convention," remarked Betsy Toole. "She didn't get a slot, but people went looking for Louise's name. That's very atypical."

Having won against tough odds previously, Slaughter commanded respect as an effective organizer, especially among her opponents. A Republican who had run campaigns against her described Slaughter as a formidable campaigner and noted her ability to cover her district with effective mailings. Another Republican added: "The people who work for me work for her, too. She has an incredible ability to attract volunteers and get them involved." With Democrats in the 30th district facing a financial squeeze, this ability to pull together an effective grass-roots organization in hostile territory was a real advantage.

In addition to an attractive political style and demonstrable campaign skills, Slaughter had good connections inside and outside the 30th Congressional District. Having long taken part in presidential primaries, she knew the Democratic activists in the county, and her work as Cuomo's upstate coordinator had broadened these contacts extensively. But the connection with New York's popular governor was even more valuable beyond the borders of Monroe County. Cuomo's popularity in Washington grew after he delivered his state to Walter Mondale in the presidential primary in April, and could help Slaughter gain access to the Democratic Congressional Campaign Committee and key PACs. Slaughter knew these organizations would take her seriously with Cuomo's backing. She had also maintained a tie with Congressman Morris Udall from his campaign in 1976 for the Democratic presidential nomination, and had friends who had been in Jimmy Carter's administration and were scattered among various interest groups. When it came time to raise money, Slaughter had access to people who could help.

Slaughter's candidacy for the House was not without disadvantages. After years of working for liberal candidates and causes such as environmental quality, women's rights, and criminal justice reform, she was clearly identified with the liberal wing of her party. This would hurt on the west side of the district, where winning Democrats often carried the Conservative party's endorsement. Although the votes on the Conservative line were not that significant, the label provided an important cue to voters that the candidate was an "acceptable" Democrat. The Conservatives made it plain that they would not even interview Slaughter for their party's congressional endorsement because of her liberal views.

In addition, Slaughter's status as a freshman in the legislature was something of a liability. She was still learning the ropes in Albany and was hard pressed for the time needed to establish a congressional candidacy. She repeatedly put off her preliminary fund-raising trip to Washington because of the demands of legislative business. And she found that whenever she was absent from sessions of the Democrats' legislative caucus to make campaign plans she became the target of sarcastic comments from the speaker. A more established member would have had the leeway to pursue other political goals, but as a newcomer Slaughter could not afford to miss meetings or drop the ball on the bills for which she was responsible.

Her lack of seniority hurt in another way. Slaughter's victory in the Assembly race had been surprising, and she needed a second win to demonstrate that it had not been an accident. By her own account, her opponent in 1982 had not campaigned effectively. "I didn't get started until mid-September, after the Cuomo-Koch primary," she said. "Hanna wasn't expecting anything, and he just did what he had always done." Whether she could pull off a similar feat when the Republicans were paying attention, as they surely would in the 30th Congressional District, was another question. The closeness of the race in 1982 and her small campaign chest of $30,000 could be a cause for skepticism among professional political organizers, especially those in Washington. Locally, some politicians simply dismissed her consideration of the congressional race as presumptuous. "Louise has only been in the legislature for one term, and she hasn't had the chance to make contacts with the various groups in town that she will have later," a fellow Democrat commented.

Slaughter's membership in the New York Assembly raised another, more subtle, barrier to her candidacy. The speaker, Stanley Fink, had made a substantial investment in her winning campaign in 1982, and he did not want to lose a seat so recently acquired. In addition, he had lost two other Democrats to House races already (as noted in Chapter 4) and was becoming testy over the possible defection of any more. Although he never pressured her directly to stay out of the race, the speaker's opposition to Slaughter's congressional ambitions was known to political insiders, and it had repercussions among those who were in a position to influence her thinking about the race.

For example, local party officials were reluctant to recruit Slaughter too aggressively, for, as one leader put it, "Fink will have a fit if we go after her too hard." The chilling effect of the speaker's disapproval was evident even in

Washington. A member of the staff at the Democratic Congressional Campaign Committee observed: "Fink didn't want Louise to do it, because he was getting worried about a Republican sweep in the fall. That put someone like Larry Kirwan right in the middle. I always wondered why he seemed standoffish about her running, and I think that was the reason." These sentiments were shared by another observer in Washington, who directed a major PAC: "The speaker was the major obstacle to Louise's running because of his influence on organized labor. They knew Fink wanted her in the Assembly, and so they didn't do anything to help her get started. Besides, they were worried about Eckert and thought Louise's chances were slim. Why cross Fink, when they thought she couldn't win anyway! I couldn't believe how negative the state labor people were when I talked to them."

Finally Slaughter's political base, in the easternmost towns of the 30th Congressional District, was small. She claimed about 8 percent of the 30th, including the Village of Fairport and the Town of Perinton. Thus only a small proportion of the congressional electorate had had any personal contact with her or actually voted for her. This and the preponderance of Republicans in the district prompted her closest political friend and advisor to warn against the race from the very beginning. "Do what's in your best interest," he told her. "The numbers just aren't there."

Despite these drawbacks Slaughter was in a strong position to run, and she had no competition from other female politicians in either party. On the Democratic side the most prominent woman, Judge Elizabeth Pine of the state Supreme Court, had no intention of leaving the bench to run for Congress. Nor did the county clerk, Pat Aducci, change her reelection plans in 1984 to undertake the House race. This left Nan Johnson, a Democratic county legislator who had campaigned throughout Monroe County in 1983 in a bid to become county executive. But Johnson lost that contest badly to the longtime incumbent Lucien Morin, and she was in no mood for another battle against tough odds. As for the three women with positions on the Rochester City Council, they were dissuaded from running by the situation of the district's political center of gravity in the suburbs, which had also kept Paul Haney out of the race. Midge Costanza, a former vice mayor of Rochester, who had given Barber Conable the toughest battle of his career in 1974, flew to Rochester from California in March, but left quickly when she discovered that her brief service as a member of President Jimmy Carter's staff did not compensate for her long absence from the district.

The list of possibilities was equally limited within the ranks of Republican women. As we have seen, Assemblywoman Pinny Cooke endorsed Fred Eckert before she realized her own political strength in the 30th district. Although she was urged by supporters to run throughout the spring, she did not actively pursue her party's nomination. Joanne Van Zandt, a county legislator from the eastern suburb of Pittsford, briefly considered entering the Republican primary, but her interest in the race grew out of a desire to give Republican women an outlet for their dissatisfaction with Eckert rather than from personal ambition to serve in Congress. At no time was she a serious candidate, even though her name began to appear in the newspapers as a possibility.

If either Cooke or Van Zandt had become an active contestant on the Republican side, she would have faced formidable obstacles in organizing for a primary against Eckert. Neither woman had ever competed in a primary, and it was clear in our interviews with party activists that neither one could raise enough money in the short span of time available to make a credible effort. One party fundraiser noted: "They just don't have the grasp of the issues to be taken seriously. If someone like Susan Robfogel or Barbara Zartman were to take on Fred, it would be different, but the others would be blown out of the water." While Robfogel, a prominent local attorney, had occupied important appointive positions in the Republican party, she had no interest in holding elected office. And Zartman, a former vice chairwoman of the party, had her eye on the Republican county chairman's seat, which would become vacant after the election of 1984. "Look, Eckert is the most qualified candidate, and I can support him on those grounds," Zartman said. "Besides, he's going to get the nomination anyway, so why not make it easy on the party?"

In the weeks leading up to the deadline for congressional candidates to file their petitions, speculation continued in the 30th Congressional District about the "right woman" running for Conable's seat. But the only woman with the ambition for a congressional career and the credentials to become a serious contender was Louise Slaughter. When she withdrew from the race, the conjecture ceased. In the end, as one Republican party leader noted, the prospect of a woman candidate "was all just talk."

Running as a Woman

When a woman with a chance of winning turns down the nomination for an open House seat she challenges conventional wisdom. Accustomed as we are to thinking of women in politics as underdogs and sacrificial lambs, the idea that a woman would pass up a real opportunity coveted by many men is startling. For years political observers have argued that a major reason for the scarcity of female legislators in Congress is the inability of women to obtain major party nominations in competitive races; Louise Slaughter's decision not to run in New York's 30th Congressional District compels us to look at women in American politics in a broader light. Slaughter was hindered by none of what is said typically to hold female candidates back, and her status as one of the few female state legislators in the country contemplating a congressional race actually gave her some advantages over her male colleagues.

Women who compete successfully for elective office have usually overcome several barriers. The demands of family life, social pressures against women pursuing their own careers, and a lack of professional credentials have all restricted their involvement in public life.[6] By the time Louise Slaughter had reached New York's state legislature she had put these difficulties behind her. Her children were grown, her husband was agreeable to moving to Washington, and her transition from helpmate to independent officeholder was accomplished when she left Governor Cuomo's staff in the middle of the gubernatorial race to run her own campaign in 1982. In addition, she had used her reputation for hard work and skillful political organization to establish herself in Albany. In Monroe County she was believed to be on the "fast track" in the Assembly, and now that she had become a full-time, professional legislator, few remembered or cared that she had begun her political career as a housewife and volunteer.

Slaughter had not only overcome the liabilities of being a woman in politics, but was free of many of the restraints that sometimes held back her male colleagues. In contrast to men we interviewed, Slaughter seemed indifferent to the monetary strain of a congressional career. Because she was a freshman in the Assembly she did not receive lulus, so her legislative salary remained comparatively low. Also, some of the constraints that led men to feel they could not go to Washington did not apply to Slaughter. She no longer had worries about educating her children and could count on a second income from her spouse. Nor would she risk forfeiting a job in the private sector or a long-term investment in a pension.

In addition, Slaughter expressed none of the concerns we heard from men about starting a new career in middle age. Although she was roughly the same age as Perry, Robach, and Nagle, she seemed to mind starting over less than they did. She had less seniority at stake and little formal power to relinquish, but she also had a different conception of time. Like most women in politics she had got a later start, and was just beginning to feel the rush of ambition at an age when many men are already losing theirs. If Slaughter had run in the 30th Congressional District and won, she would have been nearly a decade older than the average man entering the House in 1985, but considerably younger than the two women who did begin congressional careers in that same year.

Finally, Slaughter did not express the ambivalence about the value of serving in the House that we heard from so many male politicians. She saw a seat in Congress as a challenging promotion, and there was never any question in her mind about the desirability of winning it.

6. Diane L. Fowlkes et al., "Gender Roles and Party Roles," *American Political Science Review* 73 (September 1979): 772–780; Susan J. Carroll, *Women as Candidates in American Politics* (Bloomington, Ind.: Indiana University Press, 1985); Marcia Manning Lee, "Why Few Women Hold Public Office: Democracy and Sexual Roles," *Political Science Quarterly* 91 (Summer 1976): 297–314; Susan Slavin Schramm, "Women and Representation: Self-government and Role Change," *Western Political Quarterly* 34 (March 1981): 46–59; Irwin N. Gertzog, "Changing Patterns of Female Recruitment to the U.S. House of Representatives," *Legislative Studies Quarterly* 4 (August 1979): 429–445.

As a female state legislator considering a race for the House, Slaughter discovered that her gender might turn out to be a political asset. When she went to Washington in early May to explore the possibilities of raising money, she was greeted enthusiastically at Democratic headquarters. "We were looking for women to run in 1984, but we had not made the same effort nationally as the Republicans," one staff member commented. "There weren't enough female state legislators in the Democratic party to go after, and the ones we talked to weren't interested. Plus, we believed we shouldn't try to recruit women who couldn't win, especially since the party had so little money for nonincumbents. When Louise showed up, she was a state legislator, she had raised some money on her own, and she had the governor's support. She was just what we were looking for!"

The staff of the Democratic Congressional Campaign Committee spent much time with Slaughter. She later recalled: "[They] made me feel terrific. . . . No one has ever built me up like that before." She was introduced to Charles Manatt, the head of the Democratic National Committee, and Congressman Tony Coelho, the chairman of the Democratic Congressional Campaign Committee. The national party headquarters arranged for her to attend several large fund-raisers, and friends set up numerous appointments with various PACs. She talked to groups representing women, teachers, and labor, as well as the American Medical Association.

Coelho assured Slaughter that the party would contribute to her congressional campaign the maximum amount allowable. Although the support was conditional on the needs of incumbent Democrats to whom the committee would give the greatest proportion of its funds, it was important nonetheless. In addition Slaughter was told that her race would be given "priority" status, which would enhance her ability to seek contributions from other sources. "These things were done for me," she noted, "and it was made very plain that they were not transferable to the seat."

Slaughter had another advantage that drew attention in Washington: the backing of the American Medical Political Action Committee (AMPAC), a well-financed, highly professional PAC that is a leading contributor to federal candidates.[7] In addition to making contributions, AMPAC trains candidates in campaign management, finances public opinion polls, and offers a range of other "in-kind" services that PACs use to stretch the federal limits on their contributions to congressional races.[8] In Slaughter's case, for example, AMPAC agreed to pay for an exploratory opinion poll costing ten thousand dollars in the 30th

7. Larry J. Sabato, *PAC Power: Inside the World of Political Action Committees* (New York: W. W. Norton, 1984), pp. 16–24.

8. Rules issued by the Federal Election Commission regulate the valuation of in-kind contributions, which allow PACs to stretch their dollars. Sabato (1984) notes that in-kind giving gives PACs more control over their contribution and often provides a more visible token of support. For these reasons in-kind giving is on the rise among PACs. See Sabato, pp. 93–95.

district. The survey results would be held for fifteen days before being made available to Slaughter; by making the survey slightly out-of-date this would reduce its value sufficiently to bring AMPAC's contribution into compliance with regulations of the Federal Election Commission that limit contributions to five thousand dollars per electoral contest. "We'll charge that against her campaign as a primary contribution," said Sylvia Swanson, AMPAC's regional director for the New York State area. "Then we can't give to her campaign again until after the September primary, but we are planning to have a fund-raising reception here for her in Washington. Slaughter will have to reimburse us for the expenses, of course, but we can publicize her candidacy, introduce her to other groups, and help her raise money until we can make another contribution."

The backing of AMPAC was not only a financial bonanza for Slaughter's fledgling campaign, it also gave her a valuable political ally in attracting additional support. The organization's prestige and reputation for skillful political maneuver made it a bellwether for other PACs, which often relied in committing their own funds on AMPAC's judgment about prospective candidates. AMPAC's money would legitimize Slaughter's bid for a House seat and alert other contributors that a competitive race was shaping up in New York's 30th Congressional District despite the Republicans' advantage in party registration. Most important, AMPAC's preference for a Democrat, in light of the organization's longstanding conservatism and history of backing Republicans, would create an image of Slaughter as an "acceptable" Democrat with whom other trade and business associations could feel comfortable. One staff member at the Democratic Congressional Campaign Committee said: "What really impressed us about Louise was the connection with the AMA. . . . It's rare for a Democrat, and especially a nonincumbent Democrat, to get in with those business and trade PACs. The AMA's support will open doors for her all over town." And perhaps there was another, more subtle, message in AMPAC's actions that the highly sensitive political antennae of Washington's campaign professionals could not fail to pick up: something must be amiss with the Republican front-runner, Fred Eckert, if AMPAC was recruiting someone to run against him.

In fact there was something wrong with Eckert's candidacy in the eyes of some physicians. At a meeting in central New York with members of the American Medical Association, AMPAC's regional director learned of strong objections to Eckert on the part of some members. "The people in the region were unenthusiastic about Eckert because they thought he was too much of a right-winger . . . too much on the fringe," Swanson noted. These same physicians had developed a working relationship with Slaughter in the Assembly and suggested her as an alternative. "They thought she was acceptable, even though she was a Democrat, because they could talk to her," Swanson said. "They thought Slaughter would listen to them in a way Eckert never had."

At the urging of the regional organization Swanson made contact with

Slaughter and set up an appointment for May 3. Swanson had other reasons to pursue the membership's suggestion, because Slaughter was what is known among PACs as a "two-fer": she gave business and professional groups the chance to appear socially progressive, by supporting a woman, and nonpartisan, by supporting a Democrat. "We are all supposedly bipartisan, and we're always looking for Democrats we can support without hurting incumbents," Swanson explained. "I was already looking for Democrats in open seats, when I heard about Louise." AMPAC was not the only group looking to support a Democrat. "Several business groups came to me for recommendations," Swanson said, "and Louise would have been good for them. They could show they gave money to a woman in their annual report, and she was a Democrat they could support without hurting one of their friends in the House."

Slaughter's experiences in Washington at party headquarters and at the various PACs raised her expectations about the forthcoming race and diminished some of her deep-seated fears about whether a woman could run for Congress. She discovered that a woman with her credentials and connections was not only a credible candidate, but a rare commodity on the congressional futures market. Instead of worrying whether she would get a hearing in the inner circles of Washington, she found herself the object of intensive recruitment efforts by a variety of individuals and groups. "Everyone was courting her," observed a staff member at the Democratic campaign committee. But Slaughter's doubts about her acceptability as a House candidate lingered, and in the end they prevented her from taking the necessary steps quickly enough to put her campaign on a solid footing.

From the beginning Slaughter was ambivalent about whether she could run, and while in the weeks following Conable's retirement her fellow Democrats talked to fund-raisers in Washington, she postponed her visit repeatedly. She intended to go in March, then April, and finally made her first trip in early May. She did gain some vital information about the Republican opposition, particularly Eckert, whose dominance of the party she found not as overwhelming as it had appeared initially. "I would be feeling bad, now that it looks like the Republicans will have a primary, if I had decided early, when Perry did," she remarked during an interview in mid-May. But her procrastination reflected more than cautious calculation; it was a sign of uncertainty about whether she had a legitimate claim to the seat in New York's 30th district. As she told us much later, "I kept putting up barriers and thought of excuses, because in some ways I was afraid to go after it. I wasn't afraid of the tough race, but that somehow I wouldn't be considered qualified, or taken seriously."

These doubts surfaced again when it came time to design the exploratory opinion poll. "Louise wanted a lot of questions about how well a woman would run in the district," Swanson recalled. The two questions on this subject eventually included in the survey revealed few objections to a female representative in the House. Among the sample of likely voters 64 percent agreed with the statement: "It would be a good idea to elect a woman to Congress from this district, so that women's views are more strongly represented." In addition, 74 percent said that the candidate's gender did not matter, and only 6 percent said they would be less likely to vote for a woman.[9] But as Swanson observed after Slaughter had pulled out of the race, "Louise wanted assurances about how a woman would do, which just were not feasible. I don't know if the poll would have been enough assurance for her."

Added to Slaughter's insecurities about how the electorate would react to a woman running for Congress were her misgivings about whether her fellow Democrats would go all out for her campaign. From the beginning she was skeptical about the level of support she would receive from the national and local party organizations. "This is the year for women to run," she told us in early March, "but I doubt if the party will give them what they need to win. Women are still the sacrificial lambs." She was acutely aware that Monroe County's Democrats had nominated Nan Johnson to run for county executive in the previous year and had then failed to provide help for her campaign. "A lot of promises were made that weren't kept. I won't let that happen to me," she said emphatically.

Slaughter's concerns about the national party's commitment to women candidates were alleviated by the cordial reception she received in Washington. Still, the experience in the capital had another side to it, which reawakened fears that the party might let her down after all. On her second visit she was astonished to learn that a young man named Joe Fichera, a financial analyst on Wall Street who had served in Jimmy Carter's administration, was making the same circuit and saying that he, not she, was the favored candidate. "His appointments had been made by people in Monroe County," she noted indignantly, "and he was telling people that he was friends with the governor and that Cuomo wanted *him* to run."

Although Fichera turned out to be no more than what one party worker described as "a blip on the screen," Slaughter deeply resented the incident and reiterated on several occasions that the difficulties Fichera had caused figured heavily in her decision not to run. She saw Larry Kirwan's assistance to the young man as an act of betrayal, but her real trouble was with the governor, who was campaigning for Walter Mondale and failed to make the telephone calls she requested to straighten out the confusion. By the time things were clarified, Slaughter was angry and embarrassed. "I felt let down," she said. "Here the Republicans were closing ranks, and I couldn't even get a phone call

9. "Benchmark Survey of New York 30th District, May 1984" (Prepared by Public Response Associates for the American Medical Political Action Committee, Washington, D.C.). We wish to thank the American Medical Political Action Committee for making available the results of the survey.

when I needed it. The women I told this story to weren't surprised. They said that whenever something begins to look like a good opportunity, the old boy network goes to work."

The staff of the Democratic campaign committee in Washington dismissed the episode involving Fichera as insignificant. "He did make the kind of claims Louise was so indignant about," noted the party's regional coordinator for New York State, who had worked closely with Slaughter. "But everyone was so eager to get her into the race, they hardly noticed him. No, the Fichera story is only important because it reflects how unsure she was about running." But this same staff member had told Slaughter repeatedly how essential the governor's active involvement in her campaign would be. "With so little time to raise money, she needed Cuomo to make calls and give her his lists. I told her at the time that his support was more valuable than anything we could do for her, and that if she couldn't get the governor to really come out for her, she shouldn't run." In Slaughter's mind the handling of Fichera was a litmus test of how committed key Democrats would be to her campaign. Inconsequential as a rival, he nonetheless epitomized all the mistrust she felt as a woman making her way in a man's world.

Time Waits for No Woman

On June 8, 1984, Louise Slaughter announced that she would not seek the Democratic nomination for the seat in New York's 30th Congressional District. She held the press conference just a few days before AMPAC would send her the results of the opinion poll it had commissioned in May. Slaughter had planned to make her withdrawal public in the preceding week, but postponed it while she struggled over her options. "I didn't want to finalize the fact that it was over," she said. "Even then it seemed as if the race was off and on about every half hour." Exhausted and more than a little depressed about relinquishing an opportunity to run for the House, Slaughter finally came to terms with her situation. "I just ran out of time," she said wearily.

The long months of deliberation had bolstered Slaughter's confidence about running—she now understood the intensity of her own ambition and her strengths as a congressional candidate—but the delay had proved costly. She needed time to raise money and time to put together the kind of volunteer effort that had proved so formidable in past races. What she faced instead was a full schedule of fourteen-hour days in the Assembly, as the state legislature limped toward the close of a fractious and interminable session. "I have to be the one to go to Washington and raise the money," she stated, "and I can't go in June because of the session in Albany. D.C. shuts down in July for the presidential convention. And that leaves August, which is too late."

Slaughter had lost more than precious months for organizing a campaign. As she weighed the alternatives of running and not running, national and local events overtook her, making the race in the 30th Congressional District look less and less promising for a Democratic candidate. The long-awaited economic boom had finally occurred, and President Reagan was enjoying a resurgent popularity. Among Democrats the bitter presidential primary season had left the party divided and defensive about its candidate, Walter Mondale. "My friends tell me that the economy will be so bad by 1986 that I would have an easier time then rather than now," Slaughter noted. "And I believe that the Monroe County Republicans will really deliver the vote for Reagan this time. . . . Reagan, D'Amato, Eckert . . . they'll all be out there together. I'll be all alone, and I can't even get a phone call from the governor."

By then, Eckert had not only won the Republican nomination and avoided a distracting primary, he had mended fences in the Republican Party with the formation of the Women's Advisory Board. Suddenly the divisions on which Slaughter had counted to help a Democrat no longer seemed as wide or as deep as they had in March. "When all those women began to show up on Eckert's advisory panel," she noted regretfully, "I knew this time the Republicans were going to close ranks."

Perhaps time would not have been such an enemy to her candidacy if Slaughter had had less at stake. But as a state legislator she could not afford to give up her seat in the Assembly for a losing cause. As noted in Chapter 4, few members of the majority party resign from New York's state legislature, and those who do retire to run for Congress generally require favorable odds of winning. Slaughter was no exception, and she spoke enthusiastically about the rewards of serving in Albany. "I love what I am doing right now. Last year was tough, because I was too old to be a freshman. But this year it's great." Furthermore, she had every expectation of rapid advancement in the Assembly. "She's on the fast track," commented one legislative insider, "and the speaker will give her what she wants to keep her there. She'd be a fool to give that up."

Slaughter's status as one of the few women in the state legislature from outside metropolitan New York heightened the value of her position. She recognized that geography and gender might have strategic value in the future when it came time for the party to balance a gubernatorial ticket or restructure its legislative party leadership. "If I stay in the Assembly," she said laughingly, "I will be the upstate WASP woman."

The magnitude of what Slaughter stood to lose in relinquishing her Assembly seat became clear only as she talked about how far she had come in her political career. After many years of advancing the ambitions of other politicians, she was pleased that her place was no longer behind the scenes. "I like being the one who makes things happen instead of filtering ideas through someone else," she said. "I couldn't be an acolyte again." Moreover, politics was all she knew; she did not have a profession to which to return if she lost her bid for the House, and loathed the idea of having to ask her fellow Democrats for help in finding a new position. Thus for Slaughter running for Congress and losing would be more than a disappointment: it threatened her whole identity. A poignant remark she made early in our interviews made this clear: "I don't know what I would do without the public life."

This was why Slaughter made her decision not to run even before seeing the results of AMPAC's poll. Knowing that her name recognition was surprisingly high and that Eckert had some problems with a negative image would not have diminished the unattractiveness of being out of office altogether. Despite the promise of help from AMPAC and the offer of resources from others, none of those who tried to recruit Slaughter could give her what she needed most—a greater degree of certainty. As one party leader who was close to Slaughter recalled, "I kept asking her what she wanted from the Democrats before she would run. All she would say was, 'Tell me I can win.' "

In concluding her brief foray into the world of congressional election politics, Slaughter left the door open for another try. "I haven't ruled out a race in the future," she said. "I know what I have to do now: I have to think of myself in a very different way, and I have to do some long-term planning about my career. I've never done that before."

Sadder but wiser, Slaughter ended an extraordinary chapter in the story of the unseen candidates in New York's 30th Congressional District. Whether her words carried a prediction for the future was impossible to say in the spring of 1984, but whatever their meaning they had the unintentional ring of irony. As a result of the odyssey on which Slaughter had embarked in the months following Barber Conable's announcement of his retirement, she had finally become completely prepared, politically and psychologically, to run another time. Yet the opportunity that she had been urged to seize in 1984 by so many political associates would be very different in the years ahead: instead of an open seat, the district undoubtedly would have an incumbent running for reelection. At home, Slaughter would have to contend with all the advantages that House members employ to secure their seats; and in Washington, she would encounter reluctance on the part of PACs and party officials to risk resources in a bid against an established legislator. In a remarkable bit of political paradox, the very people who had been so eager to recruit her in 1984 would look on her candidacy with skepticism in 1986 and beyond. As Sylvia Swanson of AMPAC put it, "Unfortunately, Louise thought she could run again, but she's wrong. We gave money to Eckert when she dropped out, and having done that, we can't back her next time. And the business groups who were interested in finding Democrats they could support without hurting an incumbent won't be around next time. They were looking at the 30th district then, but they won't be again."

The Gender Trap in American Politics

When the 99th Congress convened in January after the elections of 1984, twenty-two women took the oath of office, and for the first time in years not a single female representative stood with New York's delegation on the House floor. Although women fared slightly better in a few other states, the only two female newcomers replaced two other women who had retired or been defeated. Thus the historic election of 1984, which saw the first woman nominated by a major party for national office and a record number of female nominees for House and Senate seats, produced no change in the number of women in the House of Representatives.

The activists who met in the aftermath of the election were angry and puzzled. How could their energetic recruitment efforts conducted over the past year produce significant increases in the number of women seeking congressional seats, and at the same time yield such disappointing results? The answer to their question lay in simple arithmetic: a record number of candidates amounted to only sixty-five women contesting House races and ten in Senate races. Of these only 8 percent ran for open seats—a figure well below the level of previous years. The lesson of 1984 was summed up by the head of the Women's Campaign Fund, a PAC in Washington committed to funding female candidates: "What we've learned for [future elections] is that we have got to start early and identify more winnable seats for women to run in."[10]

It may however be easier to find "winnable" races than to find the right woman and persuade her to run. As events in New York's 30th Congressional District illustrate so vividly, the relatively few women who are in a position to enter competitive congressional races may be reluctant to bear the personal costs of advancing a collective goal: that of representation for women in Congress. When they consider whether they can win, and whether they can bear the consequences of losing, they have to think of themselves as politicians, not as standard-bearers for the women's movement. A significant number will therefore say no to a congressional contest despite the best efforts of activists to recruit them. In this respect Slaughter's decision not to run holds a lesson that extends beyond the scope of an individual political career or a single community in upstate New York.

Slaughter's experiences draw attention first of all to the dearth of experienced female politicians, not just in New York's 30th district but in districts around the country. As the only woman in Monroe County with the credentials and ambition to consider a House race, she was the inevitable focus of local speculation about the "right woman." But the uniqueness of Slaughter's situation did not change appreciably when she went to Washington. There too she

10. *Congressional Quarterly Weekly Report* (November 10, 1984), p. 2921.

stood out—a slightly overwhelmed witness to the scarcity of female contestants in House elections. Impressive as a candidate in her own right, Slaughter caused a stir in the capital because she had so few rivals among women from other constituencies.

This was hardly surprising given the small number of offices held by women across the nation. As a group women in 1984 held 12 percent of all public positions in the United States, which averages out to thirty-nine female officials per congressional district.[11] But elected women are far less numerous at the upper levels of government. For example in the nation's state legislatures, which are training grounds for half the House membership, only 991 female lawmakers served in 1988—roughly two per congressional district.[12] The distribution of women who occupy state legislative office is skewed in a way that works against their recruitment to Congress: they are most numerous in the legislatures of the least populous states, which have the fewest House seats.[13] The mathematics of officeholding therefore hold little promise for a significant change in the number of eligible female congressional candidates, at least in the near future.

Slaughter's skepticism about the feasibility of a woman running for Congress points up a major fallacy in the conventional wisdom about women as candidates. The talk about the "right woman" in New York's 30th Congressional District rested on the assumption that women as politicians have particular characteristics that appeal to the general electorate, and that women as voters have distinctive policy preferences that set them apart from men. The facts do not support these views in Monroe County or elsewhere.

For example, the poll done for Slaughter in May 1984 demonstrated that voters accepted the idea of a female representative, but that few would support a woman solely because she was a woman. These results are similar to findings in other communities,[14] and they strongly suggest that women can compete successfully in House elections only if they possess the attributes that voters evaluate positively in men: party affiliation, name recognition, experience, and personal reputation.[15] Slaughter had some of these characteristics, but as her hardheaded friend warned her from the start, the numbers were against her just as they were against any Democrat.

11. Janet A. Flamang, "Introduction: A Reflection on Themes of a "Women's Politics," in Flamang, ed., p. 9.
12. Center for the American Woman in Politics: *Women in State Legislatures 1988* (New Brunswick: Eagleton Institute of Politics, Rutgers, State University of New Jersey, 1988); Marianne Githens, "Women and State Politics: An Assessment," in Flamang, chap. 2.
13. Diamond, chap. 2.
14. Jerry Perkins and Diane L. Fowlkes, "Opinion Representation Versus Social Representation; or, Why Women Can't Run as Women and Win," *American Political Science Review* 74 (March 1980), 92–103.
15. Clark et al., p. 146; Darcy and Schramm, p. 11.

Nor could Slaughter count on the gender gap in the electorate for help in overcoming the disadvantageous numbers. For the most part, the coalition of disaffected women that was expected to provide the winning margin for Slaughter's candidacy did not exist in the spring of 1984. As table 5.1 indicates, women as well as men were more likely to register as Republicans, even though women outnumbered men among Democrats, and on most issues the differences in political attitudes were slight. Women tended to be more pessimistic about the direction in which the country was heading, but on questions ranging from federal deficits to Social Security to military aid to Central America their views were similar to those of men. The survey did reveal a significant split along partisan lines among women, with a strong majority of Republican women espousing conservative views and supporting President Reagan. Slaughter's perception in late May that the Republicans were closing ranks was not far from the mark.

As it turned out, the gender gap did not materialize nationally either. The pattern of the presidential election of 1980 was not repeated, as women joined with men in overwhelmingly supporting the incumbent president. The gender gap has been elusive in American politics all along, appearing in some elections, such as that of 1972, but not in others.[16] Just as importantly, the electoral behavior of women appears to be rooted in education, social class, and level of occupation.[17] On some issues the differences between employed women and housewives are far greater than the overall differences between men and women. This adds up to a convincing argument against the notion that there is a women's vote on which female politicians can base their candidacies.

If women do not enjoy any particular electoral benefits from their gender, then only the number of qualified female candidates will determine how rapidly the representation of women progresses. Over the last decade the number of women holding lower public office has more than doubled, but in the same period there was a net gain of only three women in the House of Representatives. Furthermore, under the prevailing rates of election, reelection, and retirement in the Congress, the number of women serving in Congress will increase by no more than 1 percent by the year 2001.[18]

Those who wish to see greater equality between the sexes will find little comfort in these projections. Yet the urge to accelerate the pace of women's advancement to Congress poses a threat to gains already achieved. Given the shortage of female candidates with the credentials and experience to contest a congressional seat, there is extraordinary pressure on such women to carry the

16. Poole and Zeigler, p. 45.
17. Ibid., p. 89–92.
18. Kristi Andersen and Stuart Thorson, "Congressional Turnover and the Election of Women," *Western Political Quarterly* 37 (March 1984): 151.

Table 5.1   Party Registration in the 30th Congressional District

	MEN		WOMEN		TOTAL	
	Number	Percentage	Number	Percentage	Number	Percentage
Republicans	100	51	96	47	196	49
Democrats	62	31	75	37	137	34
Independents	28	14	25	12	53	13
No response	7	4	7	3	14	4
Total	197	100	203	100	400	100

Percentages may not add to 100 because of rounding.
SOURCE: "Benchmark Survey of New York 30th District, May 1984," prepared by Public Response Associates for the American Medical Political Action Committee, Washington, D.C.

torch for their sex; even if they succumb to this pressure, their advancement causes vacancies that few other women are ready to fill. In the case of Slaughter, no woman was preparing to seek her seat in the Assembly if she ran for Congress. In the short run, it appears that advancement of women to the House could occur at the cost of representation at other levels of government. Perhaps more sobering is that women who attempt a House race and fail leave the pool of credible candidates smaller than it was before. Thus Slaughter's personal dilemma in the spring of 1984—whether to contest an open seat when she felt she was not ready or wait for some future race when the presence of an incumbent would put her at a disadvantage—reflects a larger dilemma for women in general. An aggressive push now to increase the number of women in the House drains the reservoir of talent for later races.

6

Options: Lawyer, Lobbyist, Party Chief

The common aspect of democratic nations will present a great number
of small and very rational objects of ambition . . . but no such thing as
ambition conceived and regulated on a vast scale is to be met with
there.

—*Alexis de Tocqueville,* Democracy in America

Without ever going to Washington, American politicians can find many outlets
for their energies and ambitions. Because of the nation's pluralism and federal
structure, opportunities beckon almost everywhere the politically motivated
turn: in state and local elective offices, in private businesses and interest
groups, and in campaign and party organizations. With so many paths to
political power before them, many prospective congressional candidates feel no
regret at passing up a chance to move to Capitol Hill, because they are quite
satisfied with the power and prospects of their positions back home.

Elective offices in state and local government are the most obvious outlets
for the politically ambitious who turn down the chance to run for Congress. The
mayoralty of a large city, the office of state attorney general, and a prestigious
judgeship are just a few of the positions that rival the House of Representatives
in power and influence. As discussed in the two preceding chapters, service in
the state legislature is an increasingly attractive alternative to a congressional
career. The path to power in the United States does not always lead to Washington, and the number of candidates waiting to run in any given congressional
election depends in part on the number of state and local elective offices
available in House districts.

What is more difficult to comprehend is the extent to which intense political
ambition can be satisfied with the power that resides in the thousands of nonelective positions of influence scattered all across the country. These are positions of importance filled by much less visible people (campaign strategists,
lobbyists, and party leaders, for example), who instead of dealing in the cur-
rency of mass politics, electoral success, deal in that of elite politics, backroom

influence. The power these people seek is largely screened from public view, and the constituencies they serve are small, organized elites in local communities, in state capitals, or across the nation in various interest groups. These nonelected politicians help broker disagreements among competing interests, shape public debate, and allocate the money and support so vigorously sought by the more visible elected politicians.

In New York's 30th Congressional District, several of the strongest potential contenders for Conable's House seat were such nonelected politicians: local people who had traded the officeholder's starring role for the backstage role of the impresario. Although intensely political, they were engaged in promoting other people's ambitions and did not think much about going to Congress themselves. Many had said no to other contests for elective office, and their decision to remain in the background this time simply reaffirmed these earlier decisions.

Yet in the weeks following Conable's announcement, their names kept surfacing in discussions about his replacement, not as politicians who were actually active candidates, but as people who ought to be. Each of these sophisticated, well-connected players possessed the attributes knowledgeable local observers believed all strong congressional competitors ought to have: political savvy, skill at debating, deep involvement in politics as a way of life, and demonstrated respect for the give-and-take of democracy. Community leaders believed about half a dozen men operating behind the scenes in the 30th District possessed these traits (but as it happened no women), and any one of them would instantly have been a serious contender if he had shown the slightest interest in making the race. But none did; indeed even as community leaders talked to us about why this insider or that would be a strong nominee, they always acknowledged somewhat wistfully, "Of course it will never happen."

Former elected officials were at the head of the wish lists of most community leaders, followed by successful professionals who had earned their political spurs as campaign strategists or advocates of particular issues. Among the most frequently mentioned were a former Assemblyman and state government official who at the time of Conable's announcement was practicing law with a major firm in Rochester and exercising some power as a member of the state board of regents; a former district attorney whom Governor Cuomo had named the head of the state police department in Albany; a former chairman of Monroe County's Democratic party who in the spring of 1984 was the vice-chairman of the state party organization; the former administrative assistant to Frank Horton, the congressman in the 29th district; the director of the local Chamber of Commerce; and a wealthy businessman who had held office briefly in the Monroe County legislature.

Despite differences in background, party affiliation, and accomplishment, these men all held one thing in common: they were thoroughly political. By all accounts their occupations, social contacts, and even family relations revolved around the practice of politics. They were not full-time politicians in the sense of depending on the electorate for their jobs or livelihood, but they did concentrate large portions of their time and energy on public issues and to varying degrees earned a living by minding the public's business. In addition, all these insiders exercised genuine political power; they made things happen, and everyone in town knew it.

Among this small group of obviously qualified and indisputably political people, why was there no one interested in running for Congress? Was it the loss of income, as some people suggested? The frantic commuting between Rochester and Washington? The lack of privacy that accompanies being in the public eye? Or perhaps the distasteful task of raising campaign funds? Each factor figured at least to some small degree in each person's decision. But just as surely all these people already lived fast-paced lives crowded with politics, and all had considerable experience raising money for political purposes.

The more important factor in every case was that none of these nonelected politicians needed to be in Congress to have power and participate in politics at a very high level of influence. Each was already at the center of decision making in the 30th district (some were even at its center at the state level) and each could wield influence over public issues without suffering any of the drawbacks that might come with a highly visible elective office.

In examining the thinking of the unseen candidates who find themselves exercising power without holding elected office, it becomes clear that to thrive political ambition does not depend exclusively on the stimulus of popular election. For some of the strongest unseen candidates, the role of the political insider—the operator working behind the scenes—offered all the political challenge their ambitions required.

The Lawyer

When David Lovenheim, a burly, young lawyer, moved his family from Washington to Rochester in 1979, many people assumed that he had come home to lay the groundwork for a bid for Congress. It was a natural assumption, because Lovenheim had spent his entire adult life reveling in congressional politics. As a second-year law student at George Washington University he began working for Congressman Frank Horton, and upon graduation he became Horton's executive assistant, a post he held for eleven years. During this time he acquired a reputation as a skillful administrator and astute political strategist, and he developed an extensive network of contacts in the district and throughout the state. Like many other congressional aides around the country, Lovenheim was well positioned to take over his boss's seat whenever he decided to retire.[1]

Local Republicans soon recognized a potential winner in this gruff political operative, and even before Lovenheim left Washington they signaled their readiness to advance his political ambitions. A vacant seat in the Assembly (which eventually went to Pinny Cooke) and the nomination to oppose state Senator Jack Perry were among the enticements with which they sought to lure him into elective politics. But he turned down all their overtures, and when he finally decided to return to his hometown at the age of thirty-six, it was not for a party nomination but for a partnership in Rochester's second largest law firm.

Even though Lovenheim had twice declined to lay the foundation for a congressional career by running for the state legislature, he still bore all the marks of a future House candidate. He plunged into Republican politics at the state and local level and was soon caught up in a swirl of party affairs—as counsel to the Republican minority in the state Assembly, as a campaign organizer for state Senator Perry Duryea's unsuccessful bid for governor in 1978, as part of Assemblyman Jim Emery's "kitchen cabinet" during the gubernatorial primary of 1982, and finally as an adviser to several promising politicians in Monroe County. All this politicking required two telephone lines into his new home, on which Lovenheim frequently carried on two rapid-fire conversations simultaneously. He was building contacts, banking favors, and gaining campaign experience—all valuable assets in a future run for the House, which most local people were sure was coming.

Just as important, Lovenheim regularly flew from Rochester to Washington to attend meetings of the Northeast-Midwest Caucus, a bipartisan group of congressmen that he had helped to organize during his days as a House staff member. Horton was a founder and co-chairman of the group, and because of this Lovenheim had been deeply involved in the caucus's business; among other things he had established the Northeast-Midwest Institute to conduct research into regional issues, and even after leaving his job with Horton he continued to be the institute's chairman and then its treasurer.

By maintaining his role in the caucus Lovenheim remained connected to life in Washington. He was able to keep up to date on regional and national issues, maintain his friendships on Capitol Hill, and keep some ties to the interest groups that shared the caucus's agenda. Because he kept one foot planted firmly in Washington, it would have been easy for Lovenheim to resume his old life—

---

1. In 1984 seventeen former administrative assistants sought seats in the House of Representatives. These former staff members tend to be more successful than other types of candidate. See Susan Webb Hammond, "From Staff Aide to Election: The Recruitment of U.S. Representatives," in Harold D. Clarke and Moshe M. Czudnowski, *Political Elites in Anglo-American Democracies: Changes in Stable Regimes* (DeKalb: Northern Illinois University Press, 1987), pp. 209–230.

this time not as the number two man in a congressional office but as the number one man.

From 1979 to 1984, however, Lovenheim never made any moves to go before the electorate, and when Barber Conable announced his retirement Lovenheim promptly placed a call to Fiji and offered Fred Eckert his support and assistance. Throughout the spring Lovenheim worked tirelessly for Eckert, issuing press releases under the aegis of the Draft Ambassador Eckert for Congress Committee, persuading his fellow Republicans to jump on Eckert's bandwagon, and counting Eckert's delegates for the GOP's nominating convention in May. In the early weeks of jockeying for position among Republicans, when Eckert was 10,000 miles away and unable to campaign openly because he was still an ambassador, Lovenheim played the part of shadow candidate, appearing at political functions to woo supporters and keeping his eye on the developing opposition.

The two men made an odd pair: Lovenheim was liberal and Jewish, and came from an affluent neighborhood on the east side; Eckert was conservative and Catholic, and came from the modest suburb of Greece. But even though they disagreed on many issues and had very different backgrounds, they shared a passionate interest in public issues and political intrigue and had come to like and respect one another over the course of several local campaigns. In addition, their alliance in the spring of 1984 was mutually convenient. In the short run Eckert needed some loyal supporters to sustain his congressional campaign until he could get home from the South Pacific, and in the long run Lovenheim needed the friendship of the 30th district's most likely new member of Congress to complement his existing ties to Horton in the 29th. "Access to Washington is Lovenheim's stock-in-trade, you know," said one Republican insider, expressing an opinion we heard more than once. "He needs to back a winner, and Eckert will remember who was for him early in the game."

Lovenheim's knowledge of the east side of Monroe County, particularly the towns that had been in Horton's district and were now in Conable's reapportioned 30th district, was especially valuable to Eckert, whose political base lay on the other side of the Genesee River. Lovenheim's long association with Horton and other moderate Republicans also lent Eckert some connections to the mainstream of his party, which was inclined to regard some of his views with suspicion, even outrage. Eventually even Lovenheim's wife helped Eckert appear more moderate, by serving on the candidate's Women's Advisory Board. Throughout the spring of 1984, Lovenheim drew on the experience and contacts that could have advanced his own congressional career to further the career of someone else.

In March we asked Lovenheim whether he had given any thought to running in the 30th district himself. "Not one flicker," he replied. "When I was working in Washington, I had a keen sense of wanting a congressional seat, but I stayed long enough to gradually understand the heavy personal toll being a congressman takes. I decided then, I would not run until the kids were gone. A job in Congress means cutting off all family ties, and I'm not ready to do that." Later he elaborated on this theme: "We left Washington, not so I could become a congressman, but so our kids would grow up close to their family. Everyone in Washington is from someplace else . . . there is no rootedness there . . . and we didn't want that for our daughters."

Once Lovenheim settled into the practice of law in a large firm, his financial situation changed dramatically. "The income disparity between successful attorneys and public officials is much greater now than it was twenty, or even ten, years ago," he noted. Not only the money but also his professional responsibilities kept him from venturing into full-scale political campaigning.

Throughout most of American history it has been quite common for lawyers to mix their private practice with public office. Campaigning was one of the few means available to young attorneys to advertise themselves, and the ordinary pace of business allowed lawyers enough flexibility to hold elective office without damaging their clients' interests.[2] Some lawyers even benefited from the perception among their clientele that they were well-connected politically. But the profession has changed in the last decade; today the law is a highly competitive field with an increasingly corporate structure and mentality. It has become less feasible to serve the two masters—the client and the voter—to whom a lawyer who is an elected official must bow.

When Lovenheim returned to Rochester in 1979, his decision to join a partnership with more than 150 lawyers on its payroll was a sure sign that he was already steering his political career toward the shadowy world of the influential insider. Although the firm placed no formal restrictions on his becoming a candidate, none of its partners or associates had run for office in recent memory. It was fine to be active in party politics and involved in other people's campaigns; it was even good business. But actually running required a level of effort and visibility that simply was not compatible with the demands of a modern law partnership. As Lovenheim explained, "The restraints on becoming a candidate are self-imposed. When you're a partner in a major firm, you have responsibilities to your clients and the rest of the firm, which make it nearly impossible to run a campaign too. It's been done—Dick Rosenbaum ran for governor while he was with the Nixon firm—but it's rare."

This view was widely shared by members of the Monroe County Bar Association, but according to most of them the problems for lawyers in politics extended beyond the constraints imposed by increasingly complex legal practices. "In the large firms," noted one attorney who had once run for the county

2. James David Barber, *The Lawmakers: Recruitment and Adaptation to Legislative Life* (New Haven and London: Yale University Press, 1965), chap. 3.

legislature, "you can't take a public position as a candidate without injuring one of your clients, while the small firms are so badly squeezed trying to compete with the big firms that the lawyers in them can't spare the time to run." He added that his own practice in a five-person firm had been "left in a mess" just from his one brief effort to gain a county legislative seat. Another lawyer, who had been the legal counsel to the Monroe County Republican party, added, "Recruitment into elective politics now comes from people who actually earn their living that way, who have no outside lives and no outside successes. The successful businessman or professional simply cannot switch into politics. He's got to be content behind the scenes."

These attitudes have been borne out in Monroe County. Although local lawyers there have not given up politics altogether—they remain prominent in both parties, hold many high appointive positions in state and local government, work with interest groups and as policy advocates, and even occasionally set up PACs to influence campaigns—they are not running for elective office (except judicial ones) in the numbers they once did. As a result, in 1984 there were no lawyers from Monroe County in the state legislature, county legislature, or Rochester City Council, and barely a handful in the area's town governments and school boards.[3] This was not simply a local phenomenon: from the time Barber Conable entered the House in 1965 until his retirement in 1984, the percentage of congressmen with a legal background dropped steadily from 56.8 to 46.[4]

David Lovenheim personifies this trend. In him all the signs of incipient congressional ambition were present. From law school he headed straight for Capitol Hill with a roaring case of Potomac fever. After leading a life totally immersed in Washington politics, he returned to his home base and began the time-consuming process of cementing political ties among state and local Republicans, while at the same time maintaining his old links to Washington. But Lovenheim neither took the next, seemingly inevitable, step of becoming a candidate for Congress, nor made any move to run for the local or state legislature. He had so many nonelective outlets for his interest in politics that he had no need for elective public office, or for the added burdens the visibility of elected office brings with it. By adopting the role of inside deal-maker and campaign mastermind, Lovenheim had found more than enough scope for his drive for political influence.

3. State Senator L. Paul Kehoe, who obtained a small portion of Monroe County in the redistricting of 1982, practiced law in rural Wayne County.
4. Norman J. Ornstein et al., *Vital Statistics on Congress, 1984–1985 Edition* (Washington, D.C.: American Enterprise Institute, 1984), pp. 21–23; Paul Hain and James E. Pierson, "Lawyers and Politics Revisited: Structural Advantages of Lawyer Politicians," *American Journal of Political Science* 19 (January 1975): 41–51.

The Lobbyist

In the pluralist environment of the United States the line between the private and public sectors is blurred and jagged; people can easily find release for their political ambitions as spokesmen and lobbyists for private interests regulated or funded by government. Because all three levels of American government are reaching out to more and more interests, potential congressional candidates have an increasing number of these lobbying opportunities. They can become private politicians, shuttling to and from state capitals and Washington to consult with important government officials and exercise another brand of inside power in American politics.

In the spring of 1984 we talked to several of these private legislators; the one whose name came up most frequently was Tom Mooney, executive director of the Rochester Chamber of Commerce. Mooney was not on the roster of potential congressional candidates that circulated in the press, but he was on the personal lists of many Republicans who thought he would be a strong candidate for any office. "Tom's smart and he's got a lot of presence," remarked the party chairman, Ron Starkweather, "but he can't afford to run for public office."

A lifelong resident of Monroe County, Mooney had spent his entire working life in and around government. He had been a deputy county manager under Lucien Morin and a deputy city manager and city manager in Rochester. As the most visible spokesman for the major business organizations in the community, he remained involved with political decisions, particularly those affecting the revitalization of Rochester's downtown and the reinvigoration of its business climate. He had played a key role in the complex financial negotiations regarding the city's new, multimillion-dollar convention center. As someone long involved in government in both Rochester and Monroe County, he frequently mediated between these governmental units, which were often at odds.

Mooney's experience in government and prominence in the community accounted for much of his appeal to local Republicans, but he had other qualities that marked him as a good candidate, especially when compared with his friend and former high school classmate, Fred Eckert. Both men were issue-oriented fiscal conservatives, but Mooney's political style was smoother than Eckert's. Mooney would bargain when Eckert would refuse to budge, and as a result people in the community not only were more comfortable with Mooney as a politician, but believed he could be more effective in a legislature. Mooney was viewed as a pragmatic, businessman's conservative, Eckert as a diehard, right-wing ideologue.

Mooney discouraged all talk about a congressional candidacy in 1984 with a brusque "no comment" when reporters inquired about his intentions. His low profile stood in marked contrast to his behavior in the previous year, when he had been one of the most prominent individuals on the list of possible successors to County Manager Morin. "When Lou said he wasn't going to run," he noted, "I was besieged with calls, and I let it go because it didn't hurt me. You never want to be in a job where someone doesn't want you for something else." But Mooney had already made up his mind not to run for the highest elective office in the county, and he joined Starkweather and a few other key Republicans on a journey to Florida to persuade Morin, who was on vacation, to make the race.

By so doing Mooney signaled to his local supporters that he preferred the quiet influence of the insider to the public recognition of the candidate; as a result they recognized from the moment Barber Conable announced his retirement that Mooney would not set himself up as a rival to his boyhood friend, Fred Eckert. Mooney explained his reasons for staying out of the limelight of electoral politics this way: "I have the best of both worlds. I'm in politics without really being in politics. I'm in business without really being in business." It was clear that he would decline to run for Congress because he found much personal satisfaction working behind the scenes in a political position in the private sector; it was also clear that he thought he was more effective when the interests he represented were handled outside the public glare. Several times he indicated to us that he could get more done without the irritating scrutiny of the mass media and the grandstanding of elected officials who were often obliged to operate in the open. For this political man the best politics were those of the back room, and to be in Congress was to be too exposed.

The Party Chief

In the Monroe County Democratic party, Larry Kirwan was another political figure quite content to stay behind the scenes rather than step out to center stage and hold elective government office. Kirwan was thought by Democrats and Republicans alike to be a logical replacement for Conable. Although a liberal Democrat, he was seen as a gifted political moderator in the tradition of Conable, a person who would be perceived by the electorate as intellectually and tempermentally fit to follow the man who had been voted by his colleagues the most respected member of Congress. Although he had never run for government office, he was respected for his genius as a political organizer, and local Republicans were convinced that only Assemblyman Roger Robach could mount a stiffer challenge than Kirwan for Conable's seat.

As the chairman of the Monroe County Democratic party from 1972 to 1983, Kirwan was the driving force behind its enormous new success, and his inspirational leadership had gained him the intense loyalty of the party faithful. In the spring of 1984 he no longer held a post in the local party, but as the state

Democratic party's vice-chairman and the regional chairman of Walter Mondale's campaign for president, he had strong connections at every level of American politics to all the resources needed to make a competitive race for Congress. And if that were not reason enough for him to run, his concern for the broad issues of national politics, which had been manifest from his first entry on the political scene as a champion of civil rights in the 1960s, should have clinched his decision to move on to Washington.

But Kirwan never seriously considered running. Personal obligations were an important reason for this, but equally so was the enormous satisfaction he derived from his role inside the party and behind the scenes. He told us: "Some day I may change, but I never really wanted to be a candidate [for anything]. I can make more things happen and make a bigger difference through the party. As a party leader I get to play all over the field. I help to recruit candidates for the local legislature, the Congress, the courts, the mayor. I like what I do, and I know I can make a difference. I feel I get more done this way. I have my hands on the strings of social change."

To illustrate the extent of his power he told of his role in 1974 in the selection of Tom Ryan as a mayor of Rochester. Because the city then had a weak-mayor form of government, the mayor was elected by the city council and came from within its ranks. After the Democrats won control of the Rochester City Council in an upset in 1974, they had the unexpected opportunity to choose the city's mayor.[5]

Kirwan recalled: "I called each of the eight in, one by one. We talked for about fifteen minutes about who they preferred. Their first choice, second choice, etc. Then I dismissed them and went on to the next. When it was all over, I called them back in to say that Tom Ryan was the mayor. He was first on only one list. But second on everybody else's. He didn't even want it. But I got them all together and told them, 'He will be your mayor.' And Ryan has done a good job. You can use the party leader's job to get people to work together like this."

To this highly charged political activist the party is the path to power. Although Kirwan looks to others like a distinguished Wall Street banker (in fact he owns an insurance agency) he sees himself as a party organizer. In the age of the yuppie he is the functional equivalent of a party boss. And although others describe him as glamorous and charismatic, he seems not to need the political limelight. To work backstage is fine for him.

Although he declined to wage his own campaign for Congress, Kirwan nevertheless agreed to run the campaign for whoever was chosen by the Democrats to oppose Fred Eckert, and he looked forward to doing so. He told us: "I

5. In a referendum in 1984, Rochester's voters approved a change to an elected-mayor form of government, to begin the following year. Ryan was elected to the office in 1985.

respect Eckert as a tough competitor. He's no slouch. It'll be fun running a campaign against him."

Kirwan and Eckert were two professional public figures who were delighted to battle each other. In the process each satisfied a strong political drive, and each did it his own way: one would run for Congress, the other would run someone else's campaign for Congress. Each appeared equally satisfied. Less than six months later, as Eckert moved up to Congress, Kirwan moved up in the party. Right after the general election in November, Governor Cuomo named Kirwan the state chairman of the Democratic party and charged him with preparing for Cuomo's expected bid for reelection in 1986.

In many ways Kirwan and Eckert seem very similar politicians. Each got his start in local politics in the ideologically charged atmosphere of the late 1960s. Each became identified with the causes and candidates of his end of the ideological spectrum. Each entered politics by overturning established political forces: Eckert smashed the Republican party's machine in the Town of Greece, Kirwan took over the Democratic party's enfeebled apparatus in Monroe County, as he sought to control and reconstitute the local organization. Each man is ambitious, tough, and ideologically committed.

Why, then, would one of them run for Congress without hesitation and the other decline the chance without ever really considering it? At least part of the answer is that early in their careers Eckert pursued the power of government office while Kirwan pursued that of party organization. Having made these choices long ago, they had to a large degree made their decision about running for Congress many years before Conable's seat became vacant.

In a variety of ways people like Lovenheim, Mooney, and Kirwan who could run for Congress find ample governmental and political influence totally outside the realm of elective office. Without doubt such people have political ambitions to rival those of Fred Eckert. But the plethora of opportunities in pluralist American politics allows these potentially antagonistic ambitions to be channeled in so many different directions that competition for any particular place of power may not be terribly keen. Lovenheim, Mooney, and Kirwan are good examples of this; each took a different route to power, and Eckert followed still another. Once each of the four was headed in a different direction, their paths were destined not to meet in the race to replace Barber Conable.

7

Ordinary People:
The Personal Price of Power

*We are making the price of power much too high in this society. I
worry that we are making the conditions of public life so tough that
nobody except people really obsessed with power will be willing finally
to pay that price.*

—Jeane Kirkpatrick

To run for Congress some politicians from upstate New York had to risk too
much politically; others felt they had to risk too much personally. For some of
the unseen candidates, even a seat in the world's most powerful legislature did
not seem worth the sacrifice of families, friends, and financial security they
believed their election to the House of Representatives would entail. Shaken by
current stories about the frantic, disrupted lives of members of Congress, they
reined in their political ambition rather than risk the personal turmoil of a
congressional career.

Not everyone we interviewed had these personal worries, and among those
who acknowledged that they did no one dropped out of the race solely because
of them. For most of the unseen candidates it was a combination of factors—
political, personal, and circumstantial—that finally caused them not to run for
Congress. But for about half the people who thought about replacing Barber
Conable, personal costs did enter the calculations. For about a quarter, the
personal hardship they thought was tied to a House seat ended up being the
major reason they did not run. Included in this group were some of the strongest
candidates in both parties. The personal price of power is therefore a significant
part of the story of unseen congressional candidates, even though in 1984 it was
not a factor in each case in New York's 30th Congressional District.

Among those who did express concern about the personal hardships of life in
Congress, nearly every one also voiced a much more tentative, less focused,
sense of political ambition. Service in the House of Representatives was not
their primary objective when they entered politics, and they were therefore
extremely sensitive to the costs of trading their present political position in
upstate New York for a future of congressional influence in Washington. Politi-

133

cians with more intense ambitions could acknowledge the same personal costs and persevere anyway, but for others the benefits of sitting in Congress were not high enough to justify the price.

The Costs of Leaving Home

The personal costs feared by would-be candidates were all tied to leaving home: cutting off valued relationships with family and friends, abandoning established careers, and endangering their sense of self as they left behind local roots and familiar habits and entered the new world of politics in Washington.

In local politics people can serve in public office and still carry on careers, maintain a satisfying domestic life, and feel a part of the social fabric. Even state legislators can maintain outside careers and have time with family and friends if they care to. Election to Congress lifts politicians out of the local community, however, and plays havoc with their personal identities by disrupting habits that have shaped their lives for years. As a local county legislator said to us about going to Congress, "I would have to change my whole life and become a total politician. I want to keep part of myself for my family and my business, and I don't see how I could do that in Congress." Another contender expressed the same worry: "You have to think about changing your whole life. When I'm in Washington it seems very phony to me."

These established political figures had second thoughts about running for Congress because they saw too much that was negative associated with re-directing their private lives. Other politicians described the same situation from a slightly different perspective. They stressed their lives were too good just the way they were. They saw too many positive aspects in their personal lives even to consider running for Congress, and usually took themselves out of the race quickly and unequivocally. In these cases political ambition appeared at least in part to be fueled by personal discontent. "I've been interested in a seat in Congress ever since college," a local lawyer told us, "but I'm too comfortable now. Candidates can become too comfortable. You've got to have some dis-comfort to have the ambition." This candidate therefore never considered making the race, even though he was urged by several political activists to do so and promoted by the party chairman as a possible candidate. I'm just not willing to make the personal and economic sacrifices necessary to run for Congress," he said.

When politicians talked to us about personal sacrifice they were usually referring to the loss of their family life. Because they invariably saw the job of a member of Congress as requiring eighteen hours a day, seven days a week, they were certain they would have no time left for their families.

The routine they pictured was always the same. From Monday to Thursday they would be caught in a swirl of legislative and social demands on Capitol Hill, on Thursday evening or Friday fly home to the district for the year-round electioneering and tiresome contact with constituents required of members of Congress, and on Sunday night or Monday morning return to Washington to begin the grind again. They assumed that once elected to Congress their public responsibilities would be unending and their private responsibilities unfulfilled.

One of Conable's potential replacements, after describing the harsh conditions he foresaw for himself and his family if he won the seat, told us, "You know, even most of my friends serving in Congress told me not to run. They said it wasn't worth it."

Similar thoughts were expressed by another contender. Having entered elective politics because of dissatisfaction with the process of recruitment and the quality of the candidates it produced, he should have found an open seat in Congress particularly alluring. But his political concerns were no match for his ties to his family. "I thought very seriously about running for Conable's seat," he said. "And then I talked with my wife. She has her ninety-one-year-old father here and the grandchildren. After raising seven children, she's entitled to her own life. If I had really wanted to and felt passionately about having this be the capstone of my career, she would have agreed. But I didn't want to ask her."

To spare spouses and children being cut off from their friends and relatives and lessen the high cost of living in the capital, many of the politicians we interviewed planned to go to Washington alone and live in a rented room or small apartment while their family stayed in the district. Thus, in the life these politicians pictured there was double damage to the family: not only would there be the time-consuming demands of the job, but separate residences hundreds of miles apart would leave them physically isolated as well.

In addition to the strains on their family relationships, there was for many of the politicians calculating the costs of a seat in Congress a concern about the drain on their checkbooks. First, many believed they would have to maintain two residences. Even if they did not, they would have to buy an expensive home in the Washington area and struggle to make ends meet for the entire family in an economic market where the cost of living was much higher than in Rochester. In short they believed their salaries at home bought more than did congressional paychecks in Washington. The problem was summed up by the quip used by one Rochester politician to dismiss inquiries from the press about his interest in the race: "I can't run for Congress; I already have too big a mortgage here at home."

Finances were a big worry to many who considered running for Congress, because the time in a politician's life when he or she is most likely to be in a position to run for Congress (the late thirties to late forties) is also the time when the politician is most likely to encounter challenging business or professional opportunities and confront the largest financial obligations. The three political figures quoted below were each conscious of these economic barriers as they explained their decision not to try to follow Conable:

"I never really considered it. But even if the juices were really flowing to do this, I would have to take a hard look at the financial picture. I'm at a time in my personal life where I have many obligations."

"This race is four years too soon for me. My kids are too small, my business is at a critical point, and my wife has no particular desire to move to Washington, where we'd be lucky to find a house for $300,000."

"I've made a list of the pluses and minuses. With all the kids just about out of college, my wife and I are finally comfortable, and I don't know that we want to face the costs in Washington. Somebody told me eggs are two dollars a dozen; sweet corn is three-fifty a dozen. I don't know where I could live."

Beyond these clearly expressed worries about family and finances was a final concern about leaving home. Always implied, never stated directly, it was an underlying uneasiness about what life in Congress would do to the politicians' view of themselves, to their self-respect. Would life away from home change them? Would it corrupt them? Would they embarrass themselves in the "big leagues"? Could they really handle the job in the world's most powerful legislature?

This personal concern about life in Congress begins with a perception shared by politicians and voters that the congressional office is a cut above any local or state legislative job and therefore demands more character, intelligence, and judgment from the person who fills it. Ordinary politicians can serve in the lesser offices of local government, but a seat in Congress rightfully belongs to a person of accomplishment and substance. In New York's 30th district, this high-minded perception of the congressional role was enhanced by Conable's twenty-year record, which seemed to approach the ideal. Perhaps surprisingly in this age of public cynicism, there remained a sense of awe attached to a seat in the U.S. House of Representatives, even among battle-scarred politicians.

Accepting these higher standards and applying them to themselves, a few people were dogged by self-doubt about their worthiness to succeed Conable. While interviewing a public official who had spent his entire adult life in elected office, we perceived this self-doubt when we asked if he had given any previous thought to running for Congress. "Oh, sure," he remarked, "every country doctor wants to be a surgeon, even if he's better off just being a country doctor."

At another point in the interview, he gave the same message as he described the uncomfortable feelings he and his wife had recently when they took their first trip to Washington and visited the House and Senate chambers. As he recounted walking and waiting in the hallways of the Capitol he referred to himself as "rabble" and as out of place among the "vested, well-dressed congressional crowd."

Others were not as worried about their capacity to master the job as about the job's propensity to change them. The potential candidate with the greatest sense of self-doubt of those we interviewed wondered out loud if Congress would transform him. He also made explicit the role his longtime friends played in helping maintain his personal equilibrium in the topsy-turvy world of public life. "Your friends are people who know you as a person. They keep your head screwed on. They knew you before you were a big shot."

Going to Congress, where he would have much less regular contact with the people who knew him as a person, gave this politician cause for concern. All alone in Washington, would he be able to keep his head screwed on? He was not sure.

Another potential candidate showed his worry about the possibility of being transformed when he ended his list of reasons for not making the race by saying, "I didn't want to go to Washington . . . all those old guys go there and throw everything over for some chippy." For him and others there was a hint of anxiety about the seductiveness of life in Washington. To be on the safe side a person ought to stay home.

It is important to remember that these concerns were expressed by truly political people. What they feared was not the hurly-burly of political life but the trauma of leaving home and breaking up their private lives. A middle-aged, affable politician made this clear as he elaborated on his reasons for not pursuing the congressional race. Believed by local insiders to be the second or third strongest candidate his party could nominate and courted seriously by his party chairman, he still turned down the chance at Congress. After citing most of the usual personal objections to going to Washington, he hinted that a different response might be forthcoming if the opportunity for higher office arose at home, within the community, where many of his personal concerns could be mitigated.

"Three years ago I would have jumped at the chance [to run for Conable's seat]. It's a once-in-a-lifetime opportunity. At that time in my life, I would have been out in front, but not now. When I finished my MBA, I made the decision at that time not to do politics full-time, but until then politics was my life. I like my job, and I enjoy seeing my kid play basketball. I don't want to get on the plane Monday morning and come back Thursday night. I missed seeing my kids when they were small, and now I like going home at night. Besides after I lost against ——— my wife told me in bed that night, 'If you had won, I would have left you.' " After a long pause he added, "The one job that would tempt me right now, though, is the county executive's spot."

For him and many others the trouble with serving in Congress was that he could not have gone home at night. He did not turn his back on Congress because he had lost interest in politics; clearly he was still a political creature, because he held on to his local elected office. He also still had some political ambition, as was clear from his admission that he might be lured to even higher county office. This was conceivable because at the local level greater political responsibilities might still be combined with home and hearth. But in no circumstances would he go to Congress, because he was convinced that the congressional life offered no chance for politics and home to coexist.

Private People in the Public Eye

Looking at the personal reasons that prompted would-be candidates to drop out of the race to succeed Conable, it is clear that many, perhaps most, of the people mentioned as his potential successors never really intended to run. In the days immediately after Conable announced his retirement, the mass media named twenty local political figures perhaps interested in making the run for Congress. In party and elite circles, the names of several others were taken seriously as well. Even six weeks later, the field of candidates still appeared to number nearly a dozen. Why did the press report that so many were actively interested, when so few really had serious intentions for any extended period? Where did the local media get all those names? Why were so many political figures content to leave the impression that they might run, when they already knew that family obligations or political realities or simply bad timing precluded their doing so?

The field initially appeared so large because all the major players in the recruitment story had their own motives for invoking as many names as were credible and for leaving them in the public eye as long as possible.

The press had a motive: it wanted a good story. It was naturally susceptible to the idea that a tough race would develop to find Conable's successor, and a horse race is obviously more exciting if the field is crowded and all the best thoroughbreds are running.[1] In this environment the press was a willing, even eager, participant in reporting every piece of political gossip and in providing the gentle winds for every party insider's trial balloon. Soon, as the media floated one politician after another through their stories, the air was thick was political names "contemplating the race for Congress."

The press had at least an additional journalistic worry, if not exactly a motive, that helped make the list of would-be candidates progressively longer in the early stages of the race: no political journalist wants to have overlooked a story that anticipates the decisions of all the people who actually do run,

---

1. For a discussion of the role of the media in creating the atmosphere of a horse race in presidential politics see Thomas E. Patterson and Robert D. McClure, *The Unseeing Eye: The Myth of Television Power in National Politics* (New York: Putnam, 1976). See also Patterson, *The Mass Media Election* (New York: Praeger, 1980). For a discussion of how the press covers congressional campaigns see Peter Clarke and Susan H. Evans, *Covering Campaigns: Journalism in Congressional Elections*, (Stanford, Calif.: Stanford University Press, 1983).

because if the journalist misses someone his or her status as a "knowledgeable insider" will be sullied. Because in the early going so many people could conceivably have run and nobody knew who finally would, it was safer to talk about everyone, and the sooner, the safer. Finally, the idea of a free-for-all to gain a congressional seat fitted nicely into the stereotype that the press and the public have of political figures. To the media and their audience, everyone in politics is hungry for power and the opportunity to move up the ladder, and the horse race was therefore a story the press was comfortable presenting and the public comfortable reading. It upset neither's prejudices.

Party leaders also had motives: they wanted the nomination process to appear wide open, and by playing into the eagerness of the press to create a contest they not only helped form that impression but also derived some personal benefits. First, party leaders knew that contemporary democratic ideology called for open nominations and wide public participation in party affairs, and they had no desire to put their organization at odds with this ideal. In addition, some of the party leaders we interviewed subscribed to the ideal themselves and believed their organizations and the public would be better served if the nominations were seriously contested. (We should point out however that among the leaders of both parties in the 30th district, for the race to be seriously contested it did not need to have a primary. It was only necessary that the party leaders, using the organization's internal procedures, have a real choice among a range of respected political figures and acknowledged vote-getters.) To some extent, when party leaders responded to questions from the press about who would be the likely contenders in the congressional race, they were compiling wish lists—naming strong candidates they hoped would run for Congress.

Party leaders also knew that they had much to gain personally from naming as many people as they could. First, it enabled them to recognize and advertise their elected officeholders and faithful party workers. It is an honor to be thought of as a congressional contender, and party leaders were happy to spread widely an honor that cost them nothing to award. Second, they believed their name-dropping strengthened the organization's image. It said to the citizenry that many of the party's elected officials had already acquired the stature to serve in Congress, and to aspiring political figures that party service was an aid to their ambition. Third, it gave the leaders time to assess the overall political situation inside their parties before they had to take sides themselves. The longer the list of party contenders, the more freedom of action the party leaders had and the more easily they avoided the charges of bossism and heavy-handed influence. Finally, party leaders were using public reaction to the names reported by the press as a quick, crude gauge of a potential candidate's electability—a free public opinion poll. They would throw out a name and wait for the phone to ring.

The people mentioned by the news media also had a motive to keep their names before the public: the advertising was good for business. It was also good for their vanity.[2]

One politician who kept his name on the list of possible candidates for several weeks but knew almost from the start that he would not run told us, "I'm just letting my name hang out there in the breeze. It's good publicity, and it doesn't hurt anything." When his political allies offered to support him, he told them bluntly his candidacy was a sham. "I could have had several endorsements," he said. "But I told them I wasn't serious, and they should get on [Eckert's] bandwagon." Not interested in a seat in Congress, he nevertheless was eager to run for the state Assembly, and believed the publicity about running for Congress could only help his name recognition when he finally did run for the Assembly.

It was not only the elected officeholders who thought they profited from being mentioned by the news media: lobbyists and spokesmen for interest groups also believed they benefited from speculation about their potential as replacements for Conable. Anything that gave them a greater aura of being well connected was good for their reputations as influence brokers. They also thought it gave them additional leverage with their employers: reminded that their employees had other attractive opportunities, their bosses would be more disposed to placate them.

Business reasons were not the only ones so many political figures left their names in the media long after they knew their running for Congress was a fiction. For some, vanity demanded notoriety. A number simply liked the attention, even though their appetite for publicity did not always gain them the respect of other politicians. As one local political insider told us, disdaining his colleagues who gloried in having their names in the paper, "When Andropov died, I thought some of these guys would announce they were thinking about his job, too."

Whatever their motives, these political figures who did not run for Congress but were talked about in the media got what they wanted out of Conable's retirement. Their intent was not to advance their congressional ambitions but further their local ones and satisfy their egos. In these perhaps minor ways, the political figures who did not go to Washington wrung the last drop of advantage they could from their decision to stay at home.

Local Ties and National Ambitions

There has long been a deep-seated tension in the job of federal representative—a tension that arises from the requirement of House members to be both local

2. That press coverage is a form of free advertising is an old theme in studies of political recruitment. See for example James David Barber, *The Lawmakers: Recruitment and Adaptation to Legislative Life* (New Haven and London: Yale University Press, 1965), esp. chap. 3.

and national officials. The unseen candidates tell us that a congressional career requires a taste as well as a tolerance for inhabiting two very different and disconnected worlds at the same time.

Since the country's founding, men and women imbued with the distinctive values and views of their distant and disparate communities have gathered in the House of Representatives to reconcile the diverse concerns of a great nation. These lawmakers have as a rule been deeply rooted in their home constituencies, and the representation they have provided their fellow citizens has often extended beyond the intellectual plane to a more emotional, empathic one. The sense of being an integral part of the communities for which they speak in the national legislature is the great strength that members of the House bring to the institution, but at the same time their intimate connection with the people at home raises to exceptionally high levels the cost of leaving behind family and friends.[3] Recruitment of new House members therefore depends on a pool of people who have a close affinity with the rhythms of life in a particular district and simultaneously the capacity to detach themselves from the locality without losing their sense of place or self.

This dilemma is not new. The framers of the Constitution recognized, even cultivated, the conflict between local ties and national forces that pushed and pulled a member of Congress in so many different directions. The discomforts and disruptions of a modern House career, which troubled so many politicians from upstate New York in 1984, would have sounded strikingly familiar in Philadelphia in 1787. But the framers also believed that for most legislators service in the House would be short, a temporary interruption in their local pursuits rather than a wrenching, long-term break with family, friends, and profession.

Professionalization of the House during the twentieth century made the Founders' belief in the limited extent of congressional service obsolete. The length of careers in Washington is now measured in decades rather than the years or even months that the Founders envisioned. And the accelerated pace and wider scope of legislative business strains further still the weak link that is left between Washington and home. With too little time to do all that is expected of them, House members are overwhelmed by their jobs, and it is small wonder that they end up being called total politicians by their colleagues who stay home.

Perhaps some people are naturally adept at keeping their balance on the nerve-wracking tightrope stretching between Capitol Hill and the home district. Personal circumstance and past experience can also prepare a politician for the risks of a high flier. In New York's 30th district age, past mobility, and contacts outside the district all played a part in helping prospective members of the House accept the personal price of congressional power.

3. Richard F. Fenno, Jr., *Home Style: House Members in Their Districts* (Boston: Little, Brown, 1977), pp. 243–246.

In the first place, the more social and family ties people had in the district, the less likely they were to pursue their urge to go to Congress. In contrast, contenders for Conable's seat who had left the area to go to college, had spouses from other parts of the country, were divorced, had lived with their families for extended periods outside the district, or had in any way broken some of the ties that bind people to a place seemed more prepared to go to Congress.

Second, the more success people had known in business, professional, or personal pursuits outside the political arena, the less likely they were to make the race. The person who had sunk his or her roots into the community at many points, through politics, career, hobbies, or work in service organizations, was too solidly based in the community to move on to Congress. On the other hand the person whose ego was involved only with politics had fewer qualms about a future in Washington.

Thus the congressional recruitment process in the 30th district favored professionals who began in politics quite young and pursued no other career. There was even a hint that dedication to politics had to go beyond that: for persons seriously interested in going to Congress, politics could not be just their career; it had to be their whole life.

Finally, age seemed to be a factor in the decision to go to Washington. In general younger politicians seemed more comfortable with the idea than olders ones. Although Congress is frequently pictured as a home for the aged, increasingly the House of Representatives belongs to the young. Over the last two decades the influx of younger members and the retirement of many senior ones has lowered the average age of a member of the House of Representatives.

There are several reasons why the race for Congress is becoming primarily a contest among politicians in their late thirties to late forties. One is that the seniority system in Congress forces a member to serve several terms before he or she can rise to a position of importance. We believe that in several cases in the 30th district men and women who declined to run did so in part because they thought they were too old—not too old to go to Congress, but too old to wait ten years to gain some influence there. Party leaders agreed with them: although they saw some of these older politicians as very strong vote-getters, most insiders were unenthusiastic about candidates older than around fifty because their age made them a poor long-term investment.

Also linked to age were the physical demands of the job. Bridging the gulf between home and Washington is hard work: the travel, the hours, the stress. As politicians advance in age, these aspects of life as a federal representative become less and less appealing. Only the younger politicians in the 30th district were confident that they had the constitution to handle the demanding pace of the congressional life.

Age was also another indication of the likelihood that a person had put down deep roots in the community. People in their late forties and early fifties were more likely to have spent enough time in the area to have built successful careers outside of politics or have teenage children with their own, independent ties to the community. By late middle age, politicians and their families can become too established in the community to leave it, particularly if they have never lived anywhere else. By contrast, younger people tend to be less well established. Instead of finding themselves in the middle of satisfying challenges, they are just beginning careers and exploring opportunities. Young people have more mobile families that are less enmeshed in the social fabric of the community, or have no families at all. Younger candidates simply have less personal baggage to weigh them down.

Among the would-be contenders for Conable's seat it was clear that Fred Eckert, more than any other potential candidate, was prepared by experience and age to undertake the taxing balancing act of serving in Congress. At forty-three he would find the newcomers to the House in 1984 to be of a similar age.

Eckert's readiness to serve in Congress was due to far more than his age. His entire adult life had been a prelude to leaving home for Washington. A native of Rochester, he began his college career at a small Jesuit school in upstate New York and eventually graduated from North Texas State University, where he met and later married a woman from Mississippi. After college he took a job outside New York City and spent three years in the metropolitan area before returning to his hometown. His position several years later as a state senator further drew him from the community to Albany and acclimated his family to the absences of a commuting parent. In 1982 he again pulled up stakes as he, his wife, and their three children left their home in central New York to live ten thousand miles away in the Fiji Islands, where he took up his ambassadorial duties. In each case Eckert reached beyond the boundaries of upstate New York. None of his ventures severed his lifelong association with the Rochester area, but all made the upheaval of living in Washington far less threatening to him and his family than to many other politicians who were lifelong residents of one area.

In addition, Eckert's only deep involvement with the people of the 30th district had been political. A year after returning home from the New York City area he made an unsuccessful bid to attend the Republican convention of 1968 as a delegate for Richard Nixon. Shortly after this inauspicious initiation into local politics, at the age of twenty-eight he was elected the supervisor of the town of Greece, the district's largest town, where his father had been a member of the Republican party committee. By 1980, having won election to a fifth term in the state Senate, he had waged and won ten campaigns—seven in general elections and three in primaries—in only eleven years. Even Eckert's business, a public-relations firm that he had established on returning to the community, had deep political connections. Not only did it serve him well in his own campaigns, it also involved him as a media consultant and advertising man in the election efforts of other upstate Republicans. Because Eckert's whole life before going to Congress had been consumed with politics, he had been left with little time and energy for other types of community activity that might later have diverted him from a career in the House.

Eckert's participation in presidential electoral politics also gave him early, if limited, connections to life in Washington. At the Republican conventions of 1976 and 1980, where his total support for Ronald Reagan won him the gratitude of fellow conservatives around the country, Eckert attached himself to a network of people who could ease his entrance into the fast-flowing currents of congressional life. In short he had braced and cushioned himself for the disjunctures of living in two different worlds; he had allowed himself few distractions in Rochester to interfere with his plans for going to Washington, where he had cultivated a circle of friends and acquaints who would welcome him when he arrived.

Other congressional districts around the country may differ from New York's 30th by producing a larger pool of individuals who are prepared to bear the personal costs of a trip to Congress. Politicians in such areas may be less attached to their communities, because the communities themselves are not as stable as the Monroe County area or because they are too new to have any real identity. In either case, the peripatetic life of a House member may not seem as disruptive as it did in the staid environment of upstate New York. It may also be true that districts within large urban areas are so cosmopolitan that jetting from place to place and never being home for dinner is a commonly accepted way of doing business and raising a family. In such communities, the harried member of Congress who shuttles from city to city and chicken dinner to chicken dinner has much company and may feel no disorientation. Nevertheless, although the perceived price of entering the House may vary in different parts of the country, the personal cost of full-blown congressional ambitions is never low. The unseen candidates remind us that today as in the past, some would-be members of Congress are unwilling to pay it.

Part Two
Electoral Consequences

8

Political Values:
The Party's Choice

*The longer one frets with the puzzle of how democratic regimes manage
to function, the more plausible it appears that a substantial part of the
explanation is to be found in the motives that actuate the leadership
echelon, the values that it holds, in the rules of the political game to
which it adheres, in the expectations which it entertains . . .*
　　　　　　　—V. O. Key, Jr., Public Opinion and American Democracy

*The apparent independence of congressmen from party while in Con-
gress may be offset by a real dependence on party in their home districts.*
　　　　　　　—S. J. Eldersveld, Political Parties in American Society

By the time Monroe County's Republicans met in late May to select their
nominee for Barber Conable's House seat, only two serious candidates remained in the race: Ambassador Fred Eckert, an abrasive, hard-line ideologue,
and Town Supervisor Don Riley of Greece, a congenial, consensus-minded
administrator. Their starkly contrasting political styles presented the local GOP
with a striking example of the most fundamental problem faced by party organizations contesting an American election: should they offer voters a choice or an
echo? Emphasize principle or style? Move to the extreme or seek the center?

In naming Fred Eckert their congressional nominee, Republicans in the 30th
district chose the more radical course, and the ease with which Eckert gained
their endorsement underscores the advantages that ideological outsiders are
thought to have gained from electoral and organizational reforms aimed at
democratizing American parties in the twentieth century. Closer examination
reveals a different story: it was traditional party insiders who preferred the
radical, Eckert, over the moderate, Riley, not because they agreed with his
policies, but because of their perception of what would best serve the needs of
the local party organization. It was old-fashioned party pragmatism that caused
leaders of the GOP to promote Eckert's nomination, to deflect the efforts of his
more conventional opponent, and to enter the fall congressional campaign
firmly committed to a candidate who had built his image on being a party
maverick.

Our claim that party leaders exercised a crucial role in Eckert's nomination clashes with the conventional wisdom that modern party organizations are too weak to have any real influence over who their candidates will be. Lacking the resources to reward their friends and the sanctions to punish their enemies, party leaders are typically seen as spectators rather than team captains in the competition for their organizations' endorsements. As V. O. Key observed three decades ago in his classic treatment of American state politics, "To assert that party leadership develops candidates is more an attribution of duty noted in textbooks than a description of real activity."[1] Such longstanding skepticism of the extent of parties' influence on recruitment has been heightened in the past two decades by the increasing prominence of the primary election, which offers intensely committed outside minorities a legally mandated electoral weapon with which to wrest control over nominations from leaders inside the organization. Given the habitually low turnout in primaries, extremists with a small but committed following seem to have a decided advantage over the centrist candidates whom party leaders usually prefer.

In presidential politics the decline of party control over nominations has led some observers to go so far as to proclaim that "the party's over."[2] And in assessing the recruitment of new members to Congress, political analysts increasingly sing a similar refrain by noting the predominance of candidates who are self-starters and who rely on their own personal electoral coalitions to advance their individual agenda rather than the party's.[3]

National patterns of party decline noted by these observers nonetheless mask considerable variation in local partisan strength: many organizations have not been content to suffer electoral reform passively, and conditions that foster turmoil in one congressional district may not have similar consequences in another.[4] Party organizations therefore remain a vital part of political life in many communities across the United States, and despite predictions of their demise parties continue to influence congressional ambition in particular local circumstances. The story of Eckert's nomination is a story about these often overlooked particulars, which still give parties a place in American politics— even in today's antiparty era.

1. V. O. Key, Jr., *American State Politics* (New York: Alfred A. Knopf, 1956), p. 271.

2. David S. Broder, *The Party's Over: The Failure of Politics in America* (New York: Harper & Row, 1972).

3. Louis Sandy Maisel, *From Obscurity to Oblivion: Running in the Congressional Primary* (Knoxville: University of Tennessee Press, 1982).

4. For evidence of the vigor and variability of American party organizations at the national, state, and local levels see James L. Gibson, Cornelius P. Cotter, John F. Bibby, and Robert J. Huckshorn, "Whither the Local Parties? A Cross-sectional and Longitudinal Analysis of the Strength of Party Organizations," *American Journal of Political Science* 29 (February, 1985): 139–160; Cornelius P. Cotter, James L. Gibson, John Bibby, and Robert J. Huckshorn, *Party Organization in American Politics* (New York: Praeger, 1984).

The Consensus Politician

As the date for the Republican convention in May drew near, Town Supervisor Don Riley of Greece was the only politician from Monroe County still in contention with Fred Eckert for the party's nomination. Riley had been an assistant to Eckert in Greece's town hall, then succeeded Eckert as the town supervisor when Eckert moved to the state Senate in 1972. Having had twelve years' experience as the head of the district's largest town, Riley was a well-known political figure who had demonstrated strong support in his home terri-tory by repeatedly winning reelection with more than two-thirds of the vote. During his tenure he had brought modern management systems to Greece and guided it safely through a period of massive suburban growth.

In personal style Riley exudes the warmth and easy patter of the classic Irish politician, but he does it with a touch of modern urbanity. Only thirty-seven at the time he entered the congressional race, he was a bit boyish in appearance, and his easy grin and sparkling eyes gave him an engaging, disarming pres-ence. Monroe County's Republican chairman, Ron Starkweather, said, "Riley is someone who makes you wish he was your son."

Although to some he looked too young to go to Congress, Riley was in fact a seasoned public official who had been in the thick of politics all his life. He relished pointing out that the family clan had been active in local Republican politics for as long as he could remember—his uncle had served in the state Assembly and his father and mother in the Monroe County legislature—and that some of his earliest chldhood memories involved campaigning for local Republican candidates. One Republican party worker from Greece recalled Riley's "official" political debut on the night of his father's election to the county legislature. Because the senior Riley was hospitalized and unable to attend the victory celebration in the local town hall, the young son stepped to the microphone to thank party workers on his father's behalf. "It was a beauti-ful performance," she told us. "And all the party leaders recognized him as a 'comer.'"

During his lengthy political apprenticeship Riley refined a political style that stressed personal contact. The professional manager by day, he turned ward politician by night. "Over the years, Don has gone to all the wakes and fu-nerals," the leader of the Greece Republican Town Committee told us. "When one of the town committeemen's children was critically ill, he turned up at the hospital to be with the parents. People don't forget that."

Riley also knew how to practice the gentle art of persuasion. "I'm a man who works by consensus," he commented to us, and he went on to use a simple analogy to describe how a politician has to treat people as he moves toward his policy objectives. "I like to work with people over the long run and bring them along slowly. You know, I can't be going ninety-five miles an hour on the thruway and expect someone just getting on the road going forty-five miles an hour to keep up. I've got to slow down and wait for them to get up to speed."

This pragmatism gave Riley access to a broad spectrum of political interests. Although well connected to the local Conservative party and sharing many of its political views, he also had ties to organized labor. According to the president of a major local union, "Riley is acceptable to labor. When I have had to negotiate with him, he has been fair with us. And when there are strikes in his town, he doesn't hassle us. You can work with Don."

Still Riley's natural political leanings were conservative, and typically he had run for office with the endorsements of both the Conservative and Right-to-Life parties. But in recent years he had softened some of his positions. Although throughout most of his public career Riley had opposed the Equal Rights Amendment to the Constitution, his recent divorce and remarriage had prompted him to rethink the issue and resulted in a genuine change of heart. His new position moved him closer to the majority of voters in the district and provided a clear signal to women in the Republican party that he could be flexible on the social issues of importance to them.

For the most part Riley chose to emphasize issues that had very little to do with ideology. In 1983 he led a broad coalition of suburbanites, law enforcement officials, and city neighborhood activists to defeat a plan for consolidating local police departments into a single metropolitan force. Called the Metro Plan, this was backed by most major political figures in city and county government. In addition officials of Eastman Kodak, the area's largest employer, entered the political arena for the first time to urge passage of the Metro Plan. On Election Day the Metro Plan was defeated, and Riley emerged as the champion of local control. The victory earned him name recognition and political IOUs around the county, and established him as a politician who transcended narrow partisan and ideological labels.

Because Riley's style of political conduct put him squarely in the mainstream of practicing politicians, in spring 1984 he appeared to be in a strong position to win his party's endorsement to replace Conable. His political track record suggested that he would provide the kind of access and personal attention voters expected from their members of Congress. His preference for acting as a political broker also seemed consistent with the style of behavior used in the House of Representatives by many of its most successful members.[5] In addition, while Eckert was ten thousand miles away, unable to engage in partisan politics until his resignation as ambassador was official, Riley was in a perfect position to woo the party's activists around the district.

Although Riley's striving for consensus in politics was the basis for his

---

5. A legislative style oriented toward building coalitions is emphasized in John F. Manley, *The Politics of Finance: The House Committee on Ways and Means* (Boston: Little, Brown, 1970) and Richard F. Fenno, Jr., *Congressmen in Committees* (Boston: Little, Brown, 1973).

candidacy against Eckert, it also blinded him to the necessities of organizing for a contest with his former boss. He assiduously avoided open battle with Eckert and disdained scrambling for delegates in the Republican committees, which are the backbone of the party's organization. Rather than aggressively emphasize the differences that made him an attractive alternative to Eckert, Riley chose to let his supporters find their way to his campaign on their own.

"There are two kinds of people in politics: sharks and dolphins," he told us. "I'm a dolphin. I want peoples' support of me to be *for* me. When I'm old like Ronald Reagan, I'll take it where I can get it. But for now, I don't want them choosing me just because they don't like someone else. You have to have people want you for who you are, if you're going to be acceptable to them over the long run."

When we first met Riley he had just finished reading David Broder's *The Changing of the Guard*.[6] Riley shared the antiorganizational outlook of Broder's new political generation, and evoked the book in describing his own race for Congress. Like the politicians Broder depicts, Riley saw little value in political parties; in his view, a winning candidate had to have an image that appealed to the increasingly independent American voter—not to an apparatus of party hacks and hangers-on. From his perspective, not only were parties irrelevant to the conduct of modern electoral politics, but the efforts of party leaders to control decisions were actually counterproductive, creating resentment rather than support among the rank and file. Riley was sure that Eckert's steamroller tactics would fail and that pressure from the GOP's chieftains in Eckert's behalf would drive angry Republicans to Riley's side.

From the day of Conable's announcement Riley had received calls urging him to make the race. Based on this initial rush of enthusiasm and his distaste for courting the party hierarchy, he decided to play a waiting game and see how much support naturally drifted to his candidacy. He authorized some exploratory committee in his behalf and kept his name in the news as a probable candidate, but nothing more. In this way he would take an informal poll to measure his strength against Eckert; at the same time he would commission a professional one to gauge his support in the wider community. When all the evidence was in he would see if he had the necessary combination of resources to run a winning race. "It's best in politics to be a formal candidate for the shortest time possible," he told us. "The longer you are out there, the more people can take shots at you, particularly the other 'noncandidates.' "

While waiting for the evidence to come in Riley would not take shots at Eckert, who for all practical purposes was immediately in the race. Others might attack him, but Riley would not openly attack anyone. A negative campaign was not part of his style, which was marked by a striving for consensus.

6. David S. Broder, *The Changing of the Guard* (New York: Simon & Schuster, 1980).

Riley announced his candidacy for Congress on April 30 at a press conference in Greece's town hall, where many years before he had accepted victory for his ailing father. But not even then did Riley seem prepared for a fight. "[I] had no plan, no grand strategy back here," he said, pointing to the back of his head. Riley would simply continue to give low-key responses to whatever offers of support and inquiries to speak came his way. He would do next to nothing to create his own opportunities.

With this modest plan Riley believed he could win the party's endorsement, first by beating Eckert among delegates from the Town of Greece, their common base of support and the largest town in the district, and then by carrying some of the outlying towns west of the Genesee River. In the remainder of the delegations, including those representing the new towns on the east side of the river that had been added to the district by the reapportionment of 1982, he would simply hold Eckert to a draw.

Riley's refusal to play hardball within the Republican organization may have fit his consensus-oriented political style, but it worked to his disadvantage in the long run. Republican activists mistook his low-key approach for lack of interest and regarded his hands-off strategy with mistrust. Shortly before the convention, for example, a town leader on the east side told us that Riley "was not a serious candidate." When asked why not, he replied, "He's not called me or any other leader I've talked with. Not even a letter. I think he just wants the publicity."

This failure to cultivate the party's insiders caused Riley to be viewed not only as unreliable but also as arrogant and discourteous. This impression surfaced repeatedly in conversations with party activists in Monroe County. A key player in the struggle for the nomination, who had serious reservations about supporting Eckert but was never reached by Riley, described the resentment that Riley's tactics created among men and women on his committee: "My people don't like it, when I don't hear from Riley. By ignoring me, it's seen as demeaning to them."

Still another influential Republican on the east side of the district, a crucial area, told us, "There is no great reservoir of support for Eckert out here. But Riley hasn't done our people the courtesy of asking for their support. After Nagle dropped out, Riley called me once, and I was out. I tried twice returning his calls and left messages which he did not return. He came to speak to the Republican women at their instigation and to the committee meeting at ours. But he never campaigned here as people thought he should, and our local chairmen were offended and others were too because I hadn't been called. You don't just walk into a group the week before the convention and bat your eyes and expect them to give it to you."

Riley's low-key style therefore had the unintended effect of creating a widely held belief that either he was not a serious candidate or he was ignorant of the basic manners of politics. Either way, many party people were confused and angry, and had the feeling they could not trust his actions or judgment.

This damaging impression also revived memories of Riley's past indecisiveness. Two years earlier he had considered challenging the man appointed to fill Eckert's old seat in the state Senate, William Steinfeldt, for the Republican nomination. But on the evening when his supporters gathered for the public announcement of his candidacy, Riley backed out. After that experience, some people were so unsure of Riley's intentions that even after he had formally announced his congressional candidacy they remained unconvinced. Indeed, on the night Greece's party committee gathered to choose which of the town's two favorite sons it would formally endorse for the congressional nomination, at least one participant had a feeling of déjà vu. "I was prepared to have him stand up and announce that he wasn't a candidate, the way he did with the Steinfeldt seat," the party official recalled.

Although Riley's failure to court his fellow Republicans raised doubts about his ambitions for Conable's House seat, his refusal to contend directly with Eckert made him vulnerable on other grounds. Riley's image as a "nice guy" could not hide his liabilities as a politician, and as long as he was not advertising his strengths others were free to concentrate on his weaknesses.

Since losing a race for the state Assembly in 1980 he had had the slight taint of a loser. He had challenged and been beaten on his own turf by the popular, conservative, Democratic incumbent, Roger Robach. Although party leaders recognized Robach as a formidable opponent, perhaps the strongest Democratic candidate in Monroe County, they nevertheless held it against Riley that he had lost. Many insiders thought Riley had not campaigned hard enough in that race, whereas others believed that an issue that surfaced in the election had dimmed his political star forever.

During the race it was learned that Riley had used public money to pay for his graduate courses at the University of Rochester. He saw the management courses he was taking as directly applicable to his job as town supervisor, and pointed out that Greece regularly paid the tuition of other town officials who took college courses related to their jobs. Riley contended he should be entitled to the same benefits awarded other town employees, but public criticism of him continued, and he finally agreed to reimburse the town.

For many party people this episode showed a lack of good judgment and sense of propriety. "The tuition thing speaks worlds," a lawyer and party leader told us. "It goes to the core. Having done it, he passed it off with the board of supervisors as if it were nothing. You can't do that with other people's money. It showed a real failure of fiduciary responsibility. From my point of view I think it showed a lack of integrity, and I could never support him because of it."

In addition, Riley's narrow experience in government worried his friends as well as his enemies. Despite his efforts during the campaign to stress the relevance of his experience as a supervisor to President Reagan's "new federalism," and to evoke the shibboleth of local control, Riley was frequently dismissed as just a local administrator without the broad experience required of a federal legislator.

Added to his lack of contact with national issues was a sense that Riley's bid for a congressional seat was out of turn. Unfamiliar with his family history in Greece's politics, some party insiders saw Riley as Eckert's protégé. To them Riley became the town supervisor only because Eckert had brought him into the office as his assistant and before leaving for the state Senate had arranged for Riley to succeed him.

Riley hotly disputed this view and attributed his appointment as town supervisor to his reputation as an able manager during Eckert's stormy tenure. Pointing out that his family had been active and influential in politics in Greece long before Eckert came along, he contended that his own connections in the community had gained him the support of the town board in his first bid for office. Regardless of which view is correct (and we could piece together no generally accepted view of the circumstances surrounding Riley's appointment as town supervisor) to many observing the rivalry between the two Greece politicians, the protégé appeared to be an ingrate who was now sabotaging his mentor.

Finally, the major issue Riley chose to emphasize during his contest with Eckert did not enhance his image as he had intended. By emphasizing his change of position on the Equal Rights Amendment, Riley thought he was demonstrating his flexibility and more palatable brand of conservatism. Some Republicans, however, saw his use of the ERA and his appeal to the women in the party in quite different terms. Given the questions surrounding his political career, they saw the change in position as new evidence of his indecisiveness and expediency. Instead of emerging as the defender of the women's cause, he was seen as an opportunist who could not be trusted.

When all these liabilities were added together, it was Riley, not Eckert, who had the greater image problem in the minds of many party leaders and convention delegates. Contrary to first impressions, it was Don Riley, the genial candidate, not Fred Eckert, the aggressive one, who was more often viewed as an expedient politician trying to climb the political ladder too rapidly.

The Conflict Politician

Everyone knew that Eckert was in politics to advance his issues and that in pushing his conservative agenda he had angered many people. No one disputed this: not his friends, not his opponents, and certainly not Eckert.

In every one of his campaigns, he had hammered away at his issues whenever and wherever he got the chance. When early in the spring we asked one of Eckert's close aides how the ambassador would present himself in the reapportioned district, the aide quickly replied, "Eckert will use issues. He'll campaign on the issues." Much later in the summer, Eckert told us the same thing. He showed scorn for candidates who practiced what he called Kellogg's variety-pack politics. "I don't see voters as blacks or women or middle class," he said. "People are more alike than different." Throughout the interview he made plain that he did not practice the conventional political strategy of wooing segments of the electorate by appealing to their group prejudices. Instead he saw voters solely as individuals who could be united into an electoral majority by straightforward, clear-cut appeals based on the issues.

The tendency for sharp conflict that is naturally present in Eckert's brand of issue politics was heightened by his acerbic manner. Eckert could not disagree about issues with a smile, and his campaign opponents were frequent targets of his abrasive, aggressive behavior. In one election he pressed his attack so relentlessly during a public debate that his opponent finally left the hall and became violently ill. Eckert amazes his fellow politicians for his willingness to press unmercifully any political advantage he acquires. Nearly everyone we interviewed had a favorite "Eckert story" about this habit of his. Usually the stories ended with graphic comments describing Eckert's zeal for the rough-and-tumble of political life:

"Fred always goes for the jugular."

"Fred uses issues like clubs."

"He goes for the throat. He always takes you to the mat."

It was not simply Eckert's personal approach to issues that made him a politician prone to conflict. He was also seen by Republicans and Democrats as too extreme—a right-wing ideologue out of step with the district's opinion.

Eckert's background and public stands gave much support to this radical image. By the time he entered Le Moyne College, a Jesuit school in Syracuse, New York, in fall 1959, his conservative ideas were strong enough to involve him in several conflicts with one of the faculty members, the Reverend Daniel Berrigan, who became a leading figure in the radical wing of the movement against the Vietnam War in the late 1960s. Eventually, his conflicts with Berrigan in and out of the classroom forced his withdrawal from the college. Later he spent a summer writing editorials for William Loeb, the fanatically right-wing publisher of the *Manchester Union Leader*, known as one of the most rabidly conservative newspapers in the country.

This history led Republicans and Democrats alike to caricature Eckert. Shortly after we were told by a Democrat, "He's the Jesse Helms of the north," a Republican said, "The potential for him to be another Jesse Helms is clearly there. He's too conservative for this area and too inclined to pick just a few issues." A longtime Republican leader told us: "I never could understand why

Reagan appointed Eckert ambassador to the Fijis. Until I found out that the natives there had a history of cannibalism. Then everything made perfect sense."

Nearly all members of the party hierarchy whom we interviewed were troubled at least to some degree by Eckert's unbending conservatism, because it was so out of step with the district. His opposition to the Equal Rights Amendment and abortion, and his support for a constitutional amendment to allow prayer in public schools were particularly worrisome to them. On at least two of these issues, numerous public-opinion polls had demonstrated that Eckert stood squarely in opposition to the views of the overwhelming majority of citizens in the 30th Congressional District of New York. Less troublesome were his hard-line views on defense and foreign policy, but even in these areas, supporters of Eckert's positions tended to be in the minority among the area's voters.

Still, many party leaders felt they could live with Eckert's ideology, if only they did not have to cope with the abrasive demeanor that came with it. Every political figure has some weaknesses, they would point out. It was the combination of his ideology and style that was the real problem. Eckert's abrasiveness only called attention to his hard-line conservatism, and vice versa. Eckert's close associates saw his intemperate conduct as the inevitable product of his intensity about political issues. "Let's put it this way," said one political ally, "Eckert doesn't suffer fools gladly."

Eckert's political enemies were less charitable and a good deal more blunt. One Republican detractor coldly began our interview with this brutal statement: "To know Fred Eckert is to hate him." A Democrat described Eckert in equally harsh terms: "He has the personality of a barracuda. How does he get elected?"[7] For a politician Eckert was strongly disliked by an unusually large number of his peers, and even among his most devoted political supporters few expressed warm feelings toward him as a person.

In part Eckert seemed to generate dislike because of the general perception that he deliberately antagonized people who disagreed with him and perhaps went out of his way to insult them. One ally described him as "gratuitously abrasive." Another close political associate agreed. "Fred is just too fast with the quip," he said. "On the ERA, for instance, you can disagree with the proponents, but you don't have to keep taking shots at them."

No story better illustrates Eckert's fast and sharp tongue (and his tendency to take "shots" at the women's movement) than his retort on hearing that the Monroe County Women's Political Caucus had made him a target when he sought reelection in 1976 to the state Senate. He told reporters that the group's action did not trouble him in the least and that its members had little political muscle. "They are no different than the women who meet in a corner bar . . .

7. Patrick Farrell, "Fred J. Eckert: He Marches to His Own Drummer," *Times-Union* (Rochester), October 31, 1984, sec. B, p. 6.

and they have just about as many members too. But don't quote me on that. I don't want to insult the women in the corner bars."

In the year of the gender gap, the combination of Eckert's right-wing stand and macho political style inevitably led to what was usually called his problem with women. Not only did the most active women in the Republican party find Eckert's views on the issues deeply offensive, they also objected to his tendency to dismiss them as individuals. According to one woman prominent in the hierarchy, it was the way Eckert dealt with her and other women in the party that was the real issue. After she was elected to public office, she recalled, he was virtually the only Republican who made no effort to get to know her.

Despite his penchant for conflict, ideological extremism, and confrontational style, Eckert had significant political virtues that ultimately outweighed his liabilities. To begin with, many admired Eckert's aggressiveness and harsh rhetoric. It was true that his talk was often too blunt and acerbic, but people always knew exactly where he stood. And because he pursued aggressively whatever he stood for, he was seen as a decisive politician of clear convictions. Even Eckert's most intense critics acknowledged that his conservative ideology was the product of deep personal conviction, not momentary political expediency. "I don't always agree with him," said a longtime observer of Eckert, "but at least I recognize that his actions come from a well-thought-out position and a set of principles. You know, I've never known Fred to take a phony position. He always has his reasons."

Eckert saw himself in similar terms: he was not abrasive, but honest; not sharp-tongued, but candid. As he saw it he was being judged by politicians who lived in a warped world that placed a higher value on hypocrisy and double-talk than plain-speaking. Eckert described himself as a man who called a spade a spade in a profession where many of his colleagues were too cowed by the prospect of conflict to take a clear-cut stand on anything. "Other politicians call me abrasive because I say in public what other people say in private," he explained. "When everybody thinks somebody is a 'whacko,' I call him a 'whacko.' I think other politicians wonder how I can do it. They are really just jealous."

Eckert's harsh image was softened further by the view that he was informed and intelligent. He might take unpopular positions, but he was willing to discuss issues at length and treat his audience seriously when he did so. A female official in the local party, who was part of a group of women that met with Eckert before the nominating convention to discuss their opposing views about the Equal Rights Amendment and abortion, came away impressed. She had not changed her views on these issues, and she was sure Eckert had not changed his. But he had gained stature in her eyes by pointing out things about the amendment that she had not thought about before. After exhausting the original agenda, the group's discussion turned to other issues. Here she thought

Eckert was even more impressive. "He talked about the Strait of Hormuz, and I knew nothing about it. He explained it. And then later the president talked about it on TV, and I said, 'Hey, I know something about that now.' "

For her and most party leaders, congressmen are expected to be more informed and intelligent than people who hold lower office. They are supposed to lead and educate as well as provide constituent service and be personally accessible. She had learned to expect such leadership and education from Conable. "Hell, I didn't agree with Conable on everything," she said. "But I would call him up, and he would explain it to me. And then I would see why he had to do this or that." Eckert was able to meet these expectations in her and in many others in the party. At least he could explain himself in a way that made his views understandable, even if his explanation was not always persuasive.[8]

Eckert understood this perfectly. He told us: "Voters don't like to be manipulated. They like you to be what you say you are. People are much more concerned that you sound like you know what you are talking about than that they agree with you. If they trust you, they will vote for you."[9] For all his personal handicaps and deficiencies, Eckert could generate this trust in people. He did it by skillfully blending his ideology, knowledge, honesty, and acerbic bluntness to create a trustworthy reputation based on informed, principled predictability. It was a powerful political weapon.

Trustworthiness was not Eckert's only weapon. He had served an ideal congressional apprenticeship by holding office at every level of American government—local, state, and national. For nearly ten years he had practiced the legislative craft in New York's state Senate, and during his tenure in Albany had made a name for himself as the force behind the Public Pension Reform Law of 1976, which put new limits on the escalating costs of public-employee pensions in the State of New York. His success in seeing this legislation become law earned him a curious collection of accolades from the *New York Times*, his Senate colleagues, and his constituents, who saw him as a champion of lower taxes, limited government, and the little man. Having been the American ambassador to Fiji, he could even lay claim to experience in the field of foreign affairs.

In each of these arenas Eckert could point to accomplishments. Even his critics usually recognized that he was a politician who got things done, particularly if the task required stepping on the toes of powerful interests. The Public Pension Reform Law was the case most often cited, but there were

8. In her classic study of representation, Hanna Pitken argues that a legislator reconciles conflict between his or her own views and those of constituents by justifying and explaining his or her decisions. See Hanna Fenichel Pitkin, *The Concept of Representation* (Berkeley: University of California Press, 1967), pp. 209–211.

9. Richard Fenno makes precisely this point in *Home Style: House Members in Their Districts* (Boston: Little, Brown, 1978), pp. 151–157.

others: for example, he helped to close a loophole that for fifty years had enabled the residents of Greece to escape paying school taxes, thus shifting the cost of educating their children to the rest of the county. According to Eckert's sense of fair play, the cost of government ought to be borne by those who benefited from it—even if those who benefited were his own constituents.

Both these examples illustrate how Eckert's stubbornness, abrasiveness, honesty, and intelligence added up to form a picture of a "can do" politician who was in no one's back pocket. "Fred just makes up his mind, and then he does it," was how one local politician put it.

Eckert's political claims were equally impressive. First, he had never lost an election. Ten times from 1969 to 1980, in seven general elections and three primaries, Eckert had taken his case to the voters and won. Second, his ties to the national conservative movement were thought to give him access to all the money from PACs needed to wage an expensive media campaign in a hotly contested open seat. Because of his connections outside the district, Eckert was believed the only local candidate who could easily raise the $250,000 to $500,000 the race was expected to cost. Finally, his ties to President Reagan caused Eckert's stock to rise as the expanding economy in spring 1984 drove the president's electoral value steadily higher in public-opinion polls.

Over the years Eckert had made friends not only with the president of the United States but also with some important people inside the local Republican party. Despite his image as a troublemaker on the legislative front, Eckert had a history of aiding leading party figures whenever they faced difficulty on the electoral front. For example, in his initial effort to be appointed county manager in 1971, Lucien Morin received decisive, early support from Eckert. Conable also had been aided by Eckert: in 1974, after the Watergate scandal, Conable faced his toughest reelection challenge, as polls late in the campaign showed him losing. Eckert rewrote all the campaign's radio and television advertisements, and several people inside the party believe the revisions helped save Conable's career; more importantly, Conable thought they made a difference. In another election, Dale Rath, a former state assemblyman, gave Eckert credit for tirelessly providing him much-needed support in his first campaign for the Assembly.

Throughout his political career Eckert had a habit of aiding many local political figures in their moment of gravest electoral concern. It was true that in the state Senate Eckert seldom if ever came to the aid of party leaders; to them he was a constant source of aggravation. Eckert could be no party man in Albany because there he was asked to compromise on policies, which for him were matters of principle. But it was different when Monroe County's party leaders needed his help to win elections: these matters were rooted not in policy and principle but in politics. Under these conditions Eckert was a willing team player.

The Republican county chairman confirmed this. He told us flatly, "There were two people I could always count on: Conable and Eckert. You could count on [Eckert] for endorsements, for whatever help you needed. The people didn't have to pass a litmus test. He'd just do it. And he'd never say later 'I did this for you, so you should do this for me.' He was just always there."

These assets formed a big stack of chips for the kind of political poker Eckert knew would be involved in the race for Conable's seat. In the end, even Eckert's reputation as a mean-spirited street fighter was more an asset than a liability. For although he was stranded in Fiji until a month before the Republican convention, his image had a cautionary effect on his potential opponents. Even though Eckert was unable to confront them directly, his reputation as a relentless campaigner caused all of them to stop and weigh very carefully the costs of a battle against Eckert. One party insider, who was initially opposed to Eckert and looked forward to running against him, described the inhibiting effect of Eckert's distinctive style: "Fred is coasting on his reputation as a tough fighter, but I don't think he is any more. He's been away from things for two years, with servants doing everything for him. He's not going to want to get out and ring doorbells. But in politics you have to be a good bluffer. Fred's just lucky no one has called it."

Eckert had always understood the poker-playing aspects of politics, and in the weeks following Conable's announcement he did everything he could to reinforce local perceptions of his aggressive, determined nature. Although as ambassador to Fiji he could not campaign openly for Congress, he could do so privately and did. He immediately began talking by telephone to all the major political figures in the district, calling some of them repeatedly. The calls were to friends asking for support and to opponents urging them to back off. To everyone the message was the same: "I'm going to go to Congress. Are you with me or against me?" Before he left the South Pacific, Eckert admitted to running up a telephone bill of more than three thousand dollars; his campaign spending reports suggest the figure was closer to four thousand, and his detractors placed it at nearly six thousand.

From Fiji, Eckert devised a strategy to give him a presence in the district until he could return to Rochester and campaign for himself. His first move was to have several of his political allies create the Draft Ambassador Eckert for Congress Committee. The name was a joke: other potential candidates for Conable's job might need to be dragged into the race, but certainly not Eckert, who needed to be drafted for Congress no more than General Patton needed to be drafted into the army. But the title was needed to fulfill the letter of the law, which prohibited ambassadors from engaging in partisan politics, and the group gave Eckert access to the news media by serving as his mouthpiece.

The telephone calls from Fiji and the committee at home created a bandwagon effect that looked irresistible. Eckert would round up endorsements on the telephone, and the Draft Eckert Committee would release the news. Prominent local officeholders were announced as Eckert's supporters, as were well-known Republicans from outside the district, including the Congressman Jack Kemp and the Republican gubernatorial nominee in 1982, Lew Lehrman. Although many of these early endorsements, including Kemp's and Lehrman's, were quickly discounted by insiders in Monroe County's GOP, Eckert knew that news coverage of the endorsements made his presence felt in the early campaign and called attention to his eventual entry into the race.

This blitzkrieg of publicity was typical of Eckert's aggressive political style and intense ambition. He pursued everyone who could help or hurt his candidacy, first by telephone and then in person. In March, while still an ambassador, he made a brief return to Washington and stopped for a short time in Rochester. Between discussions at the State Department he busily made phone calls to important politicians in the 30th district, and during his stay in Rochester met with several party figures and talked by telephone with dozens of others. Once his campaign began officially on May 11, he stepped up the pace of his contacts with party people, meeting and calling one convention delegate after another.

One by one, Eckert reached everyone who mattered. Some were angered by the threats and pressure, but others saw in this nonstop campaign a powerful message: Eckert would be a formidable opponent to any Republican challenger for the nomination and to any Democrat in the general election.

The Party Lingers On

On May 31, 1984, Republicans gathered at the Mapledale Party House to select their nominee for the House of Representatives in New York's 30th Congressional District. It was a large, noisy convocation of the party faithful from Monroe County, with a smaller contingent of delegates from the adjacent rural counties: Genesee (Conable's home base), Ontario, and Livingston. This was the second evening the Monroe County GOP had turned out, having met the night before to choose candidates for several local offices, and their ranks had thinned somewhat as a result. But the prospect of a contest between Eckert and Riley brought about two-thirds of the party's fourteen hundred committeemen and committeewomen together with anticipation. They would listen to the nominating speeches, hear the candidates, and then write their choices on a paper ballot.

These delegates had had much time in the weeks before the convention to weigh their decision about the district's new member of Congress. Many had heard Eckert and Riley answer questions on the same platform at the candidates' nights held by their town committees, and quite a few had attended the Conservative party's annual dinner in mid-May, at which both men spoke. In

addition, a series of straw polls held around Monroe County by party committees had given the delegates a sense of how much support the two candidates
enjoyed. Riley had captured the endorsement of the Greece Republican Committee by a comfortable margin as well as that of the party's small city contingent, and had shocked everyone by tying Eckert in the large southern suburb
of Henrietta. Meanwhile, Eckert had shown surprising strength on the east side
by obtaining the support of the committee in Pittsford. And in the important
town of Irondequoit, he had had the help of the party leaders in rounding up
supporters in a closed session of the local committee. Eckert had also used his
endorsement from Monroe County's executive, Lucien Morin, and the good
offices of Ron Starkweather, the Republican chairman, to gain a favorable
reception in some of the smaller communities in the district and the approval of
the party leaders in the counties of Livingston and Ontario. By the time the
delegates met, they not only had a clear picture of the political differences
between the two men but some strong indications that the final balloting could
be very close.

The tension over the convention's outcome grew when the delegates from
Genesee County arrived en masse. Still smarting over the loss of Barber Conable, "their" congressman, and upset by having to choose between Riley,
whom they did not know, and Eckert, whom they did not like, these Republican
stalwarts had come to the convention prepared to support one of their own—a
retired state trooper named Jake Lathan. They made the most of their numbers
with a high turnout and a pledge to vote as one. This tactic had great potential,
because the party rules required a candidate to receive a majority of the convention's vote to be declared its designee. If the race were tight, Lathan's supporters might therefore force the convention to a second ballot, and they would then
hold the pivotal position between Riley's and Eckert's camps. What they might
do at that point was not at all clear, although there had been talk of an alliance
between Lathan and Riley.

The speculation soon ended when the first ballot gave the Republican designation to Eckert. Although Riley carried the Town of Greece, the portion of the
district in Rochester, and several small west-side towns, as he had predicted,
Eckert polled substantial majorities on the east side, a critical area, to gain his
narrow victory. Of the 840 votes cast, Eckert won 429 (only eight votes more
than the number needed to be designated), Riley 321, and Lathan 83. Two other
candidates, an officer of the New York State Snowmobile Association and a
committeewoman from the City of Rochester, received the remaining seven
votes.

The decision of the Republican delegates was not necessarily the final word.
Riley could try to overturn the judgment of the party regulars by going before
the rank and file in a primary in September, and he still had several weeks to file
the necessary petitions. To do so would be consistent with his antiparty outlook;

besides, Riley had known all along that if he managed to capture a majority at the convention, he would have to defend his claim to the party's nomination against a challenge in a primary from Eckert. Win or lose at the Mapledale Party House, Riley's bid for Congress seemed inextricably tied to a fall primary.

Riley had, however, made no preparations for a primary, and he had many reservations about fighting one. "If I get whipped in the convention, I wouldn't do it," he told us in early March. "What would be the point of that?" He would continue the contest with Eckert only if he gained enough support at the convention to give credibility to a primary campaign. Although he never said so explicitly, he hinted that the proportion of the convention's vote required to establish his legitimacy as a challenger was about 40 percent. The reason for his hesitancy was his perception that right-wing Republicans would turn out to vote for Eckert no matter which candidate had the party convention's blessing, while his own, more moderate supporters would not be so dependable in mounting a challenge against the organizational establishment. "Once someone has the designation," Riley told us, "those [moderates] are hard to break away." Given the aversion of mainstream Republicans to internecine warfare, he therefore had to cross some threshold of acceptability before he could challenge the convention majority with any hope of success.

This serious problem was at least partly offset by some advantages Riley enjoyed in a primary that were not available to other Republicans: he did not have to resign from office to campaign for Congress, and he had a secure political base in Greece to protect him from the ill will of the Republican hierarchy, which would be the inevitable consequence of flouting the party's unwritten law against primaries. Yet Riley's ambitions for higher office were not confined to the House of Representatives: he had entertained serious thoughts about the county executive's post and the west side's state Senate seat, both of which were held by men near retirement. These positions were closer to his interests in local government and offered him the seasoning that his detractors claimed he needed, but such opportunities would not be open to a young man who put the party to the expense and inconvenience of a primary. Running and losing could mean exile to the office of the supervisor of Greece, which he could escape only by fighting other bruising primaries. "If I were a betting man," mused Starkweather after the convention, "I'd say Don will do it. If he runs, though, he'd better kill us, not just wound us. Because if he only wounds us, he's finished around here."

This prospect gave an air of gravity to Riley's deliberations after the convention. Until then he had not invested much political capital in being a congressional candidate; he had enjoyed attention by offering himself as an alternative to Eckert without incurring any serious liabilities. "Nobody gets hurt by having me out there as a candidate," Riley told us repeatedly. But a showdown with his old boss at this point was a different matter: Could he win as an underdog? Were his ambitions for Congress intense enough to risk his place on the party's roster of up-and-coming politicians?

Riley's vote at the convention did not provide a clear answer to his dilemma. Given his low-key effort to obtain the Republican nomination, 38 percent of the vote was respectable. He had proved publicly what he had said privately: Eckert's mean-spirited reputation and abrasive tactics in seeking the congressional nomination had antagonized a large number of the party faithful despite the active promotion of his candidacy by the GOP's leaders. The dolphin commanded a significant following in the 30th district simply because his rival had a reputation as a shark. On the other hand, Riley fell just short of the threshold he had set for himself, he had lost to Eckert by more than one hundred votes, and knew that his standing among Republicans outside the county was very uncertain. To overcome these weaknesses, he would have to launch an aggressive campaign, which required a substantial financial investment and an extraordinary personal commitment of time and effort.

After a week of discussion with his wife, his political associates, and prospective supporters, Riley decided to withdraw from the race. He concluded that he could not raise the money needed to be competitive in a primary. As the challenger, Riley believed he would have to outspend Eckert to overcome his natural advantage with the more ideologically extreme primary electorate and his strategic position as the party's designee. Although he had promises of assistance from some prominent contributors in the party and some local union officials, who were willing to pursue any means to block Eckert's bid for the House of Representatives, Riley's most optimistic projection of what he could raise amounted to no more than eighty thousand dollars. He needed a good deal more than that—perhaps $100,000 to $125,000. "I don't know that Fred has as much money as people think he has," he remarked, "but I can't be sure." He was however sure of two other things: He could not match Eckert's ability to raise money from PACs in Washington, and he was finding some closed checkbooks among his usual contributors in Rochester. With few contacts outside the district and Morin and Starkweather pressuring some of his financial backers at home, Riley was stumped.

But more than money barred his entrance into the Republican primary. In a fundamental way, Riley was unwilling to do what he knew had to be done to beat his former boss. He was uncomfortable with the kind of aggressive campaign that he foresaw in September; a hard-hitting, issue-oriented battle would be jarring to a traditional politician who had built rapport with the voters through hundreds of individual contacts and personal gestures of support. And somewhere inside him was an ambivalence about whether Congress rather than some other office was what he really wanted. Before he announced his withdrawal from the race he had told his wife: "I don't know if it's my head that's saying do it and my heart that's saying no, or the other way around." As he later discussed his reasons for backing out, he paused and then said quietly: "You know, Fred always wanted it more than I did."

Without a doubt, Eckert did want the nomination more than Riley, or any of the other Republican hopefuls, for he was the only Republican candidate who did not shrink from the prospect of a primary. From the beginning this threat had been Eckert's ace in the hole, and to prove that he was not bluffing, he reportedly reserved in May his media time for a primary in September and had his advertisements already recorded. In other ways, Eckert used the prospect of a primary to increase the stakes of the contest in the 30th district; he encouraged speculation that the race would be costly, and reinforced local opinion that he had immediate access to all the money from Washington he would need. As he raised the ante, all the players except Riley folded their cards, and eventually Riley too left the table after only one raise. From the outset Eckert's image as a belligerent brawler with a key to the national bank was his most important political asset, and it became a powerful factor in driving out of the contest anyone who did not share his burning ambition, his stomach for a street fight, and his belief in a righteous cause. Party rules that facilitate primaries lend an advantage to candidates with Eckert's political style, ideological constituency, and national connections.

Despite his preparations, Eckert was not eager to fight a primary if he could avoid one, for a showdown in September could badly damage his chances in November. Not only would he lose time and valuable resources in capturing the Republican nomination, but he might suffer from the party's divisiveness and the negative exposure that are frequent byproducts of a hard-fought primary. As Republicans noted repeatedly throughout the spring nomination period, their partisans in the 30th district had a longstanding dislike of primaries and a history of letting internal conflicts persist into the fall election. Although local Democrats appeared relatively philosophical about primary conflicts, and evidence from other parts of the country suggested that they were not necessarily harmful, in Monroe County there were several precedents (described in Chapter 2) to suggest that Republicans who had to fight openly for their party's nomination suffered at the polls in the general election.

In Eckert's case particularly, poll data collected in May indicated that a primary could be a genuine threat to his candidacy. In the first place, support for a Republican candidate in New York's 30th district could not be taken for granted, even though Republicans outnumbered Democrats in the district by two to one. When likely voters were asked for which party they intended to vote in the congressional race, 45 percent named the Republicans and 24 percent the Democrats, but fully 30 percent were undecided. Furthermore, although Eckert was well-known—91 percent of the respondents had heard of him—he was regarded favorably by only 48 percent and unfavorably by 20 percent. This latter figure is unusually high and signaled that Eckert had an image problem among ordinary voters, just as his detractors claimed.

A comparison of the relative standing of Eckert and Riley among the Republican rank and file provides the most compelling evidence of the hazards to Eckert of a primary. Eckert would have been the clear winner of a hypothetical race if the primary had taken place at the time of the survey in May, but the larger number of undecided voters (31 percent) indicated that his candidacy was far from a sure thing. More importantly, Eckert and Riley received remarkably similar ratings within the GOP in spring 1984 (see table 8.1). Each man was evaluated positively by roughly half the respondents, but fewer Republicans gave Riley a negative rating, which meant that his ratio of favorable to unfavorable scores (an important indicator of the voters' reaction in the eyes of political professionals) was actually more advantageous than Eckert's. With four months to go before the primary, these figures were hardly reliable indicators of the likely outcome; they nonetheless suggested that the primary between Eckert and Riley had all the ingredients of a close and therefore dangerous battle.

The perils of a primary in the 30th district meant that Eckert had his own threshold of support to cross at the convention, just as Riley needed enough delegates to discourage Eckert from challenging him in a primary. Eckert held some aces when it came to bidding for the party activists: his experience in public office, his reputation for reliability, and his record of past electoral success; he also benefited from Riley's lack of finesse in putting his chips on the table. But Eckert could not command a majority at the Mapledale Party House by himself, and he had to turn to the leadership of Monroe County's GOP for the wild cards that would give him a playable hand. Ironically, this party maverick would owe his political winnings in the 30th Congressional District to the very people he had trumped and bluffed for so many years.

It may seem odd in this antiparty era to ascribe influence over nominations to a handful of party leaders, but Eckert benefited both from the public endorsements of prominent Republicans and from the private persuasiveness of Monroe County's chairman and other party insiders. In some respects Eckert's thin margin of victory over Riley is eloquent testimony to the limits of the power exercised by the GOP's leaders. They could not deliver a resounding win for their chosen candidate, because some of the delegates pledged to Eckert failed to show up at the Mapledale Party House to cast their votes and others defected under the protective anonymity of a secret ballot. The tally turned out to be much closer than the party leaders had expected, and as Starkweather admitted with some chagrin after the convention, he could not do much about these lapses in party discipline. Yet by means of various subtle but effective tactics, the Republican leaders were able to assemble a jerry-built coalition that was just enough to fend off Eckert's opposition.

Table 8.1   Republican Attitudes toward Eckert and Riley (in percent)

	Eckert (N=178)	Riley (N=157)
Ever heard of candidate	91	80
Opinion of candidate among likely voters		
Favorable	51	48
Unfavorable	15	10
Heard of candidate but cannot rate	24	29
Don't know or no answer	11	14

Choice of Likely Voters if Primary Held Today
(N=196)

Eckert	43
Riley	14
Undecided	31
Don't know or no answer	12

Percentages may not add to 100 because of rounding.
SOURCE: "Benchmark Survey of New York 30th District, May 1984," prepared by Public Response Associates for the American Medical Political Action Committee, Washington, D.C.

In the first place, Eckert's early endorsement by County Executive Lucien Morin carried a great deal of weight among the convention delegates. Still fresh from his resounding electoral victory in the preceding year, Morin was a veteran politician for whom many Republicans had respect and affection. He also presided over the county budget and its employees. The services and public-works projects provided by Monroe County's government were especially significant to the suburban towns, the Republican leaders of which were eager to maintain good relations with Morin, especially now that he enjoyed his own popular base rather than serving at the pleasure of the county legislature.

Morin's public support of Eckert was one of his first overtly political acts since his triumph in November, and insiders viewed it as a sign that he intended to take a more prominent role in party affairs. One well-placed Republican commented: "He's made it plain with this endorsement that he wants to play kingmaker in the party." And Morin was not simply grandstanding. About 30 percent of the Republican committeemen and committeewomen who would attend the Republican nominating convention worked in county government. They owed their jobs to Morin and the party, and it was generally accepted that they would follow his lead in backing Eckert.

Patronage in party politics is not a subject that most political observers take seriously today—outside the city of Chicago—because conventional wisdom holds that when reformers crippled the big-city machines, parties everywhere lost their capacity to reward their friends and punish their enemies. But to treat city and county parties alike is in many cases a mistake, in part because the progressive reformers who rewrote the rules of party competition made city machines their target and paid less attention to county organizations.

In recent years, however, county administration has burgeoned under the pressures of suburban sprawl, the expansion of social welfare programs, and the implementation of environmental standards. All these changes have provided significant opportunities for parties to use the county budget and payroll for organizational ends, often under comparatively unrestrictive administrative rules. These new organizations rely on the support of second- and third-generation immigrant Americans who have moved to the suburbs and have a different political style from that of the old-time party machines, but their basic structures are not all that dissimilar. Indeed the party machines that have sprung up in several suburban counties around New York State are impressive organizational specimens.

Although the patronage apparatus in Monroe County is a pale imitation of the formidable parties operating in such places as the counties of Suffolk and Nassau on Long Island, it nonetheless had some potential as an instrument of Republican leadership. Morin and Starkweather never talked about the leverage the county employees gave them at the convention, but Riley's supporters did, and they pointed in particular to an east-side town leader who they believed backed Eckert because her husband held a position in county government.

Much more than patronage was involved, however, in the coalescing of Republicans around Eckert. Also at work was a sense of reciprocity and mutual obligation that bound together people in the party. This was especially significant in bringing Assemblyman Jim Nagle, himself a strong candidate for the Republican nomination in the 30th district, into Eckert's camp.

Although Nagle initially had not been active in seeking the congressional seat, by April many party insiders gave him the best chance of winning at the convention, because he represented so much of the east side in the state Assembly and had the backing of all the party leaders in his constituency. His solid support in his own political backyard contrasted sharply with the divisions Riley and Eckert confronted in their shared political base. Once Nagle concluded that he was unwilling to stake his career in the Assembly against the uncertain outcome of a primary, his constituency was suddenly up for grabs, and much of it was expected to gravitate to Riley, whose political style presumably made him more acceptable than his right-wing opponent to the more liberal residents of the east side.

Having made up his mind about his own future, Nagle was inclined to listen to the arguments of Morin and Starkweather that Eckert was the more qualified of the two candidates and had the better chance of holding the seat for the party. He had no particular obligations to either Eckert or Riley, but he did have a longstanding relationship with the two party leaders. When he announced his withdrawal, he therefore sided with his old political friends and endorsed Eckert. He even declared that he would serve as the honorary chairman of Eckert's campaign. Nagle's eleventh-hour decision to back Eckert won no converts among the true foes of Eckert in the party, but it did sway some doubtful residents of the east side who had little personal experience of the two politicians from across the river. His endorsement also revived the flagging momentum of Eckert's bandwagon in the last, critical weeks before the convention. This gesture of loyalty to the party leadership thus contributed to the gradually accumulating delegate total that eventually gave Eckert a slender lead over his rival.

Finally, the party organization provided the mechanism for diffusing Eckert's "problem with women," which Riley had every intention of exploiting. Riley thought his newfound support for the Equal Rights Amendment would make him more acceptable to Republican women than his rival, and improve his standing in the more progressive eastern towns. But by the time of the convention, not a single prominent woman in Monroe County's GOP had come to Riley's aid. Indeed, every woman we interviewed who had vigorously opposed Eckert privately eventually endorsed him publicly. The women abandoned the party's feminist tradition, shunned Riley, and eventually embraced Eckert for two reasons: they did not have the power inside the organization to stop Eckert, and they considered more political issues than abortion rights and the Equal Rights Amendment in evaluating the prospective candidates.

As prudent politicians, Republican women did not want to end up on the losing side of the battle for the nomination. Because many believed Eckert would be the eventual nominee, and because women were a decided minority in the organization, they concluded that they ought to get on Eckert's bandwagon and gain whatever leverage they could. One woman, who ended up publicly supporting Eckert, told a local reporter, "I've taken a lot of heat from my feminist friends for this . . . But when I looked at this race, it seemed women had two choices: we could simply declare Fred Eckert the enemy, or we could have an honest give and take, because the man had this contest from the day he declared."

In addition to supporting Eckert on pragmatic grounds, women in Monroe County's Republican party were just as troubled as men by what they perceived as Riley's opportunism, and ironically some regarded his shift on the Equal Rights Amendment as evidence of inconsistency. They also believed Eckert had a better understanding of the range of national problems confronting a member of the House of Representatives.

While recognizing these political realities, some Republican women still balked at joining forces with Eckert, until the party offered them a way to pursue their political interests without losing their self-esteem. Those women who expressed anger over Eckert's apparent disregard of their concerns also resented the ridicule they received from their feminist colleagues for allowing Eckert's steamroller tactics to go unchallenged. This predicament was largely resolved when the Women's Advisory Board was formed by Eckert's campaign. The board represented a public concession from Eckert that he had to take women more seriously. It allowed his female detractors to save face, and reassured the women among the GOP's rank and file that the party was not indifferent to their views. Although it is doubtful that the advisory board brought about a change of heart on either side, it nonetheless undermined Riley's claim to be a better spokesman for women's interests in Washington. Thus it protected Eckert's most vulnerable flank by neutralizing his opponent's most salient issue.

Clearly the Republican organization added weight to Eckert's own aggressive campaign to capture the party nomination. Morin and Starkweather tapped the loyalties of convention delegates who worked in county government, drew on the feelings of reciprocity that bound to them such Republican officials as Nagle, and used the internal party apparatus to diffuse the conflict between Eckert and the women activists who opposed him. Having tipped the convention balance in Eckert's favor, they went further and helped him avoid a primary battle by persuading some of Riley's local financial backers to stay out of the contest. Thus the rivalry between these two quintessential members of the new political generation described by Broder—Eckert the ideological maverick and Riley the political personality—was decided under the old rules determined by the imperatives of party organization.

The outcome might have been very different if several circumstances had not favored the efforts of the Republican leaders to influence the congressional nomination. First, as we noted in Chapter 2, the 30th district is somewhat unusual in the extent to which a single county dominates the political landscape. The party leaders in Monroe County were able to control the flow of information about the race from the beginning, and they had the incentive often lacking in congressional recruitment to take an active role in choosing Conable's successor because the House seat so clearly belonged to Monroe County; it was their turf and they acted accordingly. Yet their plans very nearly failed in the face of united opposition from the Republicans of Genesee County, who came within nine votes of blocking Eckert on the first ballot. With a different distribution of party power, or even the balance that existed before the reapportionment of 1982, the leaders in Monroe County might very well have had less leverage over the delegates, and they might therefore have been less inclined to try dictating the outcome of the convention.

In addition, Morin and Starkweather could make effective use of their prerogatives as leaders as long as they were aiding Eckert rather than opposing him. They recognized that Riley, who continually sought consensus, did not have a following of zealots who could give him an edge in a close primary, and they were certain that Riley would not be able to raise campaign funds outside the district. But the case of Eckert was very different: his supporters had turned out for him before in confrontations with the party organization and his money could not be shut off with a few telephone calls. The GOP's leaders could play by the old rules of party politics only as long as their antiestablishment opponent was a local boy with a charming smile. Against a hard-core ideologue with a committed constituency and ties to national interest groups, their ability to circumvent a representative of the new politics with traditional methods was far from certain.

Most significant by far in the party leaders' successful intervention in the choice of the Republican nominee for the 30th Congressional District was the persistence in Monroe County of an identifiable party culture that shaped the way Republican activists viewed the two candidates. Their perceptions of Riley and Eckert grew out of many years of observation and shared experiences and were grounded in the quasi-public arena of party life. To these observers, who spent much of their time in and around politics, a candidate's reputation grew out of myriad interactions with other activists and elected officials; it had very little to do with the popular image that a politician enjoys with the general electorate. There was in effect a long organizational memory that kept track of the strengths and weaknesses of the rivals from Greece, and neither could escape its consequences. Thus Riley, the "nice guy," could not shake the label of untrustworthy opportunist; and Eckert, the experienced and reliable policy-maker, had to live with the view that he was arrogant and abrasive.

In the end, the majority of delegates at the Republican convention made their judgment in Eckert's favor. They neither embraced his conservative philosophy nor rejected Riley's consensus-oriented approach to public decision making. Instead, they closely scrutinized more than a decade of government service by the two rivals and decided not on issues or style but on reputation. Riley appears never to have understood this aspect of the Republican deliberations, for he shunned the customary courting of party officials without fully realizing that doing so might be at odds with his image of sociability or feed suspicions about his poor judgment. And he failed to perceive that his altered stance on the Equal Rights Amendment might be viewed as another sign of his indecisiveness.

What ultimately pushed the Republican delegates into Eckert's column were not Riley's deficiencies but Eckert's virtues. Ironically, the aggressive hardliner personified the values that mattered most in the Republican organization. Eckert's trustworthiness, for example, was his most highly prized political trait. Perhaps more than any other area of human affairs, the business of politics is conducted by means of the private promise and the unenforceable handshake. At the same time the environment in which these agreements are made is extremely unstable, full of unpredictable events and volatile public passions. In such a climate the temptation to change one's mind can be almost irresistible, and the knowledge that Eckert resisted the expedient about-face was critical to the men and women who would have to work with the district's member of Congress in the future. Whether they agreed with him or not, at least they knew they could depend on him to keep his word.

Republicans were also conscious of the high office their nominee would be filling, and genuinely wished to send to Washington the person best equipped to deal with the serious issues before the Congress. In their view, Eckert clearly was more knowledgeable about public affairs than Riley was, and he enjoyed a wider range of experience. They believed both qualities were truly important in a congressman.

The GOP's leaders also valued loyalty. They know how fragile a party organization is and depend on a sense of institutional loyalty to bind its disparate members together.[10] Because Eckert had been loyal to them and the Republican party in the past, by their own first commandment they felt they owed him their support when he sought the nomination.

Finally, Republicans saw in Eckert the most vital quality of all: he could win elections. He had never before lost a race, and party insiders regarded his aggressive tactics and intense ambition to serve in the House as their insurance against losing the seat. Furthermore, they knew that once Eckert had the nomination they would not have to do much else to help him: his ties to outside money and depth of campaign experience meant the party would be free to divert its scarce money and staff to close local contests for the county clerk's office and state Senate. One party leader described the most important considerations in choosing a candidate as follows: "First, who can win. Second, 'want.' How bad do they want it and how hard will they work? Third, 'need.' Does the candidate fit the bill for what the job or community needs? Fourth, past record. You can't take just anybody. You can't create a candidate . . . you have to work from something." He then explained why according to each of his criteria Eckert was the better candidate: "Look, Riley got 'schmeared' in his own backyard in the Robach race. Couldn't even carry Greece. And he still has campaign debts left over from that race in 1980. Compare that with Eckert, who's never lost an election. He can raise his own money for a primary. In primaries you have to get your money from the outside, because the party can't help you. Don can raise some money locally, but it won't be enough. Eckert can get help from the Washington PACs. On top of this, Fred has the background and qualifications: he's been out negotiating for America. Don is one of New York's best supervisors, but nothing more." He then concluded: "And it goes without saying that Eckert has the 'want.' "

10. For evidence of the importance of loyalty to party activists and the maintenance of voluntary organizations see Jeane J. Kirkpatrick, *The New Presidential Elite: Men and Women in National Politics* (New York: Russell Sage, 1976), chap 4; Samuel J. Eldersveld, *Political Parties: A Behavioral Analysis* (Chicago: Rand McNally, 1964).

For this Republican, nominating a winning candidate was the party's chief responsibility at the convention. He and others like him cared little about ideology and issues: Eckert was a winner, and his nomination improved the odds that Conable's seat would remain Republican and that the party could concentrate on winning the local offices that directly affected its viability. This was enough.

Some party regulars were not so sure, and still had reservations about Eckert's conservatism and style. These reluctant few were told to take comfort in Eckert's reputation for integrity and hard work. They were also told that by backing him, they could put themselves in a position to bring him around to their more moderate way of thinking. One reluctant supporter of Eckert admitted that Eckert had been a problem when he was in the state Senate: "During his years there, he wasn't on the team and he had to knock heads to get there. But he's on the team now . . . he's one of us."

The decision by Monroe County's Republican party to back a right-wing "barracuda" is a stunning example of the pragmatism that governs American partisan politics. The Republicans backed their leading maverick not because of his connections to President Reagan, not because they preferred conflict to consensus, and certainly not because they agreed with Eckert's conservative ideology, but because in the local context of the moment and given the options before them, Eckert appeared to represent many of the values on which the party depended for its survival. Given the rules they confronted, the collective memory they shared, the traits they valued in a member of Congress, and the candidates who stepped forward, Eckert was the better man for the job and the party, warts and all.

9

Money and Organization: The National Party and the Local Tradition

However enlightened and skillful a central power may be, it cannot of itself embrace all the details of the life of a great nation.
　　　　　　　　　　—Alexis de Tocqueville, Democracy in America

Decentralization of power is by all odds the most important single characteristic of the American major party; more than anything else this trait distinguishes it from all others.
　　　　　　　　　　—E. E. Schattschneider, Party Government

Strong congressional candidates must succeed in two very different worlds: at home in local district politics and in Washington with national parties and political action committees. Groups outside the district are increasingly important (especially in hotly contested House elections) because they control money and resources that often spell the difference between victory and defeat, and their influence grows as the gap widens between the cost of campaigning and the ability to raise money locally.[1] This outside money is not without strings. The national organizations that provide it have their own perspective on House elections and make demands on congressional hopefuls that are frequently at odds with the local political tradition.

Only a few men and women can reconcile these diverse demands and forge the ad hoc federal coalition of national, state, and district organizations required to win modern House elections. Such candidates are scarce because most politicians see the chance to run for Congress purely in the context of opportunities in the district and understand that they must campaign on the basis of personal reputations created almost entirely within the community.

---

1. These organizations are most likely to intervene in close races. See J. David Gopoian, "What Makes PACs Tick? An Analysis of the Allocation Patterns of Economic Interest Groups," *American Journal of Political Science* 28 (May 1984): 259–281; Larry Sabato, *PAC Power: Inside the World of Political Action Committees* (New York: W.W. Norton, 1984), pp. 74–75; Gary C. Jacobson, *Money in Congressional Elections* (New Haven and London: Yale University Press, 1980), p. 95.

Initial thinking about running for Congress is thus ruled mainly by local and individual considerations, and this parochialism so characteristic of congressional politics at the recruitment stage leads inevitably to tensions at the more cosmopolitan campaign stage.

Many prospective House candidates therefore lack the experience, contacts, or inclination to bridge the cultural gulf separating the activists they need in Washington from the ones they need at home. This was the case in New York's 30th district, and it cost the Democrats an unprecedented opportunity to capture a seat in the House of Representatives in 1984.

Monroe County's Democrats thought they could beat the Republican nominee, Fred Eckert, because they were certain his abrasive style and reputation for extremism were potentially fatal liabilities in the community. The Republican county chairman, Ron Starkweather, admitted as much when he commented, "The right Democrat would be a real problem." In Doug Call, the sheriff of Genesee County, the Democrats had a candidate who could have been the problem Starkweather feared. Not only had Call twice been elected sheriff by a margin of three to one in an overwhelmingly Republican area, he also fit the local tradition of moderation and public service exemplified by Barber Conable. But neither Call nor his fellow Democrats could convince the national party and PACs of his opponent's vulnerability or his own electability.

Washington's money men, hard-headed practitioners of modern, scientific politics, were accustomed to bankrolling candidates only on the basis of poll results, election returns, and voter registration data, hard numbers that could systematically and unambiguously separate winnable districts from losing ones. Lacking both a detailed knowledge of the district and an intimate understanding of the personal strengths and weaknesses of Eckert and Call, national Democratic activists had little faith in the kind of anecdotal rationale that local Democrats offered for Call's candidacy. Once these national organizations refused to underwrite his campaign, their inadequately informed expectation that he could not win was bound to be borne out.[2] Call's campaign is a telling example of the mismatch between the local criteria that still dominate the recruitment of congressional candidates and the national standards that increasingly apply to the candidates' fund-raising efforts.

The Conable Republican

Ironically, it was the Democrats who nominated a Republican much like Conable for the 30th district's seat in Congress. In personal background, political

2. The interdependence of money and votes creates a cycle of expectation: candidates who are expected to run poorly have trouble raising money, as a result of which they spend less than their competitors and do run poorly—the prophecies of skeptical contributors are self-fulfilling. See Jacobson, chap. 4.

style, and philosophy, Doug Call was more like Conable than anyone else who considered replacing him, including all the Republican possibilities.

Call had deep roots in the rural area that surrounds Monroe County and that had given the district its congressmen for seventy-five years. He was born in Batavia in Genesee County, married a woman from a neighboring community, went to college in upstate New York (at Cornell University), and returned after law school in Virginia and two tours of duty in the air force to be an attorney in the town of his birth. There he was part of a family that for several generations had been known for its service and commitment to two of the area's most important and enduring institutions: agriculture and republicanism. Most of his family—brothers, cousins, and uncles—were still farming. One uncle was the dean of the agriculture school at Cornell, another was a member of the Republican State Committee. Call's father had been a town supervisor and Republican county legislator, and remained influential in local party affairs. All members of the family were lifelong supporters of Conable who sometimes participated in regular meetings with the congressman on Saturday mornings in the backroom of Batavia's hardware store. Nothing more clearly illustrated the depth and strength of Call's rural roots than that he still lived in the old family homestead; built in the 1830s as a boarding school for girls, it had been lived in by members of his family off and on for roughly a century.

Call did not immediately follow the family tradition of active involvement in partisan politics. For eight years after his graduation from law school, he served in the air force's Judge Advocate Corps in Pakistan and West Germany. After returning home in 1973 he set up his own law practice and began attending the Colgate Rochester Divinity School, where by 1976 he had completed the course work for a master of arts in theology. In 1975, during his theological studies, Call gave up his private legal practice to become the assistant county attorney for the Genesee County Department of Social Services. In this post he provided legal counsel concerning the abuse and neglect of children, and public assistance. Not until fall 1980, when he was forty, did he finally seek elective office.

His run for sheriff was prompted as much by the urgings of his friends as by his own ambition. Call was entreated by his friends and neighbors, nearly all of whom were Republicans, to run against the sheriff of Genesee County, a long-time Republican incumbent, to bring fresh blood and a more open style to county law enforcement. Persuaded by them that he was right for the job, Call asked the local GOP to support his candidacy. He explained to local Republicans that the public was concerned about the administration of the sheriff's department and that the incumbent was in danger of defeat, and asked for their help in wresting the party's nomination from him, to ensure that the office would remain Republican. But local Republican leaders would have nothing to do with such a coup, and their opposition meant that a bloody primary was the only route to the GOP's endorsement. Call believed that if this took place a third candidate would enter the race, and the incumbent would eke out a victory over a divided opposition. "I could only beat him if I could get him one-on-one, where I would receive all the negative votes," Call told us. Faced with this problem, Call, a lifelong Republican, took the only route that would enable him to face the sheriff alone: he asked Genesee County's Democrats for their nomination. The party quickly agreed, because it was only too willing to run someone of Call's prominence against a controversial and vulnerable incumbent. This was the beginning of Call's fall from the Republicans' grace. On Election Day he ran with the endorsements of the Democratic and Conservative parties and handily defeated the GOP, winning 76 percent of the vote and every election district in the county.

In office, Call continued to exhibit the same kind of political flexibility that had marked his campaign. He abandoned his predecessor's plan to build a new county jail and attacked the problem of overcrowding by developing alternative methods of incarceration and renovating the existing facility. He advocated sentencing criminals to perform community service and provide restitution for minor offenders. Where possible he resolved disputes by bringing victims and offenders face-to-face. His liberal methods ultimately achieved a conservative goal: by reducing the number of people in jail, the county was able to save money by remodeling the old building and adding on only six new cells.

Call also employed an easygoing personal style to build morale in the department and rapport with other law enforcement agencies. "He's very good on a personal level," said Frank Repicci, chairman of the Genesee County Democratic Party. "When people listen to him, they trust him. It's like they can look into his heart. He's successful because people know how he operates. So they're willing to let him try things they would otherwise be opposed to."[3]

While employing his humanistic approach to most problems, Call took a hard-line, law-and-order stand on some others, particularly drunk driving. Under Call, Genesee County was the first jurisdiction in the nation to set up roadblocks and stop drivers randomly for sobriety tests. The program met with stiff opposition from civil libertarians, but Call refused to relent, even in the face of court challenges.

As these examples indicate, Call was no political ideologue. He retained the conservative instincts of his local roots, but his conservatism was enriched from childhood by the area's traditional commitment to human rights and further broadened in adulthood by the humanistic outlook taught in seminary. Call supported the Equal Rights Amendment, the Supreme Court's decision on abortion, and its ban on prayer in public schools. His whole approach to public

3. Mark Hare, "Doug Call's Campaign for Congress," *City* (Rochester), July 12, 1984, pp. 12–13.

questions was rooted in his trying to do the best he could. "I'm the kind of person who has doubts, who is always asking questions," he said. "But I think people want someone who's always weighing the issues, testing ideas, tempering his positions and trying to do what's the best approach."[4]

In background and style, the parallels between Call and Conable were striking. After their military service, both men were drawn home to their rural roots in the landed gentry from which they had acquired their strong sense of noblesse oblige. Each came to political office in midlife, and neither saw himself as a professional politician. Like Call, Conable in his first run for public office was pressed into challenging an entrenched Republican state senator whose arrogant use of power had clouded his reputation. Appalled by the incumbent's disregard of accepted political propriety, Conable battled him and the local Republican establishment in a primary to win election to the state Senate. But most important, at the core of both men's use of political office was a constant search for the common ground and the reasoned approach.

By no means were the parallels between Call and Conable perfect. Conable remained completely wedded to the area's partisan Republican tradition. Call obviously was no more a dedicated partisan than a committed ideologue. The two men also disagreed sharply on a number of important national issues. For instance, Call favored the nuclear freeze and Conable opposed it. Conable favored a balanced-budget amendment to the Constitution and Call opposed it. But the major difference between the two men was their approach to the marketplace. Underneath Conable's moderate image had always been a core of hard-headed capitalist thinking that observers frequently missed because they judged him mainly by his style. In contrast, Call's upstate conservatism was softened too much by his reformist leanings and humanist impulses for him to be comfortable with the streak of rugged individualism found in Conable. It was precisely this sense of social concern in Call's politics, however, that finally made him acceptable to Monroe County's Democrats.

At the heart of both Conable's and Call's approach to politics was a lack of dogmatism, a rural attachment to community, and a sense of noblesse oblige inculcated by their families; in these respects Call and Conable were nearly identical. The similarity was noted by people in both parties. A local Democrat remarked that "Call was a Jeffersonian Democrat who fits into the Conable district, since Conable was a Jeffersonian Republican." A Republican from Genesee County spoke about the similarity in more detail: "I have always supported Conable for Congress," he said. "I was always proud to have him as my congressman. He was a man of integrity. I didn't always agree with him, but at least I knew he had thought about things. When he decided to retire, I looked around for somebody like him, and Doug was that person. It certainly wasn't Fred Eckert."

4. Ibid.

Call's similarities to Conable made local Democrats skeptical of him at first. Although drawn to him by his potential appeal to a wide range of voters, they were nevertheless troubled by the twists and turns of Call's political past that made such a wide political appeal possible. What was Call's purpose in politics? Where did he see his true allies? Was he a conservative, law-and-order sheriff wrapped in the robes of a moralizing minister? (In a letter he wrote introducing himself to the party membership outside Genesee County, Call raised suspicions when he stated that "public service is a form of ministry . . . and we need to revive our moral commitment.") Or was he a liberal do-gooder who tried to keep people out of jail and thought the United States ought to be more understanding of the Russians?

Local Democrats were particularly troubled to learn that Call had voted for Ronald Reagan in 1980, and they saw his vote for Jimmy Carter in 1976 as little source for consolation. Not until he mentioned his vote in 1982 for Mario Cuomo and pledged to change his registration to Democratic were party regulars finally willing to accept him.

Because of the doubts that Call provoked, it was understandable that many local Democrats preferred any one of several politicians from Monroe County as their congressional candidate. But each of the other prospective candidates refused, for reasons we have already seen, to risk his or her current position for a chance to go to Washington. Finally, after exhausting their other possibilities, the Democrats turned to Call in the recognition that resemblances to Conable were valuable assets given the peculiar set of local forces that were shaping the contest in New York's 30th Congressional District.

Call recognized the validity of the party's preference for the other candidates, particularly Slaughter, and at least initially was not troubled by having to wait for her to make up her mind about running. He acknowledged that he had not acted decisively in seeking the nomination himself and that as a registered Republican he was in no position to threaten a primary. He therefore stood by patiently.

Call could do so because his political ambition was so indeterminate. Displaying an indecisiveness that was reminiscent of his run for sheriff, Call had first become interested in the House race at the suggestion of others, not because of his own desire for congressional office. Not until a friend invited Call to lunch to discuss his own ambition to go to Congress did Call first think seriously about replacing Conable himself. These initial thoughts of his about going to Washington were quite sobering because of his respectful view of Capitol Hill. "Congress is a big step up," he told us, and he was not certain he wanted to take it.

On reflection, Call thought the opportunity to replace Conable was one he should explore. As the idea became more appealing to him, he was first approached by friends in the Genesee County Republican Party, who were looking for a candidate to keep the seat in the hands of the rural counties. The rural

Republicans' first choice was Assemblyman Steve Hawley. When he dropped out (see Chapter 2), they believed Call was their next best hope. Call encouraged them and engaged in serious negotiations about running as a Republican who would challenge Eckert at the convention, or even in a primary. Within a short time, however, Call turned away from the local GOP: he had been persuaded that he could not beat Eckert by running as a Republican from Genesee County, given the rural area's reduced importance in the redesigned 30th Congressional District and his status as a Democratic officeholder. It was in fact Conable who made clear to Call that he could not win: "The votes just aren't there," he told him. "It was a different district when I won the nomination in 1964. Back then, 50 percent of all the Republicans who would vote in a primary lived outside Monroe County. That's not true today."

At the same time that the Republicans were pursuing Call, Genesee County's Democrats were after him too. After realizing that running as a Democrat offered the better chance to defeat Eckert, he allowed his friends in the party to tell Betsy Toole, vice-chairwoman of the Monroe County Democratic Party, that he was a prospective candidate. Toole arranged to have Call's name mentioned in the local press, and the response was so favorable that Toole immediately got in touch with him. After a long meeting with Call in her office, she began to promote his candidacy to others in the party.

Call's motivation for the congressional seat was the same as it had been for the sheriff's office. Once again it was not his own political ambition but the prodding of friends that caused him to enter the race. His wife told us, "It was friends coming to him that made him want to run. People telling him he should run. That's very important." Call himself admitted, "In the minority party, you particularly need people coming to you."

Almost as important in motivating him as his friends' urgings were his disapproval of Eckert's political style and his disagreement with him on a number of social and defense issues. In fact, he told us that if Don Riley had been the likely Republican nominee Call himself would never have considered running. Evidently, Call's attraction to the seat in Congress was rooted almost entirely in his sense of social responsibility and personal obligation. He felt obligated to give voters a real alternative to Eckert, who from Call's perspective was socially irresponsible and unworthy to follow in the tradition established by Conable. In a manner that again recalled his first run for office, Call had to enter the race for Congress because Eckert had to be stopped.

Call was thus drawn to beat Eckert, but not to go to Congress. His dream had never been to go to Congress, any more than it had been to be a sheriff. His political opportunities were always thrust on him by his friends and opponents. Even though he worked tirelessly for political success once he accepted these opportunities, he did little to create them in the first place. His wife described his passive approach to his political career perfectly when she said, "Doug is not a man who plans. He takes things as he finds them. He doesn't have a specific goal."

As early as April these vague, externally induced motivations were tested by the rigors of a congressional campaign. As Call waited for the Democrats to make up their minds and began to meet with people knowledgeable about congressional campaigns, he experienced more and more uncertainty about running. By early May he was having serious second thoughts and would have been relieved had Slaughter herself chosen to run. But he was a man of honor. He had told the Democrats he was prepared to make the race, and it was too late now to back out. "If the Democrats don't endorse me, then I'm off the hook, but otherwise I'm obligated," he told us.

In mid-June, four days after Slaughter finally announced she did not want the nomination, the party's executive committee officially named Call as the Democratic candidate in the 30th district. By then the election was less than five months off, and Call had no money, campaign staff, battle plan, or organization outside Genesee County.

That the Democrats at the last minute nominated a man who until April 1984 had been a registered Republican and who had no burning political ambition is a pointed lesson in both the weaknesses and strengths of the moderate, flexible opposition parties of the United States. Call's nomination demonstrates the openness of minority parties to outsiders and their sensitivity to the common ground, but at the same time it underlines their inability to groom and promote candidates from within, their quite casual concern about partisan principles and programs, and their tendency toward haphazard planning and lackadaisical decision making. These weaknesses of the minority party, so clearly in evidence in Monroe County, overshadowed the equally evident strengths of the local organization and its chosen nominee and contributed heavily to Call's defeat.

The National Bank

With the nomination in hand, Call's first task was to raise money, because he would have to spend heavily to overcome the weak position from which he was starting his last-minute drive for a seat in Congress. He needed a big campaign chest, mainly to increase his name recognition. Spending in congressional elections is most important in gaining name recognition, because candidates such as Call cannot get voters to pay attention to their personal qualities and political views until they first become household names. This is why the money spent by challengers produces large, demonstrable effects on Election Day, and the money that incumbents spend seems to have a much smaller, less certain impact. It also explains why campaigns for open seats, where two lesser-known politicians usually vie against each other, tend to be more expensive.[5]

To produce a winning margin in his own race, Call believed he would need at least $175,000 to $200,000. This figure was quite low compared with the average spent by winning candidates in open seats in 1984, but it still was more money than could be found inside the district.[6] Toole and Larry Kirwan, the former county chairman who was now the vice-chairman of the state Democratic party and who had agreed to direct Call's campaign, had said repeatedly that they could raise locally no more than $100,000 for even the strongest candidate. Therefore Call would have to raise on his own at least $75,000, and maybe as much as $125,000, from sources outside the 30th district.

As a Democrat, Call would have to raise most of the outside money from PACS in Washington, because as we saw in Chapter 2 the national Democrats simply did not have the resources to be of much help. In fact, they contributed only 2.8 percent of all the money spent by Democratic candidates in 1984.[7] But substantial amounts of money from these groups would be forthcoming only if the national party endorsed his campaign and pledged to him some of its meager resources. Without money from the national party to demonstrate its approval, Call would not find many open checkbooks when he made the rounds of the PACS in Washington. The national party could not itself provide Call with the resources he needed, but the Democratic Congressional Campaign Committee still held the key to the national bank.

In June, Call and Nick Robfogel, chairman of the Monroe County Democratic Party, flew to Washington to meet with representatives of the Democratic Congressional Campaign Committee. The two hoped to get the committee to make a substantial, direct contribution to Call's campaign and to have the national party designate the 30th district one of its "targeted races," which meant it would become a House seat that national Democrats thought they could win and in which they were prepared to wage an all-out campaign. Their presentation to the party people in Washington was therefore one of the most important sales jobs of the campaign.

Call and Robfogel got nowhere, however. Before the committee would consider doing anything in the 30th district, the national people wanted evidence that the Democrats were raising money locally and lining up concrete commitments to the race from area and state party leaders. Most important, the national campaign committee demanded poll results that showed Call with a chance of winning.

5. Jacobson, chap. 2.
6. The average expenditure of a candidate who won an open House seat in 1984 was $459,000. See Norman J. Ornstein et al., *Vital Statistics on Congress, 1982* (Washington, D.C.: American Enterprise Institute, 1983), p. 60.
7. Gary C. Jacobson, *The Politics of Congress and Elections*, 2nd ed. (Boston: Little, Brown 1987), p. 70.

This was a quite different approach from that which the committee had taken with Slaughter. On her initial visit it had promised her campaign $25,000 and introduced her immediately to important PACs in Washington. What accounted for the difference? In the first place, Slaughter's state legislative position and connections to Governor Cuomo and prominent PACs generated enthusiasm for her candidacy. A campaign by Slaughter also had the advantage of fitting the prevailing theory among national politicians that an attack against Ronald Reagan and the Republican party that exploited the gender gap was the Democrats' best hope in November.[8]

Call's request for aid had none of these advantages. Even though Monroe County's Democrats were now promoting him as a winner, they had earlier in the spring sent several other local politicians to Washington to ask for national money. Each had tried to portray himself as a winner and the local party as interested in his candidacy. As for Slaughter, Monroe County's party leaders had themselves made clear their enthusiastic support for her candidacy and their firm belief that she would be Eckert's strongest opponent. The national committee therefore had every reason to believe that Call, if not the local Democrats' last resort, was at least their last-minute second choice, and his late appearance in the capital did nothing to alter their presumption. Moreover, when Call visited Washington in June, he had no well-known party official like Governor Cuomo going to bat for him. Only he and Robfogel were in town to explain how the race could be won. Although they emphasized the area's political tradition, Eckert's inherent vulnerability, and Call's natural strengths, the national Democrats, removed from the local politics of upstate New York, simply could not appreciate the opportunity that Monroe County's Democrats saw so clearly.

Even though Call had a better record as a vote-getter than Slaughter, a more acceptable ideological stance to upstate New Yorkers, and a larger political base inside the district, the national party was as unwilling to help him as it had been eager to help her. It would have to be persuaded on its own terms, by convincing data, that Call could be a winner too.

As soon as he returned home, Call commissioned a professional survey that he could show in Washington. It was his first major campaign expenditure, and it would amount to nearly seven thousand dollars. The poll's preliminary findings were available in late July and of course documented Call's lack of name recognition and his definite status as an underdog. Not surprisingly, the poll showed Eckert was well known and had a commanding early lead. When Call

8. This is an example of how national thinking can affect local congressional races through the deployment of resources and recruitment of candidates. National elites put their money into local races when national circumstances cause them to think the money will be particularly well-spent. For an elaborate treatment of this argument see Gary C. Jacobson and Samuel Kernell, *Strategy and Choice in Congressional Elections* (New Haven and London: Yale University Press, 1981).

was pitted against his opponent in a standard question designed to gauge voter preferences four months before Election Day, Eckert was the choice of 50 percent of the voters and Call of 23 percent; the rest were undecided or did not respond.[9]

The survey also confirmed another commonly held local view, one that had also surfaced in Slaughter's poll: Eckert had serious problems of his own. Although he was well known, respondents who had a very favorable opinion of Eckert outnumbered those who had an unfavorable opinion by a margin of only four to three. Voters had far more favorable opinions of the three other Republicans included in the survey—Ronald Reagan, Lucien Morin, and Barber Conable. Morin received roughly four very favorable evaluations for every unfavorable one, and Conable received ten.

On the other hand, of the 29 percent of the respondents who recognized Call's name he had four very favorable responses for every unfavorable one. In addition, the survey showed that none of Call's positions on issues would cause him trouble with the electorate. Only if Call attacked the president and his economic recovery (which he had no intention of doing) would he be sharply at odds with the voters. Eckert, on the other hand, was clearly on the wrong side of public opinion on the issues of abortion and the Equal Rights Amendment.

The survey's most interesting aspect was the respondents' choice after they had been read one paragraph describing each candidate. The paragraphs were intended to portray the candidates accurately and fairly, yet do so in the way an aggressive political campaign would. The idea was to determine what voters would be inclined to do if both candidates were able to communicate their campaign themes to the voters before Election Day.

The paragraph the respondents heard about Eckert was as follows:

> Let me tell you about Fred Eckert. Once a state senator from Monroe County, Eckert resigned his position in order to become U.S. Ambassador to the Fiji Islands. Known as a brash individual with very conservative political views, Eckert has voted against the Equal Rights Amendment, supported a constitutional amendment to outlaw abortion and supported tax cuts, has voted for the death penalty and is considered to be anti-labor. He has been endorsed by such people as Lucien Morin, Barber Conable, Jack Kemp and Lew Lehrman. Once compared to Napoleon because of his divisive and obstructionist manner, many believe Eckert will alienate much of the 30th Congressional District rather than work to bring its widely varied communities together. Eckert is a staunch supporter of President Reagan and his policies.

9. All the data in this chapter come from the poll taken for Call by GFM and Associates, a survey firm in Albany closely tied to the state Democratic party. The poll encompassed 603 telephone interviews conducted between July 10 and July 21, 1984, and was typical of surveys congressional candidates use in their campaigns. Call's campaign turned over to us all materials associated with the poll and gave us unqualified permission to use its findings.

The paragraph the respondents heard about Call was as follows:

Now, let me tell you something about Doug Call. Doug Call is the elected Sheriff of Genesee County, an attorney and former divinity student. Raised on his family's farm, Call entered the Air Force after law school, reaching the rank of Captain while working in Pakistan and West Germany. He has extensive foreign affairs experience having been head of the Air Force's International Law Section in West Germany. Critics of Doug Call say that he is too liberal and not tough enough to represent the 30th Congressional District. They also feel that his lack of *legislative* experience will hurt his effectiveness in Congress. Call's innovations as Sheriff include STOP-DWI checkpoints, drug-tip lines, victim assistance, and restitution, and have attracted nationwide attention. Call has a reputation for being a problem solver and wants to bring this skill to such problems as arms control and federal deficits.

The order of the two profiles was reversed for half the respondents so that the ordering would not bias the survey. After being read the profiles, the voters were asked: "Now, after hearing about both candidates, for which do you think you will vote: Fred Eckert or Doug Call?" In this trial heat, Call won 48 percent of the vote and Eckert 37 percent; the rest was undecided. In the first trial heat, where voters were given no information about the two candidates, Eckert was favored by a margin of two to one. It seemed that the more information the voters had, the better Call's chances.[10]

Call's camp thought the poll's findings confirmed dramatically the campaign's fundamental proposition: Eckert was vulnerable. First, there was substantial negative feeling against Eckert on which Call could build, and, just as important, much of Eckert's initial support was quite tentative. Second, Eckert had been away from the area for a couple of years, and voters in more than half the new district had never had any direct contact with him. If the Democrats could get across to voters their message about Call and Eckert, Call could win. All he needed was the money to deliver the message, and the 30th Congressional District of New York was the ideal place to wage a campaign oriented toward the issues because of its extraordinarily efficient position with respect to media markets. Call was in the perfect congressional district to get himself known quickly, and Eckert's record and the sizable number of voters who still knew nothing about him meant there was a real opportunity for the minority party's media message to be decisive.

With all these data, local Democrats believed they now had the ammunition

10. This is not an uncommon survey technique. Walter Mondale's vulnerability as a presidential candidate in 1984 was documented when the pollster Pat Caddell began matching Mondale with a fictitious candidate in surveys conducted before primary elections and using a technique similar to this one to gauge the characteristics a politician would need to challenge Mondale effectively for the nomination. The profile arrived at by this technique was said to have been a guide to Gary Hart's campaign against Mondale, which nearly succeeded.

necessary to persuade the party in Washington to jump on Call's bandwagon. This time Kirwan, not Robfogel, would make the local party's pitch. Although Kirwan was no longer directing Call's campaign, having taken the position of upstate coordinator for Mondale's troubled effort, he agreed to ask the national party to fund the race in the 30th district. Because of his role in Mondale's campaign and his position as the state party's vice-chairman, he was a powerful advocate. Kirwan enlisted Governor Cuomo's pledge of support, and at the Democratic National Convention he won over to Call's cause Senator Daniel Patrick Moynihan and state labor leaders. With this array of state supporters, with local fund-raising picking up, and with the positive results of the poll, Kirwan thought he had a good case.

For two months in August and September, Kirwan tried to persuade the members of the congressional campaign committee to support Call. He met with them in Washington and called them repeatedly on the telephone. He arranged for Moynihan and Cuomo to telephone the committee on Call's behalf. When the committee wanted letters from both men, Kirwan had them delivered immediately. Kirwan also enlisted the support of two Democratic congressmen from upstate New York, Matt McHugh and Stan Lundine, to lobby the committee in support of Call. Each time he thought he was close to getting a commitment, the national party would add another condition. "They kept giving me one more task to do in the expectation that I couldn't do it," he told us. "When I'd do it, they'd think of something else. It was one of the most frustrating experiences I've ever had."

In late September, Call's fate was sealed when a national poll was released that showed Democrats would lose forty seats in the House. The survey suggested the election was turning into a realigning landslide for the Republicans. After this bombshell, whatever money the congressional committee had left in reserve for challengers such as Call quickly dried up. All available funds were shifted to protect the large number of supposedly vulnerable Democratic incumbents. Once again, success in Monroe County's race was undermined by national party leaders' reliance on survey data and their tendency to predict the outcomes of House elections solely on the basis of trends revealed by national data. On Election Day this forecast, like the many other predictions of realignment and of gross shifts in congressional seats in previous years, was found to have been in error; it failed to take into account the local, idiosyncratic elements that still persist in House elections.

In early October, Kirwan was told that Call would receive no help. This meant that money promised to Call by Kirwan's many contacts in organized labor groups would not materialize either; they had agreed to help Call only if the national committee made the 30th a "targeted district." "I failed," Kirwan admitted. "We had raised $100,000 locally. We had a plan and the mailings and the ads to do the job. But we just couldn't come up with the resources."

The final campaign spending reports filed by the two candidates with the Federal Election Commission documented Kirwan's point. Eckert raised $234,293 and spent $259,457. Call raised $102,417 and spent $102,544 (see table 9.1). To wage his campaign, Call had less than half the resources available to Eckert. Even more important was Call's failure to raise even the minimum amount of money he believed a challenger needed to wage an effective campaign.[11]

Call did not reach his goal because of the unequal success of the two candidates in raising money from outside the district. The candidates did raise roughly equal amounts in small, local contributions, and in local party contributions. As for local contributions of $200 or more, Eckert held a noticeable edge. But this advantage was slight compared with the extraordinary difference between the two in raising money from national sources. At national fundraising, Eckert had an overwhelming advantage. From all sources at the national level—individuals, economic and ideological groups, and party committees, Eckert raised nearly four times as much money as Call, who raised almost none from individuals, party sources, or ideological groups. Only from PACs tied to economic and professional interests (mostly organized labor) was Call able to generate a sizable sum—$29,075, or 29.4 percent of all his funds. Even this figure exaggerates the national presence in Call's campaign, because most of the money he raised from groups outside the district was obtained through efforts in his behalf by organizations and individuals inside the district. He ended up getting only 32.3 percent of his funds from national sources.

Eckert's fund-raising was quite different. He got 55.7 percent of his money from national sources, of which more than $85,000 came from national PACs tied to economic and professional interests. (The most conspicuous givers in this category were PACs aligned with builders and developers.) These large, national contributors, crucial to Eckert's campaign, together accounted for 8 percent of all the money he collected.

Eckert also got more than $30,000 (13 percent of the total) from ideological PACs.[12] Five times as much money came to Eckert from such groups as came to Call, and the ideological PACs tended to make larger contributions than the economic ones. For example, the conservative PAC formed to support President Reagan, Citizens for the Republic, gave Eckert $10,000, the maximum allowed by law. (It is a strange twist in American politics that the president of the United

11. For a discussion of winners' expenditures see Jacobson, chap. 5.

12. By getting more than half his campaign money from PACs, Eckert was considerably more dependent on these groups than the average House candidate in 1982. See Gary C. Jacobson, "Money in the 1980 and 1982 Congressional Elections," in Michael J. Malbin, *Money and Politics in the United States: Financing Elections in the 1980s* (Washington, D.C.: American Enterprise Institute, 1984), pp. 38–69. Early figures from 1984, current at the end of October, show him again to have been well above the average. See Michael J. Malbin and Thomas W. Skladony, "Campaign Finance, 1984: A Preliminary Analysis of House and Senate Campaign Receipts," *American Enterprise Institute Public Policy Week*, December 2, 1984, table 3.

Table 9.1　Sources of the Candidates' Campaign Funds

CALL'S CAMPAIGN

	NATIONAL	LOCAL	TOTAL	PERCENTAGE OF ALL CONTRIBUTIONS
Group Contributions				
Ideological	$ 2,023	$ 668	$ 2,691	2.6
Party	200	3,551	3,751	3.7
Professional and Economic	29,075	1,050	30,125	29.4
Total	$31,298	$ 5,269	$ 36,567	35.7
Individual Contributions				
Large ($200 or more)	$ 1,726	$20,567	$ 22,293	21.8
Small (less than $200)	100	43,457	43,557	42.5
Total	$ 1,826	$64,024	$ 65,850	64.3
All Contributions	$33,124	$69,293	$102,417	100.0
Percentage of All Contributions	32.3	67.7	100.0	

ECKERT'S CAMPAIGN

	NATIONAL	LOCAL	TOTAL	PERCENTAGE OF ALL CONTRIBUTIONS
Group Contributions				
Ideological	$ 30,600	$ 200	$ 30,800	13.1
Party	9,819	3,685	13,504	5.8
Professional and Economic	85,169	3,775	88,944	38.0
Total	$125,588	$ 7,660	$133,248	56.9
Individual Contributions				
Large ($200 or more)	$ 4,990	$ 49,445	$ 54,435	23.2
Small (less than $200)	—	46,610	46,610	19.9
Total	$ 4,990	$ 96,055	$101,045	43.1
All Contributions	$130,578	$103,715	$234,293	100.0
Percentage of All Contributions	55.7	44.3	100.0	

Dash denotes zero.
SOURCE: Federal Election Commission.

States is in effect allowed to be the single largest contributor to the campaign of a member of Congress!) The National Rifle Association Political Victory Fund contributed $5,150, the National Right to Life PAC $5,000. Among groups of this kind, the average contribution to Eckert was more than $2,000. The average contribution to his campaign from the economic and professional PACs was slightly more than $750.[13]

13. That the economic PACs gave Eckert smaller contributions and the ideological groups larger ones is typical of a more general pattern. See Theodore J. Eismeier and Philip H. Pollock III, "Political Action Committees: Varieties of Organization and Strategy," in Malbin, pp. 122–141.

It is however clear from Eckert's financial reports, and from our interviews with him and other local political leaders, that the national cast of his campaign cannot be attributed solely or even mainly to the presence of a vigorous national party organization in Washington; more important is the proliferation of economic and ideological PACs that have emerged to support congressional candidates nationwide.[14] These groups provided roughly half of Eckert's campaign money, and it was his connections to them as much as his ties to President Reagan and the national party that made him an attractive candidate to Monroe County's Republicans. Obviously, the Republican Congressional Campaign Committee's direct contribution to Eckert of nearly $10,000 was important to his efforts to raise money from the national PACs, as was the considerable amount of coordinated expenditures it made on his behalf. Also, the national GOP quickly found an experienced, young party tactician from outside the upstate area to be Eckert's chief of staff and sent Eckert to a training session on how to wage a modern congressional campaign. But it was the money from the PACs themselves that made the big difference.

Eckert was a politician whose style and background were completely suited to the new congressional environment of national money and local media, and for this reason his candidacy itself intensified the nationalizing effect of other factors. From the beginning of his political career he had reached out to a national, ideological constituency, and appealed to voters by using the mass media rather than the more traditional techniques of campaigning face-to-face and door-to-door, on which most of his rivals in both parties had built their careers. When the 30th district was reapportioned so that it became essentially one media market, Eckert was the ideal person to exploit the situation. Eckert's abundance of money, provided mainly by national sources, was used quickly to influence local voters. During the fall campaign, Eckert spent $162,173 on direct appeals to voters through the news media and the mails. On the other hand Call, who spent about half as much getting his message to the voters, was forced to cancel his last series of television commercials and abandon a planned districtwide mailing because he ran out of money.

Reports of the Federal Election Commission, which itemize the two campaigns' expenditures, also show the effect of Call's failure to raise money and Eckert's success at it (see table 9.2). Whereas Eckert spent $87,400 on media advertising, Call spent only $59,735. The two biggest differences in spending were in direct mail and staff: Eckert spent nearly $75,000 on direct mail and postage, Call slightly more than $20,000; Eckert spent nearly $60,000 on his

14. See Sabato. For a discussion of the Republican party's efforts to increase the effectiveness of its national organization see John Bibby, "Party Renewal in the National Republican Party," in *Party Renewal in America: Theory and Practice*, ed. Gerald M. Pomper (New York: Praeger, 1980). For a broader discussion of party renewal see Yandra Kayden and Eddie Mahe, Jr., *The Party Goes On: The Two Party System in the United States* (New York: Basic Books, 1985).

Table 9.2   Candidates' Campaign Disbursements

| | CALL | | ECKERT | |
	Amount	Percentage of Total	Amount	Percentage of Total
Media, Advertising	$ 59,735	58.3	$ 87,400	33.7
Printing, Mailings, Postage	21,614	21.1	74,773	28.8
Polling	6,760	6.6	11,650	4.5
Office, Payroll, Supplies, Equipment	6,708	6.5	58,462	22.5
Fund-raising	4,722	4.7	16,745	6.5
Travel	2,227	2.2	2,084	.8
Miscellaneous	778	.8	8,343	3.2
Total	$102,544	100.0	$259,457	100.0

Percentages may not add to 100 because of rounding.
SOURCE: Federal Election Commission.

office and staff, Call a little under $7,000. A volunteer in Call's campaign told us how outgunned she felt: "We were all volunteers. We worked as hard as we could, but we all had other responsibilities, including Doug. Eckert worked full-time and had that huge paid staff looking after everything. We just didn't have that, and it made a big difference."

Her assessment of Eckert's advantage was shared by nearly every observer of politics in Monroe County. One local politician with a keen sense of campaign dynamics assessed the election results this way: "If Call could have gotten started early and not had to wait quietly while those [Democratic] legislators fiddled around, I think it would have helped him a lot. He could have won it, if he had the time to raise money. His volunteer organization was excellent. It was his media campaign that was not very good."

If the 30th district is at all typical of others around the country, then the large national dimension that has been added to House campaigns is due not only to the vigorous intervention of the national party organizations. At work also is reapportionment, which sometimes places at a disadvantage politicians with a more local orientation, or makes new district boundaries more compatible with media campaigning, or even makes media campaigning essential. In this altered environment, the presence of the national PACs becomes critical. Because they are ready sources of the money needed for these new expenditures, PACs make a media campaign all the more attractive, particularly to local politicians who have cultivated the necessary national ties that make access to money from PACS somewhat more certain.

There remains one observation about the role of money in this congressional campaign, and it relates to the unequal ability of the two candidates to raise money from national sources while at the same time they raised similar amounts from local contributors. This pattern is important because it suggests that the political leaders in Washington and Monroe County were making two different predictions about the likely outcome of the race. Contributors give money to the candidates they expect will win, and turn their backs on those they expect will lose.[15] In the case of Call and Eckert, those who appropriated funds for the national Republican party saw Eckert as a sure winner, and their money flowed to him accordingly. Democrats in Washington viewed the race the same way, and therefore put no money into Call's campaign. Local contributions to Eckert and Call were not nearly so lopsided, because professionals in the 30th district believed the race to be competitive; ultimately they were of course right, as the election turned out to be much closer than had been expected.

That political contributions can reflect such different opinions of an election's outcome argues against certain commonly held assumptions: first, that the total amount of money raised during an election is always an accurate measure of the views of political insiders of the election's likely outcome (it can be, but only if the political activists at the national and local levels are making the same predictions); second, and perhaps more importantly, that the money raised for a race simply reflects the relative strengths of the candidates at the start of the campaign and has little effect on the outcome. Certainly neither assumption would have been correct in the 30th district. The more accurate view of the candidates' strength was reflected by the distribution of local contributions, not by that of national contributions or by the total amount of money raised. By improperly assessing the race, the Democrats in Washington who refused to bet on Call's candidacy let the cash provided by PACs tip the balance in Eckert's favor. From this perspective, the national money provided to Eckert takes on a more decisive role.

The Local Issue

Even with all the factors working to nationalize congressional elections, there remain counterbalancing tendencies that also keep them local. For one thing, we have seen that the candidates are local political figures judged mainly by their local public records. For another, a successful candidate from the minority party in a congressional race usually rides to victory on a local issue, not a national one. It was therefore just as important for Call to have a strong local issue to use against Eckert as it was to have a lot of national money. But although he tried throughout the campaign to stress his compatibility with the

15. See Jacobson, pp. 72–101.

local congressional tradition typified by Conable, he never latched on to a local concern that could give his argument specificity and immediacy.

Lacking a burning local issue, Call sometimes tried to campaign on the differences between him and Eckert over national policy. But this tactic was not particularly effective, because Call often appeared uncertain and talked in broad generalities. He was after all a local politician more comfortable discussing problems of local law enforcement than the nuances of nuclear-arms treaties. Eckert, on the other hand, who had ambassadorial experience and was long absorbed in national politics, was full of well-rehearsed, detailed explanations. A close observer of the campaign told us, "It took Call a long time to get command of the issues. Eckert always had all the facts and figures and names. 'My good friend Cap Weinberger,' he would say. It was sickening and got to be just too much. But Call talked too much in generalities. There are just so many issues in a congressional election that it takes a long time to get on top of them."

When not campaigning on national issues Call tried to stress the differences in style between the two candidates, as a way of linking himself to Conable's tradition and giving the campaign a local focus. But this strategy fared little better, and in the end actually backfired.

In the first place, differences of style are best stressed face-to-face with voters, but the size of modern congressional districts makes this almost impossible for a challenger. In Call's case in particular, the late start of the campaign gave him too little time to present himself in person to large numbers of voters. His next best way of communicating differences in style was through televised political advertising, but for this he lacked the money. The local newspapers were of some help in his effort to emphasize style, because Eckert had always been a favorite target of the press, and his blunt campaign comments still made good copy.[16] But the newspapers gave only intermittent attention to the campaign and tended to stress Call's status as an underdog.

Most newspaper coverage of the race after Labor Day concentrated on campaign mechanics and the question of which candidate was ahead, and this focus always put Call on the defensive.[17] His staff was smaller than Eckert's, his campaign ws not as efficient, and he started the race clearly behind; he always seemed a sure loser. Toward the middle of October, a poll conducted by the marketing department of the local newspaper the *Democrat and Chronicle*,

16. For a discussion of the emphasis on style in press coverage of congressional campaigns see Peter Clarke and Susan H. Evans, *Covering Campaigns: Journalism in Congressional Elections* (Stanford, Calif.: Stanford University Press, 1983), chap. 4.

17. This sort of coverage is typical; see Clarke and Evans. The coverage of presidential campaigns is similar. See Thomas E. Patterson and Robert D. McClure, *The Unseeing Eye: The Myth of Television Power in National Politics* (New York: Putnam, 1976). See also Thomas E. Patterson, *The Mass Media Election* (New York: Praeger, 1980).

and prominently displayed to readers, showed Call 20 percent behind Eckert. The next day, the newspaper endorsed Eckert. "For the rest of the campaign, Fred whipped out that endorsement every chance he had," Call told us. "It really hurt."

The biggest hurt to Call's campaign was inflicted by another endorsement: Conable mailed a letter endorsing Eckert to every voter in the district and repeatedly went on television and radio in Eckert's behalf in the final days before the election.

If there was a local issue in this congressional campaign, it was the question of which candidate was more in the tradition of Barber Conable. Call's campaign suggested that he was, and as long as Conable did not act the claim was credible. But when Conable so forcefully and visibly endorsed Eckert, Call's basic issue—his one genuinely local appeal—was cut out from under him.

In his endorsement, Conable praised Eckert for being "more experienced and better trained for Congress than I was when I was first elected." He also singled out Eckert's strong support of the balanced budget amendment and noted, "I feel very strongly about the amendment. . . . The man who is running as the Democratic candidate opposes it."[18]

Conable's sweeping public endorsement of Eckert took Call's campaign by complete surprise. Although Conable had endorsed Eckert quietly in July in a perfunctory press release, that had been expected by everyone. He had always been helpful to the party's candidates, but never before had he thrust himself and his prestige into the very center of local politics. His endorsement of Eckert was an abrupt departure from his past behavior.

In speaking with us after the election, Eckert tried to play down the impact on the campaign of Conable's endorsement. Although he told us it was not critical to his election, he did admit, "Its absence would have been important. People were starting to ask, especially out in Genesee County, if Conable had endorsed me. I would say he had. And they would say they hadn't seen it. Still I think we went a little overboard on those radio and TV ads."

In the heat of the campaign Eckert must have felt differently, for he probably spent more money publicizing Conable's endorsement than any single fact about himself or his campaign.[19] A look at his campaign expenditures suggests that his large expense for mass mailings was related to getting out Conable's letter of endorsement, and to airing Conable's announcement in televised political advertisements.

Call's camp thought Conable's endorsement was the biggest single reason they lost the election. When Call's closest political confidant and campaign

18. From Conable's letter to all registered voters in the district.
19. In the mailing containing the letter from Barber Conable was also one endorsing Eckert from Lucien Morin.

treasurer was asked what were the main reasons Call lost, he said without hesitation, "First, Conable's endorsement. We thought he would stay out of it. It particularly hurt us here in Genesee County. I think it cost us 4,000 votes in this county alone."

Another important campaign volunteer was equally certain that Conable's endorsement had been the big blow. A woman had told her shortly before the election that she intended to vote for Eckert. When asked whether this was because she disliked Call, she replied, "Oh, no. Call is very good. I want to keep him as sheriff. It's just that I have been voting for Mr. Conable a lot longer than I've been voting for Call. And Conable tells me Eckert is the best man for the job."

In other places at other times, endorsements in American politics have seldom translated into votes. Even the most popular incumbent presidents have not been able to transfer their popularity to the congressional candidates they have supported. But the endorsement in the 30th Congressional District of New York in 1984 may have been different. Conable was an extraordinarily well-respected local figure, as Call's own poll demonstrated. In addition, he had served for twenty years in the office about which he was offering voters his advice. Because Conable was leaving the office he was not motivated by self-interest. Thus the woman in Genesee County who paid attention to what "Mr. Conable" told her may not have been the only voter to do so. In fact, we are convinced that Conable's endorsement was the final example of the power of local tradition in the race to replace him.

Why did Conable do it? Why did he break his usual pattern of noninvolvement in local elections? Why would he deliberately undermine the campaign of a politician who shared his deep attachment to the values and people of rural upstate New York and endorse a man with whom he had a number of fundamental differences? Throughout our interviews we heard from many sources in the Republican party and outside it that Conable was not pleased to be succeeded by Eckert. It rankled him that he was being replaced by the very kind of new Republican politician who had given him so much trouble in his last years in the House.

In the end, however, Conable's displeasure over his successor's political style was not equal to his deep sense of party loyalty and feelings of political obligation to Eckert. Throughout his career in Congress, Conable had been a party man: accommodating, loyal, and a good soldier. Indeed his only serious electoral scare in politics was in 1974, and this was due in part to his being one of the last Republicans to abandon Richard Nixon during his Watergate troubles. Later, in Ronald Reagan's era, Conable again carried the burden for his party on taxes and Social Security, which led him often to express his annoyance in private but seldom in public. In addition, Conable was indebted to

Eckert. Eckert had helped him win the election in 1974, and Conable could not resist Eckert's heavy pressure to return the favor. Also, on the fiscal issues that mattered to Conable, such as the balanced budget, he felt Eckert was right and Call wrong.

When Election Day came Conable got what he wanted: a Republican victory, but only a narrow one. Call won slightly more than 45 percent of the vote and ran 5 percent ahead of Walter Mondale. After the election it was clear that Eckert's vulnerability had probably been underestimated by both the national Democrats and the local GOP. Eckert's victory seemed narrow in light of all his advantages: a large campaign treasury, a paid, professional staff, heavy use of the mass media, endorsements from prominent politicians, an extraordinarily popular president at the top of the ticket, and a disorganized opposition party. Even with these pluses Eckert's share of the vote (55%) was lower than that of Ronald Reagan (60%), of Conable in 1982 (68%), a difficult year for Republicans, and of Frank Horton in the 29th Congressional District, adjoining the 30th. Call, on the other hand, carried Genesee County, a Republican stronghold, by a comfortable margin of 2,500 votes and generally did far better than the published polls and most of the local pundits had predicted.

In fact, by the rule of thumb used by professionals in Washington, Eckert had taken a safe Republican seat and by failing to gain 55 percent of the vote had turned it into a marginal one. Of the twenty-seven districts that were open in 1984, the 30th of New York was one of only ten where the winner failed to cross this threshold. On the morning after the election, what many local Democrats had known all along was becoming increasingly clear to all: had the Democratic party nominated its strongest candidate and waged a sustained, coordinated campaign against Eckert he would have lost, because he had too many liabilities and the president's coattails in the Rochester area were nonexistent. On election night, as the returns came in, a party insider who was one of Eckert's early supporters observed, "It's a good thing the Democrats didn't know how close this was." They had in fact known all along but were unable to do much about it. The race was over before it began only because the Democrats were unprepared and unwilling to make a fight of it.

Campaign Federalism

Given his lack of support from national PACs and the national party, Call came surprisingly close to beating Eckert. His defeat came by such a narrow margin that one is tempted to attribute it to his lack of money alone; clearly Eckert's use of his huge financial advantage to dominate the mass media in the two weeks before the election hurt Call badly. But Call's money problem was only a symptom of a larger organizational failure: he failed at the critical task of joining together national and local political organizations in a common campaign effort.

Making this linkage is however difficult for political parties, which have traditionally operated autonomously.[20] While signs point to increasing attempts by local, state, and national party organizations to integrate their efforts, there are not many well-established mechanisms for doing so.[21] Such mechanisms are also easier to establish in presidential and senatorial elections than congressional ones. Whatever integration is achieved in congressional elections is likely to result from one level of party organization doing what it can ad hoc to entice another to follow its lead. But in 1984 the enticements from Democrats in the 30th district failed to produce genuine cooperation.

In the recruitment of House candidates, it is more likely that local parties will understand the strengths and weaknesses of congressional nominees. But once again the federal system tends to cause problems. Distracted by too many other responsibilities and thwarted by too many other centers of power, congressional politics often gets pushed aside.

This clearly happened to Monroe County's Democrats in their battle against Eckert. In February and March, just when they needed to give their undivided attention to naming a congressional candidate and getting an early start against their Republican opponent, they were putting all their effort into New York's presidential primary of April 13. Because of Governor Cuomo's strong endorsement of Mondale and Kirwan's connection with Mondale's campaign, the preoccupation of local Democrats with presidential politics may have been unusually great. Nevertheless, the long presidential primary season has a similar effect across the country, by obliging local parties to emphasize presidential politics at a time when the minority party in particular needs to put its energy into congressional races, if it is to have any chance of winning them. Certainly, Monroe County's Democrats were unable to afford the distraction in 1984 of Mondale's battle with Gary Hart.

These Democrats were distracted not only by the presidential politics at the center of the federal system, but also by several local races on its periphery. American party organizations grew up around the numerous power centers that the federal system leaves at the city and county levels.[22] Today, elections for these offices still have the most direct impact on the organizational vigor of

20. See Samuel J. Eldersveld, *Political Parties* (Chicago: Rand McNally, 1964); E. E. Schattschneider, *Party Government* (New York: Holt, Rinehart & Winston, 1942).

21. See Cornelius P. Cotter et al., *Party Organizations in American Politics* (New York: Praeger, 1984), chap. 4. See also John S. Jackson III and Robert A. Hitlin, "The Nationalization of the Democratic Party," *Western Political Quarterly* 34 (June 1981): 270–286.

22. See Schattschneider, chap. 6; James Bryce, *The American Commonwealth* (New York: Macmillan, 1941), vol. 2, pt. 3.

local parties. Monroe County's Democrats understood this fact of federal life and were already heavily involved in preparing for several such contests when Conable made his announcement. Local Democrats were particularly interested in retaining the county clerk's office, which they had won in an upset in 1981. They were also poised for a major effort to take William Steinfeldt's state Senate seat from the Republicans and to defend Jack Perry's against yet another tough Republican challenge. In addition, several local races for judgeships were deemed important. Democrats were unable and to some extent unwilling to push aside their natural concern for these races and focus most of their attention on the congressional race.

The Democratic experience in New York's 30th Congressional District illustrates that to a local party the congressional office falls into the cracks of the federal system. It lacks the glamour of the presidency, and no party rules mandate that the same special attention be paid to House nominations as to presidential nominations. When compared with many local offices, such as those of county executive or even county clerk, the position of congressman is both more remote and less important. The attention paid by party leaders to congressional nominations and campaigns is therefore subject to pressures from both the top and bottom of the federal system.

As a result of these federal strictures and the organizational weakness that persists in many American local parties, the early recruitment of congressional challengers has sometimes been taken over by the national party. But this has its limitations also, because as Call's experience shows, the national party has a difficult time being sensitive to local traditions.

Finally, no matter which level of an American party tries to take the lead in planning a congressional campaign, it soon runs into difficulty communicating its intentions to the others, because there is no mechanism to facilitate coordinated, long-range thinking. In fact the more forceful level of party organization finds not an established forum for cooperative planning, but a tradition of hostility and suspicion.

As a result of these organizational weaknesses caused by federalism, the task of creating a successful campaign for a seat in the U.S. House of Representatives tends to fall to the would-be candidates, and usually only those with the most burning ambition to go to Congress start early enough and plan carefully enough to link successfully the necessary local, state and national elements. By force of will these ambitious politicians build their own federal campaign apparatus, and the extraordinary difficulty of doing this is the final barrier to the recruitment of congressional candidates.

This fact also sheds light on why the impact of national tides on congressional elections is so episodic, idiosyncratic, and unpredictable. For the national tides to affect the outcome of a local race there must be a candidate able to link the national and local forces of a congressional campaign. Many politicians are not suited to the task, and those who are must have time to put together the necessary organization. The national tides must start running early and persist strongly for these strategically placed politicians to emerge and to have a chance to assemble a winning effort.

10

New Choices: From One
Election to the Next

*Most serious candidates operate, of choice and necessity, as individual
political entrepreneurs. The risks, rewards, and pains of mounting a
campaign are largely theirs. They instigate their own candidacies, raise
their own resources, and put together their own campaign organizations.*

—Gary C. Jacobson, The Politics of Congressional Elections

Before Fred Eckert ever took the oath of office in Washington, speculation had
begun in Rochester about his bid for reelection. Could such an unconventional
politician convert his suddenly marginal House seat back into a safe Republican
stronghold? Would his strongest Democratic rivals now decide to challenge
him, or would they sit on the sidelines once again? A lot depended on Eckert's
ability to consolidate his support and win over his detractors. But his future
depended as well on the actions of others—on the 30th district's unseen candidates—who were again rethinking their ambitions and assessing the new congressman's liabilities.

Along with other freshman lawmakers in the 99th Congress, Eckert confronted two possibilities with respect to his reelection: either he would increase
his winning margin in 1986 and show a "sophomore surge," which would
signal his tightening grip on the district and dissuade strong challengers from
running against him in future elections, or he would slide further into the depths
of vulnerability, perhaps even losing his seat at the end of a single term.[1]
Eckert's incumbency gave him all the perquisites needed to engineer a "sophomore surge," and his years in the state legislature gave him enough political
savvy to put them to good use. As one professional told us right after the
election, "Eckert has got to answer people's calls and get things done for them.
He's got to get his franking machine going in Washington. If he does that, and I
think he will, then nobody can touch him. Fred is a smart man, and he knows
what he has to do."

---

1. The term "sophomore surge" is Robert Arsenau's. Quoted in Gary C. Jacobson, *The Politics
of Congressional Elections*, 2d ed. (Boston: Little, Brown, 1987), pp. 29–30.

Yet even as Eckert set about deploying the resources of his new office, he faced the prospect of a tough reelection challenge. After Doug Call's strong showing against heavy odds in the campaign of 1984, Call had become a rising star in Monroe County and was likely to run again. Louise Slaughter had raised her political standing and self-confidence by beating back an aggressive opponent in her bid for reelection in 1984. Other potential Democratic contenders for Eckert's seat simply took comfort from the election returns of 1984, which showed a continuing decline in the Republican party's hegemony throughout Monroe County. The GOP lost a state Senate seat and a judgeship in county court, and failed by an embarrassingly wide margin to recapture the position of county clerk.

These startling losses made the political leanings of the 30th district far clearer than they had been at the time of Conable's surprise announcement of his retirement ten months earlier. There now seemed to be much convincing evidence that the district was truly competitive. Eckert had to reckon with changes in the political atmosphere outside the district as well as within it. Because President Reagan was in his last years in office, and because the party of an incumbent president traditionally lost House seats during off-year elections (particularly during the incumbent's second term), freshmen Republicans all over the country would be especially vulnerable in 1986. More importantly for Eckert, the Democrats in Washington were ready to go on the offensive; the first-term legislators they had struggled to protect in 1984 were for the most part safely reelected, and the party could now afford to turn its attention to capturing new seats rather than holding on to the ones it already had.

Finally, the next congressional election coincided with Governor Cuomo's bid for another four-year term. Already widely discussed as a possible presidential candidate, Cuomo was looking for a big win in his home state to launch a national campaign in case he decided to seek the Democratic nomination. Every resource available in the state party organization would be directed at getting Democratic voters to the polls, and in an off-year election, when turnout traditionally is low, such efforts would benefit other candidates on the party's line as well. Just as circumstances had so clearly favored Eckert in 1984, they were certain to work strongly against him two years later.

A hard-fought race would not just happen. Challenging an incumbent who enjoys a partisan edge in the district requires exceptional entrepreneurship by his opponents. To beat Eckert, the Democrats would need an individual with the skills and connections needed to exploit the newly competitive nature of the district and to take complete advantage of the more hospitable environment beyond its borders. Would Doug Call be the one to harness these local, state, and national tides to a single, formidable campaign? Would Louise Slaughter? Would others among the community's strong unseen candidates take up the challenge? Eckert's task from the moment he assumed office was to ensure that the answer to each of these questions would be no. The Democrats' task was to get busy persuading Call or Slaughter or some other heavyweight to give immediate direction to the party's new, promising possibilities.

Smoke Signals

Eckert seemed to understand what he had to do, and initially he set about doing it. His first moves to establish his presence in the district were organizational. In talking to us a month after the election, he was eager to underscore that he had spent some of his campaign money in 1984 to make a capital investment in computer equipment and software for use in future elections. "We have the names of everyone who even had a sign on his lawn for us or did anything—all sorts of information that we can pull out of the computer now or any time," he told us. From his reports of campaign expenditures, it appears that he used as much as thirteen thousand dollars for this purpose. In addition, he kept leading members of Conable's administrative staff on his payroll in Washington to persuade his constituents that the new regime would not be so very different from the old. Finally, Eckert opened a district office in Genesee County, where he had lost unexpectedly to Doug Call.

Eckert also worked hard to demonstrate that he could be as influential a member of the House as his predecessor was by securing a valuable assignment on the Energy and Commerce Committee. Although more freshman lawmakers sought membership on this committee than any other, Eckert was the only Republican in the 99th Congress to succeed. With the assistance of Monroe County's other congressman, Frank Horton, who used his influence as New York's representative on the Republican Committee on Committees, as well as through the good offices of Conable, who was still influential, Eckert was able to launch his career in Washington with a flourish. In the months following his election he often boasted of this coup and went out of his way to remind his constituents that the House Energy and Commerce Committee had jurisdiction over the Superfund, used to finance the disposal of toxic waste. This was of interest not only to the large number of environmentally conscious voters in upstate New York, but to the district's largest employer, Eastman Kodak, which uses hazardous chemicals in its manufacturing operations.

Membership on the Energy and Commerce Committee was more than a signal to the community that the new congressman was on the rise; it was also an indication of his willingness to play down his conservative ideology in the pursuit of reelection. After his victory in November, Eckert's fellow conservatives urged him to seek assignment to the House Foreign Affairs Committee, where he could bolster the president's hard-line foreign policy. "They were telling me that there were a lot of yahoos on that committee that needed to be dealt with," he noted. They also tried to persuade him that his ambassadorial experience would give him some advantages on the committee and that his work there would serve the larger conservative cause. But in the end Eckert ignored their advice, choosing to serve the interests of his local constituency rather than the passions of his national one.

The assignment to the Energy and Commerce Committee was by no means the only evidence of Eckert's preoccupation with his standing back in the district, for early in his term he began an ambitious public-relations effort to improve his negative image. The first big story about him in the Rochester newspapers, for example, described how he spent two full weekdays in Genesee County dealing personally with constituents' concerns only a month after Congress had gone into session. Eckert, who left those chores to others when he was in the state Senate, was himself tending to the voters at home once he got to Congress. It was surely no coincidence that Eckert chose Genesee County, his Democratic rival's home base, for the first display of his more open political style. This appearance was followed by a series of meetings in town halls around the district, at which Eckert would sit down with one voter at a time and discuss the issues. In describing these sessions in a newsletter sent to residents of the district, Eckert observed: "The one-on-one approach gives everyone an equal opportunity to bend my ear—and it's much more personal. Yes, it's very time-consuming . . . but it does give me a far better 'grass roots' feel than anything I can think of . . . and, of course, these personal meetings give me a good understanding of the sort of problems people can encounter with the federal government—and often we are able to help." The newsletter closed with an invitation to "stop by!"

In addition to reaching out to his new constituency by mail and in these meetings, Eckert faithfully attended local party gatherings, showing up on one occasion in the middle of a blizzard. But perhaps the most telling sign of his early determination to hold on to his seat was a press release that appeared in the local newspaper, outlining legislation he had introduced in the Energy and Commerce Committee that would require more complete labeling of prescription drugs for senior citizens. This free-market, antiregulation conservative had apparently caught the fever of consumer protectionism in his very first term in the House.

Observers who knew Eckert as a shrewd politician believed that he would be in electoral danger in 1986 only if he became tangled in the national agenda of his right-wing friends. "If the Republicans in Congress emphasize their social agenda, that could make it tough on Fred," an ally of Eckert's told us. "Certainly it would cause him a lot of trouble on the east side." But the president's emphasis on tax reform and Eckert's own actions quickly dissuaded people in the district from thinking that he would get into difficulty on this front. At the start of Reagan's second term, the GOP's more militant conservatives were overshadowed by the pragmatists in the White House. And the freshman representative from upstate New York seemed to have no desire for a moral crusade of his own.

Given Eckert's quick moves to consolidate his position in the 30th district and his lack of emphasis on the right-wing social agenda, the Democrats would have to get behind a candidate early and work relentlessly to construct the kind of federal campaign that would be necessary to beat the new incumbent, especially one whose party held an edge in party registration of two to one. Call seemed the obvious choice, for by running in consecutive elections he would have the benefit in the second one of the increased name recognition and organizational experience he had gained in the first. Yet even if the Democrats could commit themselves to challenge Eckert aggressively in 1986 and agreed to support Call, they would still have to persuade Call to run.

After the election of 1984, Call had expressed little interest in running again. When asked if he planned to challenge Eckert again in 1986, his reply was cautious: "If the economy goes bad or if I think that some of the crazy things Fred talked about in the campaign actually start to happen, then I might do it. I care deeply about the issues. I know some people didn't think that about me, but I do. And if the things I care about are jeopardized, I'd think about it. But Eckert will be the incumbent." He then added, "Besides, the commitment and excitement that was there at the end this time . . . I don't know if I can create that again. The sacrifices that people close to me made. Can I count on them for that again? I just don't know if that other 6 percent is there. I don't want to chase something that can't be done. . . . I just don't know."

Call's wife shared his reservations: "Maybe next time it can be done by a Democrat, but Doug's not the one to do it," she said. "I am not sure this is an experience worth repeating. We learned from it, but there are a lot of other things to think about. It is a matter of priorities." When we asked Call's closest political confidant if Call would run again in 1986, he waited a long time and then said, "Doug would like to be a congressman." But when we pressed him by asking whether Call really wanted to be a congressman, he again thought for a long time before reluctantly admitting, "Yeah, but less so."

Although Call was a reluctant rival for Eckert's House seat, Assemblywoman Louise Slaughter seemed increasingly eager. Despite her late withdrawal from the race in 1984, she was careful not to close the door on a future congressional candidacy. Although Slaughter never said publicly or privately that she intended to run in 1986, she had told many people in Washington and Monroe County that a future race would be possible if she had more time to organize and would not be bucking a Republican tide. As we saw in Chapter 5, some of her backers dismissed such talk as mere rationalization to justify her having pulled out of the race at the last minute. Yet others took her explanation seriously, and they began to telephone Slaughter almost immediately after the election urging her to challenge the new incumbent.

While Eckert went about the business of securing his hold on the 30th district, Slaughter deliberated over whether she might try to take the seat away from him. On March 10, 1986, only two years after she first thought about serving in the House of Representatives, she filed as a candidate with the Federal Election Commission. Conable's seat was no longer vacant, but this time she was ready to accept the risks of running. What made her change her mind?

The Return of the Right Woman

There was no single compelling reason behind Slaughter's decision to make the race she had rejected earlier—no catalytic event, no scandal, no damaging mistake by the freshman incumbent. Nor were there obvious turning points in Slaughter's personal circumstances that might have stimulated a change in direction. Her career in the state legislature advanced on a steady course, and her family life followed its established pattern. Nothing had altered except her own ambition, and her willingness to act on it.

This transformation was something more than a personal conversion; it was fostered in myriad ways by family, friends, and political associates. After deliberating so long about attempting to replace Barber Conable, Slaughter finally came to recognize the full extent of her congressional aspirations and accept that savvy politicians viewed her as a respectable candidate for higher office. Her reelection to the state Assembly against determined Republican opposition reinforced this heightened confidence.[2] Despite these changes in her self-image, it is doubtful that Slaughter would have challenged Eckert without the cumulative effects of persuasive individuals and activist groups pledging their support. These external validations of her inner desires eventually convinced Slaughter that her candidacy was founded on something more than private ambition, that it had the beginnings of what eventually became a formidable campaign organization.

Slaughter's transition from state legislator to congressional candidate began in earnest with a letter in fall 1985 from the Women's Campaign Fund. Disappointed by its failure to increase the representation of women in Congress after fielding a record number of female candidates in 1984, the group was bent on finding winnable races and identifying the right women to run in them. As part of this effort, the fund's field staff had organized a campaign school in October to recruit candidates and sent invitations to hundreds of women, including all the nation's female state legislators. Slaughter was on the list by virtue of her

2. Conventional wisdom holds that women are inherently less ambitious politically than men. Recent research on women holding elective office suggests, however, that much of this thinking is based on faulty data. See Susan J. Carroll, "Political Elites and Sex Differences in Political Ambition: A Reconsideration," *Journal of Politics* 47 (November 1985): 1231–1243.

position, but she already had connections to the group because of her exploratory trips to Washington in spring 1984.

Slaughter's contact with the group was however not enough to interest her in attending the campaign school. "At that point," recalled Celinda Lake, the staff member who directed the school, "she had to be persuaded that it was worthwhile. She still had questions about whether she would run, and wasn't sure that a candidate's school was relevant." Lake described Slaughter's reservations as follows: "Raising money. Could she get enough? Incumbency. Was Eckert really vulnerable? Risking her state legislative seat. Did she want to give it up when she was successful at it? Having run in such constituencies before, she knew how hard it would be. And finally, the depth of commitment among the people who were recruiting her. Would they follow through on their promises?"

Eventually, Slaughter did participate in the school, although this still did not persuade her to run. Yet while she was meeting with other women from all across the nation to discuss their chances of moving to higher office, she was getting powerful signals from other quarters, particularly from her friends in organized labor. Some unions, such as the National Education Association, had tried to persuade Slaughter to run for Conable's open seat in 1984, though most of the labor movement had remained neutral during her deliberations, in part because of their preoccupation with the presidential race and, to some observers, out of deference to the Assembly's Speaker, Stanley Fink, who was not eager to have his stable of Democratic legislators raided for congressional campaigns. In addition, such state labor leaders as Norman Adler, the head of New York's chapter of the American Federation of State, County and Municipal Employees, were skeptical that the district could be won by a Democrat, and had been unwilling to invest their scarce resources in a losing cause. Finally, labor had grown accustomed to having a lawmaker in the 30th district antagonistic to their cause: how much worse could Conable's successor be?

All this had changed by fall 1985, and the labor PACs were now ready to talk seriously about a challenge to Eckert. For one thing, Fink was less opposed to Slaughter's departure than he had been previously. As one Democrat observed, "The speaker had a heavy investment in her, but she's served four years now, and he's amortized." (Perhaps there was another reason: several months later Fink would announce his retirement from the Assembly to resume the full-time practice of law.) Call's performance in 1984 provided a further indication that the seat was competitive and not the lost cause that labor had judged it to be. There was also the added stimulus of Eckert himself. "They've got religion now," remarked Monroe County's Democratic chairman, Nick Robfogel. "Eckert has turned out to be everything we said he was, and they are after him in earnest."

Labor's newfound enthusiasm for Slaughter's candidacy soon became tangible, as several groups joined forces in November to commission an opinion survey of the district. Completed in December 1985, the poll turned out to be an ambiguous guide to the prospective challenger.[3] Slaughter's name recognition outside her Assembly district was predictably low: only 54 percent of respondents in the congressional district recognized her name, compared with 88 percent for Eckert. Eckert received a positive rating from 62 percent of the respondents and a favorable evaluation of his job performance from half of them. Finally, in a trial heat between the two politicians, Eckert outpolled Slaughter 56 percent to 24 percent, with 20 percent of the likely voters undecided. These were hardly numbers to propel a candidate into the electoral arena.

On the other hand, the summary report that the polling firm prepared for Slaughter was quite positive in tone. It stressed that Eckert's numbers were not as strong as they should be given his incumbency. For example, Eckert's unaided name recall (the proportion of respondents who could name their congressman without being prompted) was only 29 percent, a relatively low figure. His negative rating, 15 percent, was unusually high. (This figure, incidentally, was the same as that uncovered by the American Medical Political Action Committee's poll conducted for Slaughter in May 1984.) In addition, the report concluded that Eckert's majority was unstable because it contained a high proportion of "movable" voters: 52 percent of the respondents said that they "didn't know much about Eckert" and only 42 percent agreed with the statement that "Eckert has done a good job and deserves to be reelected." At the same time, the pollsters pointed out that Slaughter was extraordinarily well liked by the voters who knew about her and that she enjoyed a positive rating of 70 percent in the southeastern suburbs, even though Republicans there outnumbered Democrats 46 percent to 32 percent.

On these grounds Slaughter's consultants judged Eckert vulnerable and that Slaughter could be an acceptable alternative to him. The pollsters were in effect saying that they had seen similar numbers before, and that they knew them to be more favorable than they might at first appear. That the firm had an excellent record of advising successful Democratic challengers made its optimistic assessment particularly credible.

Slaughter observed later that even if the polling data had been less favorable, they would probably have made little difference in her decision to run. "I really don't trust polls all that much," she said. "They are only true for today. Actually, Betsy Toole and others in the party have told me since then that if they had seen the numbers they would have advised me not to run!"

Although the poll taken in December was not decisive in Slaughter's think-

3. The poll was conducted in December 1985 by Cooper Secrest Associates of Alexandria, Va. The results were made available after the election by Slaughter's campaign.

ing, it did reinforce what she had been hearing from many sources and what her political instincts were telling her. If the results had shown the voters to be overwhelmingly supportive of Eckert or revealed serious weaknesses of her own, her decision might have been different. By the time the poll was completed Slaughter was close enough to becoming a congressional candidate that it would have taken such unexpected negative findings to deter her.

Still, the poll was important in one respect: that it was commissioned in the first place demonstrated a genuine commitment to her candidacy among those recruiting her. The ease with which the money was raised and the quality of the firm commissioned to survey the district were proof of intent. One early participant in the deliberations noted: "We were all very conscious of the fact that we had lost her last time. Having been unsuccessful in persuading her to run once before, people came to the table prepared to make commitments and put things on the line. One of the unions put someone on full-time to raise money for her poll and get things organized. That sent a powerful signal, as did the fact that the money itself was forthcoming so early." In the language of modern election campaigns, polls can be an expression of purpose as much as an assessment of public opinion.

There is one more lesson to be learned from labor's provision of seed money for Slaughter's candidacy. An examination of the list of donors indicates that half of the ten thousand dollars raised for the survey came from unions in New York State, that is, local chapters in Buffalo, Utica, New York City, and Rochester of national organizations. Just as the impetus within the American Medical Association to fund Slaughter's campaign in 1984 came from the organization's members in New York, much of the critical support for her campaign nearly two years later originated outside of Washington. This is hardly surprising, given that so many successful congressional candidates come from the state legislature, but it is worth noting for two reasons.

First, it shows how the decentralized structure of many PACs facilitates their early involvement in the recruitment of candidates. These groups have sufficient knowledge of the local context and connections to the district to be active in encouraging congressional ambition. At the same time, they have direct ties to Washington that enable them to transmit their political intelligence to a national audience. Second, the active role of PACs at the state level (and the apparent autonomy of some from national headquarters) provides a bridge between the district and Washington that aspiring candidates can use in constructing their federal campaigns. One consequence of having this third group of activists is that the organizations of budding congressional campaigns are made more complex. Yet the burden of this increased complexity is offset by the support and information that the professionals at this intermediate level can provide to aspiring candidates at the initial stage of their deliberations, when they so desperately need it.

The PACs were not the only political organizations encouraging Slaughter to run for Congress. The Democratic party was also part of the decision making. After the local elections in November, Monroe County's chairman, Nick Robfogel, met with Slaughter to talk about the coming congressional race. He wanted an early decision so that the party could find someone else if she decided not to run, and she wanted guarantees that she would have a solid local effort behind her. Both politicians got what they wanted. Slaughter decided at the start of the election year to challenge Eckert; Robfogel pledged that the party would raise $100,000 for her campaign by June 30.

More than the chairman's promise was involved in the party's backing of Slaughter. In addition to the private urgings of her Democratic friends, Slaughter was caught up in a burst of enthusiasm among local committeemen and committeewomen. As she met with party activists around the county, she could see that the nomination was hers for the taking. No one else was courting the local committees, and as far as she could tell the party organization had already fastened on her its hopes for an upset. Eventually, a young county legislator did challenge her in the primary, as did a follower of Lyndon LaRouche, a right-wing figure known for his bizarre conspiracy theories, and she beat both handily. But during the winter months leading up to her formal announcement, it appeared she was the unanimous choice of her party and that she was free to concentrate her energies on defeating Eckert.

One local Democrat perhaps more than any other was instrumental in getting her to run: Doug Call. "I never would have run, if it weren't for him," Slaughter observed. "When I saw how well he did with so little support, I decided that perhaps my worries about whether the party would come through as they promised really didn't matter that much." In addition, Call had been very encouraging and indicated his willingness to help Slaughter in Genesee County, where she was unknown and had few contacts. Call's campaign treasurer ended up with a prominent position in Slaughter's organization, and Call figured prominently in some of her campaign literature.

Finally, the national party organization added its weight to the balance, which was tipping steadily toward a candidacy by Slaughter. She went to Washington to talk to Tony Coelho, the head of the Democratic Congressional Campaign Committee, and asked him whether the offer of assistance he had made in 1984 still held. Coelho's reply was affirmative, and this time there were no reservations about needing to put incumbents first. As Robfogel later observed: "There was a different mind-set in Washington—more interest after Doug Call did so well. They made commitments this time without any conditions."

Added to the encouragement of political people in and outside the district was the personal support from Slaughter's family. Her husband and grown children had urged her to run for Congress in 1984, but this time they were even more enthusiastic. For many women in politics, juggling household responsi-bilities during an all-out campaign generates enormous emotional and physical strains, and those who appear to deal with these distractions most successfully are the ones, like Slaughter, whose families participate in their election effort.[4] But the demands of a contemporary congressional campaign also drain severely the energies of men, and as we have seen throughout this book, many ambitious male politicians were reluctant to impose the costs of a congressional race on their wives and children. The enthusiasm of Slaughter's family for her can-didacy cannot be overlooked as a significant reinforcement of her ambitions for higher office.

Most important was that Slaughter's own attitudes toward running for Con-gress had shifted. After three and a half years in the Assembly, she could see that her fast advancement was bound to decelerate. The Assembly's Democrats had been so successful reelecting their members in recent years that the party was entering a state of political gridlock, with too many senior legislators in line for too few positions of genuine influence. Slaughter's hopes were neglig-ible of obtaining the chairmanship of a major committee after two terms, as her upstate colleague Roger Robach had done earlier. As one Democrat from Mon-roe County observed: "Louise has done well down in Albany and she is well thought of, but there is a lot of seniority now and fewer slots to open up. So she may be better off running for Congress. . . . Perhaps she's not giving up so much after all."

Perhaps the greatest change in Slaughter's thinking about running for Con-gress was her new willingness to go it alone if necessary. Recalling her fears that the party would abandon her candidacy once she had decided to run, Slaughter had not forgotten an embarassing episode in Washington two years earlier. In an interview she recalled the story of the young man who claimed to be connected to Governor Cuomo and who had been circulating in Washington with the help of Larry Kirwan: "I know you don't agree with this, but that incident with Fichera was a terrible hurt to me. I have never had the political rug pulled out from under me quite like that before." This time, however, she felt less need of Cuomo's backing and less threatened by Kirwan's lukewarm support of her candidacy. Recognizing that she was courted for her strengths as a candidate rather than her connections to other political heavyweights, Slaugh-ter concluded that she could put together her own political organization from the loose coalition that congregated under the Democratic umbrella. As Rob-fogel observed, "She has the confidence now that she didn't have then."

With firm commitments in hand and a solid record on which to build, Slaughter had completed her pasage from state legislator to congressional chal-

4. Ruth B. Mandell, *In the Running: The New Woman Candidate* (New Haven: Ticknor & Fields, 1981), chap. 3.

lenger. She was ready to become a high-flying entrepreneur in the risky business of running for Congress.

The Upstate Uprising

The electoral donnybrook that everyone in the 30th district had expected when Barber Conable retired finally did take place—two years later. As Eckert and Slaughter went head-to-head, the voters witnessed the tough, expensive, high-profile battle they had been denied in 1984. It was a race that brought hundreds of thousands of dollars of money from PACs pouring into the district, a race that involved both national party organizations heavily and sparked substantial coverage in the national news media. The campaign became the first in local history to cost more than a million dollars. And until the winner was announced, the outcome was too close to call. Conable's seat, once a comfortable Republican bailiwick, was now one of the most competitive in the country.

Did Slaughter's entrance into the race bring about this metamorphosis? To the extent that her talents as an organizer and ability to attract dedicated volunteers generated a formidable presence in the district, the answer is yes. The breadth of her personal connections outside the district also ensured that her efforts within it would be adequately funded. Finally, her distinctive political style appealed to many voters. These attributes alone would not have been sufficient to galvanize opposition to Eckert had he himself not been an issue. His seeming vulnerability and persistently negative reputation energized the disaffected elements in the district. At the same time, his preoccupation with national issues in Washington and his lack of rapport with his own supporters hampered his ability to counter the aggressive tactics of his opponent. Ultimately, the battle in the 30th district came down to a test of two individuals— a contest of political skill, electoral image, and the will to win. It was a classic example of the growing trend toward personalized electoral politics in congressional campaigns.

The race began quietly enough, with the announcement in early March that Slaughter had filed notice with the Federal Election Commission of her establishment of a finance committee. Then Slaughter's campaign went underground, as the candidate turned her attention to creating an organizational structure and raising money to support the lengthy battle that lay ahead. "I'm going to run the kind of campaign I always run," Slaughter declared. This meant recruiting volunteers, putting together mailing lists, and soliciting contributions in the community. The main objective in these early months was to raise $150,000 by June 30, much of it locally, to demonstrate that the candidate had the local backing and political know-how to interest national investors.

Democratic activists provided the nucleus around which these early efforts were built: they sponsored wine tastings, dessert parties, and barbecues, obtained signatures to submit to the Board of Elections, and helped distribute literature to boost the candidate's name recognition. In early June, the executive director of Monroe County's Democratic party, Fran Weisberg, became Slaughter's full-time campaign manager. In commenting on her involvement in the race, Weisberg observed: "The party has not gotten together in the past on congressional races. As executive director, I saw this as the most important race we had, and I took a leave to do it in order to demonstrate that the party was totally committed to her campaign. This effort has been a real shift: it brought all segments of the party together in an extraordinary way." Indeed, some of the early fund-raising events held for Slaughter had the flavor of revivalist camp meetings, with participants stepping forward to write large checks in front of the assembled crowd and declare their intention to raise a thousand, two thousand, or even five thousand dollars for the cause.

Despite this unprecedented show of unity, the Democrats were unable to guarantee their chosen candidate an uncontested nomination, and she was soon embroiled in an ugly primary. Charging that the party leadership had railroaded Slaughter's candidacy through the local committees, County Legislator William Bastuk decided to take his grievance to the primary electorate. He did not look like a serious candidate, and his reasons for taking on a seemingly lost cause remained a puzzle throughout the campaign. Bastuk never made good on his promise to move into the district, nor did he raise much money for the race: of the roughly twenty thousand dollars he spent, about seventeen thousand dollars came from his own pocket. But whatever his intentions, his negative campaign caused Slaughter considerable aggravation and distracted her attention from the coming battle with Eckert.

Although Bastuk accused Slaughter of favoring child pornography and being too liberal for the district, Slaughter tried to remain above the fray. She was advised that to respond to such charges would only legitimize them. But she believed that some of the mud slung in her direction had stuck, and, more important, that her silence during the summer months leading to the primary in September had given Eckert an opening. Thus when Eckert launched his first salvo, contending that Slaughter had avoided a tough vote in the Assembly on hydropower and then claimed that she had misrepresented her attendance record in the legislature, her response was low-key. "You can run, Mrs. Slaughter, But you can't hide," screamed the headline of one of Eckert's early advertisements. Trapped into a defensive posture by Bastuk's attacks, Slaughter had to ride out these storms as best she could and concede the first round to her opponent, who now had a campaign theme that would play to his strengths. For the remainder of the election season Eckert returned repeatedly to the issue he had raised with impunity that summer: he would make the tough choices his opponent lacked the courage to face; he would not lie to the voters as she had done.

The primary season was by no means wholly negative for Slaughter. By keeping a low profile and concentrating on her organizational strategy, she did score some points of her own. Her first victory was financial: by the end of June she had exceeded her fund-raising target of $150,000 by a healthy margin and raised nearly 70 percent of her campaign money from individuals. More important, she had outdistanced her opponent by some $50,000. This news quickly made headlines in the local newspapers and galvanized the PACs in Washington. More than anything else Slaughter could have done, this fact made Eckert's vulnerability clear to the whole political world.

Slaughter also had some unexpected help from her Republican antagonist. After focusing the attention of the press on Slaughter's questionable voting record and running a series of damaging advertisements, Eckert fell strangely silent in August. His campaign was short of funds, and the candidate himself was in the middle of family turmoil. Having decided to move back to the Rochester area because his wife and daughter were unhappy in the isolated suburb in Virginia they had chosen for their principal residence, Eckert suddenly had to deal with numerous real-estate transactions: he sold his house in Virginia and bought a small condominium unit across the river from the Capitol, then turned around and purchased a new home in Greece and sold the smaller one he had acquired before going to Washington; the sale of a recreational cabin added to the confusion. "It was wild," Eckert recalled after the election. And it slowed his campaign to a standstill: there were no appearances, no press conferences, and very little evidence of fund-raising in his financial reports for August.

Finally, the primary was a dress rehearsal for the volunteer effort Slaughter was putting together throughout the district. She had telephone banks to mobilize her supporters, automobile pools to get voters to the polls, and people distributing leaflets in key areas. According to newspaper accounts, some two thousand volunteers took part in the election in September—roughly one of Slaughter's workers for every four primary ballots cast in her favor. It was an extraordinary grass-roots effort that won Slaughter 81 percent of the vote.

The pictures of the triumphant, smiling candidate in the newspapers the next day and the continuing accounts of her success in raising more money than her opponent dispelled whatever doubts may have lingered about the competitiveness of the race in the 30th district. "We're going right on from here," Slaughter told reporters on primary night. "We have had even more people sign up to help tonight. I think it looks good."[5]

On Wednesday, September 10, the real campaign began. Eckert led Slaughter in the polls by at least 20 percent, while he trailed her in fund-raising by more than $50,000. He had his incumbency and Republican connections to

5. Michael Clements, "Slaughter Triumphant: Eckert Is Her Next Foe," *Democrat and Chronicle*, September 10, 1986, sec. A, p. 1.

protect his comfortable lead; she had the momentum of a win in the primary and the resources to go on the offensive. In only a few weeks, the two opponents would be racing toward a photo finish.

As the candidates began vying for public support, they appeared relatively well matched. Eckert brought in the big guns from the Republican administration: Vice President George Bush had already paid a spring visit to the district and Treasury Secretary James Baker arrived in September. Slaughter responded with Governor Mario Cuomo and Senator Daniel Patrick Moynihan. Eckert was the host of a campaign luncheon with Guy Vander Jagt, the head of the Republican Congressional Campaign Committee; Slaughter retaliated with his Democratic counterpart, Congressman Tony Coelho, and Congressman William Gray, chairman of the House Budget Committee. Slaughter was also assisted by the musician Peter Duchin and the film actor Richard Gere, who spent a day touring the district with her. But Eckert outdid her when he aired a television spot by President Reagan, who urged voters to "reelect my good friend, Fred Eckert." One exchange dutifully reported by the press typified the public-relations flavor of the race: Eckert belittled Slaughter's support from a film star, and she retorted that the president was a movie actor, too.

Their seven public debates were also fought to a draw: Slaughter won some, Eckert others. Slaughter stressed her accomplishments in the Assembly and her accessibility to the voters, while chiding Eckert for being out of touch with the mainstream of the district and failing to be an effective lawmaker in Washington. He pointed to his success in reforming New York State's pension system, the high rating by the State Department of his performance as an ambassador, and his having been named by *Reader's Digest* as a legislator who had the courage to say no to special interests. At the same time, he accused his opponent of misleading the public about her own record and distorting his.

By the end of September it was clear that Slaughter had won the battle of the airwaves. After a series of "soft" advertisements that stressed her positive attributes, she began a series of highly negative ones, the most successful of which showed an actor who resembled Eckert stamping a big, red "NO" on Social Security, environmental cleanup, student loans, and military reform, while martial music blared and harried aides rushed to get more items under his pounding stamp. At the same time, President Reagan had met with the Soviet leader Mikhail Gorbachev in Iceland to discuss arms control and come back empty-handed, looking as if he had bungled the negotiations. This combination was devastating, and Eckert's standing in the polls plummeted.

Eckert did not respond initially to Slaughter's attack. He was low on funds, which he decided to save for the last weeks of the campaign, and he rejected his campaign staff's advice to take out a loan to cover the cost of rebutting Slaughter's accusations. Besides, he thought he was sitting on a large lead, and his pollster was advising him to let Slaughter have her say, then come back hard at the end. By that time the damage was done, and when Eckert finally did counterattack, he charged his opponent with lying to the voters. Rather than hitting the mark, this last-ditch effort seemed to affirm the mean-spirited image that Eckert had begun to acquire.

While the public battle between Eckert and Slaughter raged in the media, the two rivals were locked in a far more serious test of strength at the grass roots. This involved taking their message directly to the voters through personal canvassing: letters, leaflets, contacts with volunteers, and of course meetings with the candidates themselves. Slaughter had the tougher task as the challenger, but in the end she was the victor in this less visible struggle. She had simply created an organization for reaching out to the voters that was vastly superior to Eckert's, despite his advantages as the incumbent.

The contrast in organization was most apparent at campaign headquarters. Whereas Slaughter had a large, noisy office suite crammed with telephones and volunteers, Eckert's operation was eerily quiet. She had a professional, full-time campaign manager in Fran Weisberg; he had selected a local lawyer, Lonnie Dolan, who valiantly strove to run the campaign while simultaneously carrying out her responsibilities as an associate in one of Rochester's largest law firms. Dolan, an intensely political woman with considerable experience in electoral politics, got some help from the manager of Eckert's campaign in 1984, who was now a legislative aide to Eckert in Washington, but she was clearly in over her head. Eventually, she prevailed on the congressman to put a person in charge of the campaign's daily business full-time, but to an outsider it was sometimes hard to tell who was actually running things in Eckert's camp.

The most telling difference between the two campaigns was evident in the streets. Slaughter had a phalanx of volunteers going door-do-door and campaigning at the suburban shopping centers, whereas Eckert could count on no more than a handful of people to spread his message. Reportedly the Republicans even had difficulty getting his election petitions circulated and signed. It was a question of intensity, and all the issue activists in 1986 seemed to be on the left end of the political spectrum rather than the right. As one Republican commented, "We have businessmen who show up at a luncheon to be seen and they write a check. But they can't put two people on the streets. That's where elections are won, and we don't have the people with the fire to do it."

Eckert had outraged various constituencies with votes against legislation to impose sanctions on South Africa and against the reauthorization of the Superfund. He had angered senior citizens by supporting a Republican budget resolution in 1985 that would have reduced the cost-of-living increase paid to recipients of Social Security, and antagonized educators by attempting to cut support for student loans and other programs. On many of these issues, he was the sole legislator from New York opposed to bills that passed with huge majorities. Added to this was his advocacy of aid to the contras in Nicaragua and his having voted with President Reagan 94 percent of the time—more often than any other lawmaker in Congress. There was also Eckert's "problem with women"—not the rank-and-file female voters, but the activists who viewed him as a threat to their aspirations to equality. Even law enforcement organizations objected to Eckert on the grounds that he had supported several amendments to weaken the nation's gun control laws. Eckert's position on these highly charged issues brought Slaughter a spate of widely publicized endorsements from an assortment of groups, such as environmentalists, retirees, teachers, and veterans of the Vietnam War. More important than these expressions of public support, however, was that many of Slaughter's supporters saw themselves engaged in what can only be described as a crusade. For the men and women on the streets in Slaughter's campaign, Eckert was the enemy: he personified all they detested about Reagan and his policies, and readily made large personal sacrifices to bring about his defeat.

No comparable fervor ignited Eckert's camp. The candidate had not drawn on his right-wing supporters in 1984 because he had not needed them to obtain the Republican nomination, and because he had been eager to portray himself as acceptable to party moderates. Although he had the Conservative endorsement in 1984 and 1986, he did not seek the endorsement of the Right-to-Life party in either election. More importantly, Eckert chose to emphasize broad issues, particularly the deficit and Soviet expansionism, which did little to galvanize intense groups on the far right. In pursuit of his predecessor's statesmanlike image, Eckert had cut himself off from those in the community who might have taken to the streets on his behalf.

Eckert did have an organizational resource in the local Republican party, but the GOP did not stretch itself for his reelection as it had for his first campaign. Not only was the local Republican organization in dire financial straits when its new chairwoman, Barbara Zartman, took over in spring 1985, but it was heavily committed to recapturing the west-side state Senate seat now held by a Democrat. Town Supervisor Donald Riley of Greece, Eckert's former rival for the seat in the 30th Congressional District, was the party's candidate in that race, and he led the Republicans' list of priorities. Eckert, as the incumbent in a heavily Republican constituency, presumably could fend for himself.

Nor was Eckert's status as a Republican as useful to him this time as it had been in his first election. Although the national GOP once again contributed to his campaign the maximum allowable amount, the Democrats offset this, as they had not in 1984, by giving a comparable amount to their candidate. And though the president came to the assistance of his most loyal supporter in the House, the voters seemed to be looking at the congressional election through a prism of local concerns.[6] Despite the efforts of Eckert to nationalize the election by drawing attention to Republican successes and attempting to link Slaughter

6. E. J. Dionne, Jr., "GOP Going National with Reagan as Democrats Take Local Approach," *New York Times*, October 26, 1986, sec. 1, p. 24.

with Jimmy Carter and Walter Mondale, much of the electorate seemed more interested in personality than federal policy. Finally, Eckert had to contend with a lackluster gubernatorial candidate at the head of the Republican ticket. After many prominent Republicans declined to challenge Governor Cuomo in his bid for reelection, the party ended up with a politician from Westchester, Andrew O'Rourke, whose lack of name recognition and absence of funds crippled his campaign. When Cuomo refused to debate him, O'Rourke was reduced to debating a cardboard cutout of the governor. Eckert did share the Republican ballot with Senator Alfonse D'Amato, an incumbent, but because he had never won the senator's forgiveness for some slighting remarks he had uttered six years earlier, he could not look to him for help. In short, Eckert would have to lure voters to the Republican line largely through his own efforts.

Eckert's campaign in 1984 had drawn heavily on local party loyalties to compensate for the candidate's weak personal appeal. The highly visible support of County Executive Lucien Morin, the endorsements and mailings from Barber Conable, and the public support of other Republican notables had rallied the party faithful to the GOP. But this time Eckert did not ask for such help from the party's big guns until the very end of the campaign, and his last-minute effort to invoke the magic name of Conable unexpectedly brought a polite rebuttal. Conable, now head of the World Bank, refused to involve himself in the race or even confirm that he had made a favorable comment about Eckert that Treasury Secretary Baker had attributed to him during a visit to Rochester. Telling reporters that it would be inappropriate for someone in his position to become involved in electoral politics, Conable coolly dismissed the race, leaving doubtful Republicans to make their own decision about their party's candidate.

There were indeed many doubters among Republican voters: residents of Genesee County who remained unreconciled to the idea of Eckert as their congressman, supporters of Riley in Greece who still held a grudge over Eckert's defeat of their candidate in 1984, women eager to elect one of their own who were willing to overlook Slaughter's Democratic label, and progressives who found Eckert's stance on particular issues too extreme to be acceptable. There were also individuals who had stories of Eckert's lack of responsiveness to their concerns. The most dramatic example involved a woman named Peggy Say, the sister of a journalist held hostage in Lebanon, who charged that Eckert had ignored her requests for help in obtaining her brother's release. Say not only pressed her case against Eckert in the press, she eventually made a highly emotional television advertisement for Slaughter's campaign.

Eckert had to give his wavering partisans a reason for staying with him, but his method of going about it was a dismal failure. With Congress in session until October 18, he was unable to campaign full-time until Election Day was close at hand. Yet when he did get back to the district, he resisted the efforts of his staff to schedule press conferences with groups that were supporting him and to arrange appearances for the candidate at local functions. Often he would cancel planned events at the last minute or, even worse, just fail to show up. He confessed after the election that this was a side of politics he found both distasteful and rather pointless. "The angel Moroni makes appearances," he joked. "The Virgin Mary makes appearances. A Congressman should accomplish something, not just be content with making appearances." Thus instead of reassuring voters that their representative was interested in their well-being, Eckert seemed compelled to reinforce their fears about his inaccessibility.

In addition, he let his opponent put him on the defensive with a public-relations stunt worthy of the best of Eckert's own. Eckert's greatest strength as a politician, even his enemies conceded, was his ability to get things done. But by the conclusion of the campaign, he was parrying Slaughter's charges that he was ineffective. Her argument was simple: in four years as a state legislator, she had been instrumental in enacting 112 pieces of legislation, while over the course of an entire term Eckert had not a single bill to his credit and had sponsored only three. "The score, sports fans," Slaughter would say triumphantly, "is 112 to zero. It's clear that I will stand up for the district, while my opponent has accomplished nothing." Eckert's explanations about being a freshman and a member of the minority notwithstanding, the charges stuck. Instead of making his incumbency work for him, Eckert allowed it to be used against him.

By the last week in October, Slaughter had edged ahead of her opponent in the polls. Republicans in Washington now conceded privately that their man would lose. On Election Day their gloomy predictions proved accurate. Slaughter defeated Eckert by 51 percent to 49 percent; her margin of victory was 3,300 votes. Eckert was one of only eight members of the House to be defeated in 1986, and Slaughter was the only woman in the country to beat an incumbent. She had outspent him by some $75,000 (raising more than half a million dollars), outmaneuvered him in the media, and outorganized him at the grass roots.

Ambition over the Long Run

In the wake of Slaughter's stunning upset, startled Republicans searched for reasons for their nominee's defeat, and almost all blamed Eckert. "Slaughter didn't win, Eckert lost," proclaimed the banner headline in one highly partisan suburban weekly following the election. Among the armchair quarterbacks who took this view, the favorite topics of conversation were Eckert's strategic mistakes. There was some truth in what they said.

"Eckert didn't use his incumbency the way he should have," noted one Republican activist. "He only sent out three newsletters this year, and he didn't do a questionnaire the way he had in the first part of his term." Another Republican noted that when constituents visited Washington, "Eckert wouldn't give them the time of day." He recalled an incident involving a family of stalwart Republicans who came back from Washington so angry about the way they had been treated that they promptly wrote a check for Slaughter's campaign. "These little things don't cost you anything to do," commented the former party chairman Ron Starkweather, now Monroe County's elections commissioner, "but Fred just wouldn't make the effort. Over and over, I kept hearing Republicans saying, 'I just don't like this guy.' "

In addition, many observers of the race felt that Eckert had not paid sufficient attention to the mechanics of the campaign. He started late and never caught up. When raising funds, for example, Eckert neglected to court the PACs in Washington, choosing instead to hobnob with the ambassador to China and other notables in the foreign-policy establishment. Having done little to broaden the narrow base of contributors on which he had drawn in 1984, Eckert had neither the cash at the start of the election season nor the good will of PACs on which to fall back when it became clear that he was in financial difficulty. In contrast to New York's other marginal freshman Republican, a representative from Westchester County named Joseph DioGuardi, Eckert did not appear on a list of incumbent House members who had raised large sums of campaign money by winter 1986.[7] And he reportedly had more than one PAC turn him down outright when he did get around to asking for its support. In discussing the election, Eckert conceded that he should have made more time for fund-raising early in the campaign. "I was just wrapped up in the issues," he remarked. But he also indicated that outside of his conservative base, it would have been difficult for him to attract funds regardless of when he started. "If you do things that matter to the general public, like pension reform, that's only going to put a few dollars in the pocket of the taxpayers, but the municipal employees will hate you forever." The municipal employees' union had in fact been among the earliest groups supporting his opponent.

As a result of his money troubles Eckert not only appeared vulnerable, but also could not afford to match Slaughter's media barrage at a crucial stage of the campaign. He ended up withdrawing advertisements in the outlying, rural areas of the district, where he thought he had a comfortable lead, to put more resources into Monroe County. The final returns indicated that he did not have as large an advantage outside Monroe County as he had supposed, and giving up easy votes in the GOP's heartland proved costly to his overall margin. Equally damaging was his inability to pay for telephone banks to mobilize his own supporters. Eckert relied instead on the telephone system the Republicans

7. Richard E. Cohen, "House Incumbents Gain Edge," *National Journal*, February 22, 1986, p. 453.

had installed to rally west-side voters for Don Riley's race for the State Senate. Riley's workers were however turning out some Democrats who said they supported him, and these apparently voted for Slaughter while also voting for Riley. Eckert got fewer votes as a Republican in Greece, the district's largest town and his home base, than Slaughter received as a Democrat, and he carried the town by some nine hundred votes only because of the votes he received on the Conservative line. To experienced observers this lapse was symptomatic of what one Republican termed a breakdown in the election mechanics. "That's where we lost it," he argued, "not on television, but at the grass roots."

Finally, Eckert relied too heavily on his polls. They had been wrong in 1984, predicting an easy win in what turned out to be a much closer race. It is thus surprising that Eckert relied again on a forecast that he had a comfortable lead, when all the other signs in the district suggested otherwise. According to one campaign insider, even when later survey data showed his victory clearly in jeopardy, Eckert apparently believed the polling firm's assertion that it must have oversampled Democrats and that the results could not possibly be accurate.

These examples of Eckert's inattention to the fundamentals of campaign management, coupled with the candidate's demonstrated lack of enthusiasm for making appearances and engaging in the other rituals of contemporary election-eering, led some Republicans to conclude that their nominee had not wanted to win. Eckert surely knew better, they reasoned, and therefore must not have cared about the outcome.

As Eckert spoke about the campaign and his stint in Washington a week after he had lost the election, it appeared that his Republican colleagues were partly correct. He had not set out to lose, but neither had he been willing to do all that was necessary to win. The man who had dreamed of going to Congress since he stood on the steps of the Capitol with his bride no longer had the fire in his belly needed to defend a House seat against a determined challenger. Why did Eckert's lifelong ambition for a career in the House of Representatives disappear in the brief span of a single term?

In the first place, he found the personal costs of serving in Congress much higher than he had estimated. The members of Eckert's family were experienced in coping with the strains of political life after his years in the state Senate and their tour in Fiji, but were unprepared for the disruption and alienation that greeted them in Washington. Being a closely knit family, they found the change far more painful than they had anticipated. Coupled with these worries were genuine financial strains, which had not been forestalled despite Eckert's having had the foresight to set up educational trust funds for his two sons of college age. Having lived relatively well in Rochester, the Eckerts now enjoyed fewer of the little luxuries they had taken for granted before they went to Washington. The loss of income hurt, but what seemed to bother Eckert more was the realization that his financial situation would never be any different. "Before, if I ever decided we wanted to do something, I would just work harder—get another client, put in extra hours. But in Congress, there is no room to grow. You're up against a limit on your income, and there is nothing you can do about it if you are conscientious about the job." As he reflected on the emotional and monetary drawbacks of congressional life, Eckert paused and said: "I keep remembering a remark my wife made one evening as we were leaving a reception at the White House. As we walked across the East Lawn to the car, she turned to me and said, 'You know, you left the best job you ever had . . . for the worst job.' "

Eckert's disappointment with his experience in Washington was not confined to his personal life; Congress as an institution was also something less than he had expected. In truth the House was far too similar to the legislature in New York State for his liking. Just as he had in Albany, Eckert found the pace of lawmaking to be unconscionably slow, the compromises made in drafting bills too unprincipled, and the unwillingness of his colleagues to deal with such broad public concerns as the deficit inexcusable. "I just can't compromise," he told us exasperatedly.

Worse still was the chaos that he saw reigning in the House. He recalled a conversation with a fellow lawmaker from New York: "We were standing around and waiting for something to happen, and I said to my colleague, 'This is just like the old days in Albany.' " His colleague replied: "Except then the leadership was trying to wear us down or round people up. Here, there's no point to it, and nothing is going to happen in the end." Perhaps even more telling was Eckert's dismay over the conduct of his fellow House members at the end of the legislative session. "Here was Tip O'Neill retiring, after giving his whole life to the House and serving as Speaker for ten years, and nothing happened. Nobody could think of anything but going home to campaign, and the session just died." Although Eckert, the passionate conservative, was no supporter of O'Neill, the quintessential New Deal liberal, his sense that the Speaker had been treated shabbily raised questions in his own mind about whether service in the House over the long run would be worth all the sacrifices he would have to make to stay there. These incidents offended Eckert's conservative sensibilities because they bespoke an absence of organization and dignity, which he believed essential to the proper functioning of a national legislature.

Given these pressures and doubts, the trait that distinguished Eckert most strongly from his political rivals in 1984—his single-minded desire to be a Congressman—did not survive the day-to-day realities of the job. He had no patience for tending to his constituents and fewer opportunities than he had hoped to pursue his national agenda. It appears that Eckert went to Washington with the idea of following in Barber Conable's footsteps, but without realizing that Conable had spent many years laying the groundwork for the trust and leeway he enjoyed in the district that enabled him to be a statesman in Washington. "I don't think Fred ever understood how much person-to-person stuff Conable did," one Republican said. Eckert also lacked the patience for the grind of committee work that was the foundation for Conable's policy leadership in the House. Indeed his attendance at meetings of the Energy and Commerce Committee fell significantly in his second year in Washington. Eckert seemed as unwilling to invest in close relationships with his colleagues on the committee as he was with his constituency. It seems likely therefore that Eckert would have stayed in Congress only if weak Democratic opposition had permitted him the comfort of serving on his own terms. Slaughter denied him this luxury, and he had too little desire for a bruising battle with her to hold on to a position that had lost so much of its allure.

Thus after the election of 1986, Eckert immediately ruled out a rematch with Slaughter in a later election and instead stated his intention to seek other opportunities in Washington. Before the year was out, he had secured a new ambassadorial appointment, this time in Rome as the American representative to the United Nations Food and Agriculture Organization. As Monroe County's Republican chairwoman observed wryly, "Fred has landed jelly-side up."

Although Eckert's ambition for Congress was now spent, Slaughter's was white-hot. While attending to the business of securing committee assignments and setting up her office in Washington, her first priority was to consolidate her campaign organization into a permanent coalition. Busloads of workers from her campaign went to Washington for her swearing in, and thousands more received notes of appreciation from her. Slaughter made appearances throughout the district and even sent messages on videotape to functions that she could not attend in person. She held her first fund-raising event in winter 1987 and in spring began a series of newsletters to her volunteers and contributors. Having endured one nasty primary Slaughter sought to discourage any Democrat who might covet her seat, and having upset an incumbent, she took pains to ensure that she would not be upset herself.

These precautions may not have been enough, for two weeks after the general election Eckert's campaign manager met with a group of young Republicans to search for a challenger to Slaughter in 1988; the GOP's leadership also began prospecting for recruits. With the disappointment of the recent election to spur them on, activists in the party reentered the quiet world of recruitment politics to find Barber Conable's "true" successor.

Thus, the tide of ambition for Congress continued to course through New York's 30th district, flowing for some and ebbing for others. Among the potential contenders in 1988 would be some familiar Republican names from 1984 and some newcomers whose success in various local races over the past two years had elevated their standing in the community and their political prospects.

Missing from the list would be other hopefuls from two years earlier, most notably Supervisor Don Riley of Greece, who lost his bid for the New York state Senate in the same lackluster Republican showing that cost Eckert his seat in the U.S. House of Representatives. Whether the Republicans would find the political entrepreneur they needed in 1988 to join local and national elites in a cause to defeat Louise Slaughter, and whether someone would step forward with a desire to go to Congress that exceeded Slaughter's to stay there would depend on the chance confluence of personal and local political circumstances that lure strong unseen candidates into the open.

As for how long both parties and the district's political activists will keep up such an intense effort to find the right candidate for New York's 30th district, and how long the district will remain a marginal House seat and a major political battleground, this excitement and intrigue will continue until one local politician finally dominates the district as Conable once did. It wil continue until someone puts a personal stamp on the district and clearly makes it his or her own turf. Then the flow of political ambitions throughout the House district will have found a new equilibrium, and congressional politics in the district will return to a calmer, steady state.

11

Recruitment: Ambition
and the District

*To slight the role of ambition in politics, then, or to treat it as a hu-
man failing to be suppressed is to miss the central function of ambition
in political systems. A political system unable to kindle ambitions for
office is as much in danger of breaking down as one unable to restrain
ambitions. Representative government, above all, depends on a supply
of men so driven; the desire for election and, more important, for reelection becomes the electorate's restraint upon its public officials.*
—*Joseph A. Schlesinger*, Ambition and Politics

The search for Barber Conable's successor in New York's 30th Congressional
District did not turn out as we thought it would. In 1984 we followed a low-
cost, low-key campaign—without even a primary—that met none of our expectations about a race for an open seat, but still managed to convert a safe
Republican district into a highly competitive one. Two years later we saw a
modern election involving big money and the mass media, in which a liberal,
Democratic woman defeated a right-wing, incumbent Republican in a district
with a conservative tradition dating back a century. We could not have invented
so many unlikely twists and turns, much less expected them. But this extraordinary chain of events served our purposes exceptionally well, because it drove
home the basic premise of our book: results on Election Day depend on decisions made by prospective candidates months or even years beforehand.

When we began this inquiry into congressional recruitment, we assumed
prospective candidates would approach their decisions about running for higher
office as relatively straightforward calculations of personal costs and benefits.
Like many others we thought potential House members would judge the probability of winning, estimate the relative value of the House seat, and then decide
if the risks of a campaign were worth the expected gains. Whether they made
these calculations with their heads or followed their hearts, we were sure that
ambitious men and women who held lower offices would be drawn to Congress
as the next step up the political ladder.

The unpredictable events in New York's 30th district did not fit such a
simple model. To explain the events of 1984 and 1986, we were compelled to

look beyond immediate personal calculations and to examine long-term, external factors as well. When we did, we saw how individual desires for a career in the House varied across time and how many competing options diverted potential House candidates in other directions. We also discovered that these external regulators of congressional ambition—the power and rewards of local offices, the restraints imposed by state and local election rules, and the habits fostered by community traditions—so pervaded everyone's thoughts about who could or should be the local representative in Washington that everyone in the district simply took them for granted. Thus as we sorted through the puzzles surrounding the selection of Barber Conable's two immediate successors, we came to view recruitment decisions as resulting from a distinctive combination of individual motivation and the district's circumstance. As has so often been the case in the study of congressional politics, personal political goals were found to be intertwined with institutional constraints.

We came to realize that modern House campaigns required both an extraordinary level of personal political ambition and a local environment that allowed these aspirations to be directed toward Congress. Having observed a single district over the course of more than two years, we do not think either condition can be taken for granted. In most districts, would-be candidates have few organizational supports to ease the heavy burdens of running for Congress. Their route has so many roadblocks and sharp detours that it is not at all surprising that the number of individuals entering House races has declined.[1] Most observers of congressional politics have attributed this dwindling interest in the House to the difficulty of unseating incumbents, even though incumbents are not noticeably safer today than they were thirty years ago—despite their impressive margins on Election Day.[2] But with the veil of entrenched incumbency pulled aside, as it was for us during the House elections of 1984 and 1986 in New York's 30th district, we clearly see many other influences governing the recruitment of congressional candidates. Using these observations as a backdrop for some freewheeling speculation, we conclude our story of the unseen candidates with an assessment of the private and political factors governing modern decisions to run for Congress.

The Private Side of Congressional Recruitment

The men and women who run for Congress have one thing in common: an intense desire to serve in the House of Representatives. Some congressional

1. See also Alan Ehrenhalt, "Campaign '86: Few Real House Contests," *Congressional Quarterly Weekly Report*, January 25, 1986, p. 171.

2. Gary C. Jacobson, "The Marginals Never Vanished: Incumbency and Competition in Elections to the U.S. House of Representatives, 1952–82," *American Journal of Political Science* 31 (February 1987): 126–141.

candidates catch Potomac fever early in life, others develop it later. Whenever this drive to serve in the world's most powerful legislature begins, it is deeply rooted in the perceptions candidates hold about themselves, both as politicians and as individuals. At a minimum, a bona fide congressional aspirant is someone interested in local and national affairs, who tolerates living simultaneously in sharply different worlds and who navigates through life without intimate personal connections (or lives in a family that can withstand great stress and long separations). A viable congressional contender also feels a strong sense of public approval and is confident that the voters see him or her as qualified and competent for national office.

No one possesses all these attributes at the beginning of the long road to Congress; individuals add bits and pieces to their political identities as they gain experience. Fred Eckert, for all his lifelong ambition to serve in the House, required many years to gain the skills and contacts to get there, and in 1984, at the age of fifty-four and with a decade of political work behind her, Louise Slaughter still needed additional seasoning before she was ready to present herself to the electorate as a congressional candidate. It is no accident that most men are in their late thirties and early forties, and women even older, before they have the polish, confidence, and connections to undertake a grueling campaign for Congress.

As ambition to hold a seat in the House is tempered and honed through experience, some men and women drop by the wayside, while others wander off in other directions. To understand recruitment completely, we therefore have to look at the decisions candidates make about their political careers over the long run. As they acquire new information about themselves and the district, they may see their political futures in a different light—just as Louise Slaughter did. This dynamic aspect of recruitment means that a district's roster of potential candidates is constantly expanding and contracting. At some points, it may be a good deal larger than the field of would-be contenders we observed in upstate New York, at others quite a bit smaller.

Two additional factors seem to be at work in the surge and decline of ambition for Congress. First is the rhythm of an individual's career. For some people the chance to participate in a competitive race comes too late in their political lives, while for others it arrives too early. Repeatedly, individuals with an acknowledged interest in running for Congress find themselves concluding, often with considerable regret, that an opportunity has appeared at the wrong time for them to move up the ladder. As we examined Conable's district in 1984, Assemblyman Steve Hawley's observation that "you can't pick your time or place in politics" echoed through our interviews like a poignant refrain.

Furthermore, prospective candidates constantly compare their own desire to go to Washington with that of their likely opponents. "Who wants the seat most?" they ask themselves. "Who can mobilize the largest personal coalition of supporters?" Against a determined foe such as Eckert or Slaughter, some potential candidates recognize that their level of commitment to Congress simply falls short of what is demanded. Eckert's presence in the race had an effect of this kind in 1984, and the same can be said of many districts across the nation with entrenched incumbents. From the perspective of the unseen candidates, incumbency per se is not the chief deterrent to congressional ambition, as Slaughter's successful candidacy demonstrates. What matters more is the fierce tenacity of sitting House members to hold on against all comers—which very few challengers can match.

We became attuned to the ebb and flow of personal ambition in a House district because we were able to follow prospective candidates in upstate New York from their very first thoughts about replacing Barber Conable in 1984 until they made their final decision to get in or drop out, in some cases two years later. In retrospect, it seems the choices made in 1984 were influenced heavily by the relatively short period of time Conable's surprise announcement gave the prospective candidates to weigh their options. There was little opportunity on the Republican side, for example, to examine the weaknesses behind Eckert's facade of invincibility, and by the time some Republican politicians recognized the strength of their own claims to the 30th district, it was too late for them to act. Among Democrats, it appears that Slaughter's flirtation with the PACs in Washington in 1984 might have blossomed into a serious relationship much sooner had she had a few more months to assess her situation. Under the pressures of time, Eckert's highly focused ambition, which lured him back from Fiji and immediately into the campaign, provided him with an enormous head start. While his potential opponents deliberated, consulted, and tested the waters, it became apparent that his most telling advantage (although by no means his only one) was that his longstanding desire to go to Washington enabled him to move promptly and aggressively into the vacuum created by Conable's retirement.

Thus incumbents themselves affect a district's supply of potential candidates. Whether there is a surplus or scarcity of individuals who have the required fire in their bellies for a race for Congress depends on the length of the incumbent's tenure and the timing of the incumbent's announcement (or hint) that the seat will fall vacant. For example, Speaker of the House Thomas "Tip" O'Neill announced his retirement two years in advance, giving numerous contestants in his district in Massachusetts the chance to organize. Competitors for Congresswoman Geraldine Ferraro's seat in Queens, New York, knew even before she was nominated for the vice presidency in 1984 that she intended to run for the U.S. Senate in 1986, and accordingly some were already planning to succeed her.

It is difficult to imagine a district held by a vigorous, respected incumbent bent on staying in office being rife with congressional ambition. Challengers are most successful at the very beginning of an incumbent's career and at its very end; during most of a legislator's tenure few individuals in the district will think about Congress as an outlet for their political ambition.[3] Having made other choices and other plans, men and women who might have thought about a seat in the House find it difficult to redirect their careers, particularly on short notice. We should therefore not be surprised at the scarcity of congressional contenders in New York's 30th district in 1984 and in other districts like it: Conable was at the peak of his career, with every prospect of serving several more terms, and he gave little notice of his intention to step aside. In districts around the country held by similarly secure incumbents, we think an unexpected retirement, death, or scandal would find potential candidates for Congress as unprepared as they were in upstate New York. This is one reason why a House district should not be assumed to be competitive simply because it involves an open seat.

If we are correct in asserting that congressional ambition is tied to the career cycle of incumbents, then sitting House members have a good deal of discretion over the process of recruitment in their districts. By the timing of their decision to retire or seek another office, for example, they may place some of their would-be successors at an advantage and others at a disadvantage; certainly Conable's announcement in February 1984 had this effect. Because many House seats become vacant when their occupants run for the Senate, and because the dynamics of Senate races are in turn equally complex, the ambitions of politicians at the state level affect the pool of potential candidates at the district level. In addition, it is likely that local customs for filling vacancies that occur in mid-term may influence the level of ambition that politicians harbor for the House. In the South, for example, where it is still common to appoint the spouse of a deceased member to fill out an unexpired term, the calculation about running or not running may look very different from the way it does in regions where special elections are the norm.

The impact of incumbency on the supply of would-be House candidates makes it possible to identify interesting districts for future studies of candidates' decisions. Although we cannot be sure of just when seats will become open, we can easily identify incumbents who are approaching retirement. We can also figure out likely vacancies in the Senate that will create new openings for prospective House members. In this fashion, we might reasonably construct a set of districts to serve as the basis for a much broader inquiry than this one into the politics of congressional recruitment.

In addition, we should recognize that the natural life cycle of incumbents' careers has a particular influence on the advancement to Congress of women. Despite the easing of many of the barriers that have denied women access to the House in the past, the number of female legislators in Washington has remained

3. Jacobson, p. 130.

static and is likely to show little change in the foreseeable future. In 1986, for example, only six women ran for open seats, half of whom were successful, and only one, Louise Slaughter, defeated an incumbent. With four women entering Congress and four leaving, the number of female legislators was exactly the same as it had been in 1984 and 1982. Given the small (although slowly increasing) number of women holding and seeking state and local public office across the country, the reservoir of female talent ready to move to Congress will continue to be quite limited. Therefore, the chance that a woman who has the credentials and desire to win a House seat will also reside in a district with a vulnerable or retiring incumbent is exceedingly small.

When we look into the districts ripe for congressional turnover, we need to keep in mind that the decision to run for Congress is not simply the product of careful calculations about the timing of a move up the political ladder—the exchanging of one place of power for another. The thinking of most politicians also involves considerations about family, friends, personal needs, and private insecurities. Outside observers will always misunderstand and misinterpret the career decisions of people in politics if they fail to view political men and women as ordinary people as well as candidates for public office.

We found in our discussions with the unseen candidates that they are often deterred from moving on to the nation's capital by the fear of losing part of their personal and private identity. It is not just the relatively low salaries and high cost of living in Washington that cause them to stay home, but the sense that their lives will be reduced to a single, all-consuming, unsatisfying political dimension. Unwittingly or not, the popular view of House members as people with no life but politics, which is fostered as much by House incumbents as by journalists and academics, has the undeniable effect of raising the price of congressional ambition to unacceptably high levels for people who value their ties to family, friends, and community.

For all these reasons, what sets many congressional politicians apart from their ambitious contemporaries in other political positions is their consuming urge to go to Washington and stay there. This highly focused objective directs them to the state legislature for training and moves them to cultivate allies in Washington's parties and PACs for future support. As in many other areas of American life, specialization has reached the realm of political ambition, and individuals who have a well-understood, deep-seated goal of sitting in Congress, and who work to acquire the skills and background to achieve it, have a decided edge. In the era of disciplined parties, individuals might serve in several different capacities over the course of their political careers; in the modern era each level of public office has its own network of influential leaders, its own body of knowledge and expertise, and its own rewards, making it difficult to run for Congress if a politician has not already got on the fast track and been warming up for the big race for a long time.

The Local Setting of Congressional Ambition

In New York's 30th district we found a constituency that seemed to have relatively few congressional candidates among its 525,000 inhabitants. From the time of Conable's announcement in February of his retirement until the formal designation of party nominees in June, the number of people who actively considered the race never rose above a handful. Despite the lengthy list of names that circulated in the community, Monroe County and its surrounding areas contained few individuals with both the experience and the ambition to make a serious bid for the House seat being vacated. The dearth of candidates had little to do with national conditions, for as we noted in Chapter 2 the partisan and economic tides that might have swept more players into the electoral arena (or encouraged others to stay out) did not run long enough or strong enough to influence the thinking of potential candidates. The lack of desire to go to Congress in this particular constituency was purely a local phenomenon.

In other districts with open seats, competition for the nominations of the major parties in 1984 varied a great deal. Sometimes it was intense, as in Texas's 19th district, which had hotly contested primaries in both parties, while in other parts of the country, such as the 7th district in Virginia, the number of recruits appeared as limited as in upstate New York. The very existence of these differences and their occurrence in a single year suggests that the ebb and flow of candidates in congressional elections has something more behind it than the surge of national events. Exactly what these local factors may be and how precisely they function at the district level to determine the number of would-be congressional candidates are questions involving relationships that we do not fully understand, and we do not presume to generalize about them with great confidence on the basis of our observations in a single constituency. But we do believe that the recruitment decisions we chronicled in New York's 30th district allow for some useful speculation about the influence of the local context on individual aspirations for a career in the House.

Each district obviously has inherent advantages and disadvantages for different kinds of candidate. In a given district members of one party, ideology, ethnicity, or class will automatically be rewarded and others will be hindered. But these simple realities of a district are not always easy to interpret: the 30th district, for example, was perceived locally as potentially competitive even though it looked heavily Republican on paper and was viewed that way by most outside observers. Beyond these sometimes opaque political demographics are the further complications of political geography—size, configuration, number and type of media markets, number and type of channels of communication—that make a constituency more or less accessible to would-be candidates. For politicians interested in Conable's old seat, the political geography meant that a foothold in suburban Monroe County was a significant asset, an urban or rural base a significant liability.

In addition to these obvious givens of a district's landscape there is a hidden geographic factor: the congruence of a congressional district's boundaries with those of lower offices that have traditionally been stepping stones to Congress. Some districts' boundaries define natural political communities and overlap significantly with important local offices, so that politicians are able to assess their future prospects and plan their career with a fair degree of certainty. On the other hand, districts lacking this overlap, such as the curious one produced by reapportionment in upstate New York, hold so many unknowns for would-be congressional candidates that the candidates are forced to channel their political ambitions in other, more certain, directions.

We often saw these distinctive demographic and geographic influences at work in New York's 30th district. Although the situation of Conable's old constituency with respect to media markets was a candidate's dream, most other features of the district deterred prospective candidates from thinking seriously about the race. The combined effect of the negative factors was to limit severely the number of individuals who could see themselves competing successfully for Conable's seat.

Another local influence on congressional ambition in a House district is the availability of other political opportunities, particularly seats in the state legislature. The state legislature prepares prospective House members for life in Congress first, by providing them with the skills and experience to wage a successful campaign, and second, by socializing them to think of themselves as career lawmakers. Yet state legislatures vary widely in their capacity to train future federal representatives.[4] Some states, such as Maryland, maintain the tradition of the citizen lawmaker who serves part-time. Obviously, the pool of congressional recruits will be smaller in these states than in those with a more professional legislature. Still others, such as New York, provide such desirable sinecures to their more senior members that life in Washington loses much of its allure. The timing of state legislative elections in relation to House races undoubtedly figures as well in the calculations of state lawmakers interested in Congress. When the two types of contest occur in the same year, running for Congress requires a politician to give up a seat in the state legislature. How much more sustainable the risks of running for Congress must look when the electoral schedule in a state does not demand this sacrifice!

Finally, it seems likely that there is some connection between the size of state legislative districts and the number of state lawmakers who wish to run for

---

4. In statistical studies intended to predict the emergence of serious candidates, scholars have used a dichotomous dependent variable to distinguish between individuals who have political experience and those who do not, which clearly is an oversimplification.

Congress.[5] For example, in large states with small legislatures, such as New York and Texas, a state legislator will represent a relatively large portion of a congressional district, but few men and women will have experience in the state capital. On the other hand, in small states with large legislatures, such as Connecticut, there will be little overlap of state legislative districts with congressional ones, but more people with state legislative experience. There is little evidence at present about the capacity of different state legislatures to nurture congressional ambition in their members, and this topic clearly deserves attention.

The state legislature is not the sole institution affecting the pattern of officeholding in House districts: the entire network of opportunities in the private sector, in state and local government, and in party organizations and interest groups creates many paths of advancement for politically motivated people. In New York's 30th district, we observed a particularly rich mix of options that attracted those who might otherwise have considered running for Congress. Business and professional people (notably lawyers), who typically swell the ranks of prospective candidates in other communities, seemed to find much in Rochester to keep them at home. Those who did crave a public arena often found it in high-paying positions in Albany, in the state judiciary system, or even in the management of county and municipal affairs. We doubt that most districts around the country have so many diversions for politically ambitious men and women; New York is, after all, a large, wealthy state with a sophisticated public sector, and Rochester is a prosperous community. But there must be many such districts in California, Texas, Florida, Illinois, and Massachusetts—all affluent states with a rapidly growing public sector. These are the districts where it would be useful to know if the supply of congressional candidates has dwindled as it has in upstate New York.

All these private and local factors remind us again of the pervasiveness of federalism in shaping the career of American politicians. In recent years, as political power has shifted to Washington, many politicians have seen their ambition connected to events there, and state and local governments have obligingly offered a ladder for their advancement. But a federal system lodging real power in state and local governments also provides many separate and satisfying avenues to political influence. For this reasons, some individuals may never focus their energies on a congressional race. Particularly as state and local governments become more modern and professional, it will be a mistake to see them as hinterlands and as mere staging areas for politicians marching

---

5. David T. Canon, "Political Conditions and Experienced Challengers: 1972–1984" (Paper prepared for delivery at the Annual Meeting of the American Political Science Association, New Orleans Hilton, August 29–September 4, 1985). Canon reports that the more state legislators there are in a district the higher the probability that one will run for the House. His measure of district overlap is however seriously flawed.

toward Washington. Ambition in the American polity is much more complicated than that, and it contains many satisfying paths in public life that too
frequently are overlooked by everyone but the ambitious politicians themselves.

The role of Republican leaders in selecting their nominee in New York's
30th district provides a final, cautionary note about the influence of local party
organizations on the recruitment of candidates. Although modern congressional
candidates operate in an antiparty era, not all prospective House members
pursue their ambitions for Congress in a partisan vacuum. The variation in
organizational strength of parties at the district level thus commands our attention as an important determinant of the depth and size of the pool of candidates.

Although County Executive Lou Morin and County Chairman Ron Starkweather were unable to dictate to the Republican rank and file their preference
as to who would be nominated in New York's 30th district in 1984, or prevent a
challenge to their choice at the party's convention, they nonetheless were able
to tip the balance of delegate votes in Eckert's favor and create enough barriers
in the community after the convention to discourage Don Riley from mounting
a challenge in the primary. Several features of the district pushed the Republican leaders to take such an active role in the selection of a House candidate,
among them the preeminent position of a single county within its borders and
the potential for a Democrat to exploit a divisive primary. But even though
these special concerns may have prompted their actions and given them added
force, the two Republican chiefs still made their presence felt by drawing on the
traditional instruments of party cohesion: patronage, personal loyalty, ties to
local contributors, and a pervasive antiprimary culture in the GOP.

On the Democratic side, we saw a similar drawing together of party leaders
in 1986 around the candidacy of Louise Slaughter. They too were unable to
forestall a primary challenge, but they did facilitate her early fund-raising
efforts and provided her with crucial organizational support throughout the
campaign.

Party organizations in New York are probably stronger than in many states,
and even within New York there is considerable variation in how much influence party leaders can exert over the recruitment of congressional candidates.
We would therefore not expect to find such strong indications of party activity
in House districts generally as in the particular case of the 30th district, where a
strong party tradition remains. But even when party organizations are relatively
passive in the final choice of House contestants, they almost always have
another, more subtle, more pervasive role to play in the winnowing process that
precedes congressional elections. In this role party activists in the district create
"the street talk" about who can run and who should. They provide cues to the
press and to other political elites that some candidates are more serious than
others. They become the primary source of intelligence about the district to

outsiders, particularly members of various staffs in Washington who actively recruit candidates to run in House elections. Most significantly, they reinforce or dampen the ambitions of all the men and women who are thinking about a seat in Congress. Even in their weakest form, parties are still a forum for people to meet and discuss politics, and the conversation at these gatherings invariably centers on candidates, not only for the House but for all sorts of offices. Beneath the speculation and banter at these occasions is a constant weighing and testing of the potential of various individuals for public office or advancement to another rung on the ladder. When an opening suddenly arises, the party activists have already decided which candidates are serious and which are out of the running.

When these myriad contextual factors in a district are viewed together, we see that House constituencies have their own peculiar structures for promoting congressional ambition. Whether the pool of prospective House members is large or small depends on the particular politics at work on the local level— politics that we believe are not easily understood from a distance.

Nurturing Congressional Ambition from Washington

Although the decisions of would-be candidates for the House in New York's 30th district were mainly the product of personal preference and local influences, national organizations and elites were visible throughout the two election cycles we observed. Their presence was not strong enough to alter significantly the climate of the two races, but their involvement did suggest how the parties and PACs in Washington sometimes enter the calculations that prospective House members make about running.

Money more than any other factor heightened local sensitivity toward organizations in Washington. People we interviewed in upstate New York believed without exception that the cost of a modern congressional campaign exceeded the amount that could be raised in their community, and saw outside groups as the only remedy to their expected shortfall. Inevitably, this perception raised the stock of any candidate who could quickly and easily tap outside contributors. Access to national money heightened Fred Eckert's status as the Republican front-runner in 1984, and it fueled Louise Slaughter's hopes in 1986 as well.

Despite the emphasis on attracting contributions from national groups, outside money was not the principal reason why so few candidates stepped forward to claim Conable's seat. The necessity of raising money outside the district did eliminate weaker candidates, such as Paul Haney, and inhibit Republicans like Riley from contesting a primary. But potentially strong contenders, such as Jack Perry, Roger Robach, Lou Morin, and David Lovenheim, could have raised what they needed had they begun the job immediately. And Slaughter had actually obtained the backing of the American Medical Political Action Committee and other important groups before she pulled out of the race in 1984 for other, more personal, reasons.

The races in New York's 30th district are nonetheless instructive about how financial backing from national parties and PACs can intrude into House races, for they demonstrate how much forethought and planning are essential to a congressional campaign dependent on national funds. Candidates who seek help from organizations in Washington have to meet outsiders' expectations about what makes a winner. They have to educate potential donors about the district and sell their expected opponent's weaknesses. All this effort takes time and organization, even for seasoned candidates; for the less experienced politician it is a discouraging task of many months. Although strategic connections or a highly visible consultant can ease the strain on candidates, even the ablest politician assisted by the most advanced tricks of the trade cannot realistically hope to raise half a million or a million dollars overnight.

In the short run, the logistical problems of managing a congressional race make unexpected openings like the one in the 30th district in 1984 unattractive to prospective candidates who need more time to mobilize a national base for their campaigns than retiring incumbents allow them. We think this is particularly true for Democrats, who draw fewer resources from their party and hence depend more than Republicans on contributions from PACs. In the longer run such obstacles clearly heighten the potential influence of both parties' talent scouts in Washington, because to the extent that they begin recruiting early and can streamline the business of prospecting for contributions, they may be able to lure some individuals into the arena and discourage others from running. In this respect, Louise Slaughter's experiences in Washington in 1984 and 1986 may be a sign of what lies ahead.

There remain some real constraints on how much national parties and PACs can nurture congressional ambition. In the first place, House elections do not head the electoral agenda of many elites in Washington. Recruitment of House candidates among Democrats in 1984, for example, took a back seat to the struggle over the presidential nomination. The attention national parties can pay to House races in one year also depends to some extent on what happened to the party in the previous election. Democrats in 1984 had the defense of vulnerable freshmen as their top priority and allocated resources accordingly. But only two years later they were in a position to go after marginal incumbents such as Eckert. Although Republicans do not have to husband scarce resources quite so carefully—they have more "take-a-chance" money for risky House races—they too were limited in what they could do for their candidates in 1986 by the necessity of trying to preserve their majority in the Senate. Because a large class of Republican senators were seeking reelection for the first time, the party and its allied PACs could not give Fred Eckert as much help raising money outside the party as they might have done in another year.

Finally, organizations operating from Washington have limited intelligence about what is going on in the hinterlands. With the benefit of hindsight, it is easy to see that Democrats and Republicans both misjudged what was going on in upstate New York in 1984. Their stereotypical notions of what makes a good candidate had something to do with these misperceptions, but they also lacked understanding of the race's local contest. As a result, they interpreted the district's numbers—party registration and the like—very differently from those who knew the constituency intimately. Until parties and PACs create organizational structures that allow them to reach into House constituencies with greater sensitivity (some already have, as we saw with Slaughter's candidacy in 1986) we think their success in recruiting congressional candidates will remain modest.

These remarks suggest that we need to know a great deal more about how the national parties and PACs behave in the months and years preceding a congressional election before we can explain their impact on the decisions of prospective House candidates. Until we have that understanding, we should not invest too heavily in recent theories of "strategic politicians" as the principal source of competition in congressional elections.[6]

Ambition and Popular Control of Elections

Before a congressional campaign begins, it could conceivably be fought by any number of candidates in any number of combinations and scenarios, with all sorts of possibilities open to the district's electorate. Each candidate in this wide array of possibilities would offer voters a unique combination of traits and experiences: a distinctive record of accomplishments, a facility with certain types of issue, and his or her own style of political presentation. Each of these potential entrants into a congressional race would also have a different capacity to mobilize support and manage the complexities of a contemporary House campaign. But as Election Day draws near few of those once seen as real possibilities actually enter the race, and voters' options are narrowed drastically. What voters hear in November and how persuasive the messages turn out to be depend in large part on who decided many months earlier to run and who chose to remain on the sidelines.

6. In a recent paper Gary C. Jacobson, who helped formulate the theory of "strategic politicians," reached the following conclusion: "How national forces impinge on individual voters remains uncertain; but local candidates and campaigns clearly play an important mediating role." See "National Forces in Congressional Elections" (Paper presented at the Annual Meeting of the American Political Science Association, Washington Hilton, August 28–31, 1986).

The elections in New York's 30th district provide ample proof of this simple fact. The contest in 1984, for example, was not the hard-fought, issue-oriented battle that everyone had expected. Freed of the negative baggage that a primary would have produced if some of the strong unseen candidates had chosen to challenge him, Eckert had the luxury in the general election of running a positive campaign essentially without issue. The dogfight that so many politicians in Monroe County told us was the hallmark of a campaign by Eckert simply did not happen; there were no personal attacks on his opponent, no ingenious public-relations ploys, no calls to arms for the agenda of the New Right. The man who reportedly used issues like clubs was strangely silent, choosing instead to emphasize his service in office, his prestige as a diplomat, and, most important, his endorsement by Barber Conable. Eckert could afford to do this, because the ambivalence and latent hostility toward him that were so evident in the poll conducted in May 1984 and again at the Republican convention remained unarticulated by the few people who finally challenged him. Indeed it was these widespread but inchoate reservations about Eckert as a person that allowed Doug Call to do so much better at the polls than one would have been led to predict by his poorly organized campaign. Two years later, when these previously undiscussed shortcomings were given a full airing by Slaughter, who was tough-minded and had a campaign rich in resources, Eckert was defeated.

As we survey these events we cannot help speculating about what might have been. Would Call have been the Democratic candidate if other Republicans had tested Eckert in spring 1984? Would Call have won as many votes against a different Republican opponent? Would Slaughter have been recruited so intensively by the Democrats in 1986 if Don Riley rather than Fred Eckert had been the incumbent? Would she have had the confidence to go it alone if necessary without the galvanizing effect of Eckert's negative image? Although these questions are all unanswerable, even to pose them highlights the profound effect on the final outcome of congressional races of the decisions of unseen candidates.

With the discretion of voters so limited by this hidden winnowing process, what do the election results actually reveal about the electorate's policy preferences? Judging from the radically different politicians who held a mandate from the people of New York's 30th district in the span of only four years, the will of the majority is almost incomprehensible. The progression from Conable to Eckert to Slaughter, from conservative to ultraconservative to liberal, is inexplicable if we view it apart from the recruitment decisions that preceded each election and that ultimately defined the very narrow options presented to the district's voters.

The outcomes of congressional elections have some meaning if we focus on candidates rather than policies. From this perspective, congressional elections fulfill their democratic purpose so long as voters are presented with good candidates to send to Congress. But what is a good congressional candidate? In purely instrumental terms, the good candidate is the one who can win. This definition conforms nicely to our ideas of legitimacy in a democratic system, for under majority rule the better candidate ideally wins the most votes. Yet how are we to recognize a strong contender if our only test is the outcome after the polls have closed? Clearly, in evaluating prospective House members we need to understand which attributes inspire public confidence before citizens enter the voting booth, not only after the ballots have been counted.

Professional observers of politics—campaign consultants, staff members in parties and PACs, and some academics—have produced some effective predictors of the quality of candidates simply by focusing on winners. Not surprisingly, the attributes they identify are membership in the majority party, money, visibility, and experience—in short, all the characteristics that Eckert had in such abundance. Despite Call's strong showing and Slaughter's victory these traditional indicators remain sound measures of part of what constitutes a good candidate; they simply fail to reflect all of it.

We believe the most important missing attribute in the profile of a strong congressional contender is his or her ability to fit the district, not simply in a partisan or ideological sense, but in a more personal, empathic one. Although Eckert fit his old state Senate district, where his constituency in Greece was homogeneous and his uncompromising, abrasive nature much admired and taken for independence, he was unable to find such a common denominator with the larger, more diverse electorate in Conable's congressional district. Both Call, who had a claim to upstate New York's rural progressivism, and Slaughter, who had the style of a populist from Kentucky, were more successful than Eckert in establishing this essential personal connection with the district's voters. Judging which of these candidates was best therefore meant, to borrow a phrase from the statisticians, estimating their goodness of fit with the local political culture and customs. By this standard the best man was never Eckert.

Without an intimate knowledge of the district, it is difficult for observers of congressional elections to know in advance which politicians will be good candidates and will be able to establish this bond with the electorate. Nevertheless, public-opinion polls offer some clues, especially the questions that probe voters' negative attitudes toward potential candidates. The higher a politician's negative rating, the less likely it is that he or she will fit the district. At the very least, a high negative rating suggests just how far a politician will have to travel to gain acceptance by the district. By this measure, Eckert was a misfit in New York's 30th district, because polls showed him having the highest negative rating of any local politician.

There was another measure of Eckert's mismatch with the 30th Congressional District. Buried in the campaign finance reports filed during the early phases of each election with the Federal Election Commission were data revealing that Eckert's campaign drew its contribution from a narrow base. This was a strong indication of his lack of fit with the constituency, because the breadth of a candidate's financial base (not just the total amount raised but the number and distribution of donors in the district) gives a reliable estimate of the amount of local enthusiasm a politician can generate at home. By this rather indirect measure, Call and Eckert competed on roughly equal terms for Conable's seat in 1984, and Slaughter clearly outmatched Eckert in 1986.

Political activists in a community have yet a third standard by which to measure a candidate's fit with the district. Drawing on their past experiences, the men and women who participate most directly in the nomination process perceive characteristics in prospective candidates that the public at large has little opportunity to observe and may care about even less. In 1984, this collective memory of the local elites proved decisive in New York's 30th district, as the "shark" and the "dolphin" battled for the Republican designation. The elite's standards of fitness prompted the Republican faithful in Monroe County to support Eckert as the better candidate even though their policy preferences and personal feelings dictated otherwise. Among Democratic elites two years later a similar collective memory fueled a conviction that Slaughter could upset Eckert.

In districts lacking the rich party culture of New York's 30th, a candidate's reputation and the elite's judgment about fit may lie in other hands. But whether it is the party or some other group of activists that applies the yardstick to prospective candidates, we cannot overlook that the district's political insiders, whoever they are, usually understand how candidates fit a district far better than the pollsters and politicians outside its boundaries.

Beyond this sense of fit, a good congressional candidate must have a burning desire to serve in Washington. The voters need to see such focused ambition to have some assurance that a politician will assume the burdens of congressional life and surmount the barriers that mark the route to power on Capitol Hill. In a sprawling democracy like the United States, such ambition helps tie federal lawmakers more closely to their distant constituents. Without the politician's ambition driving him or her to capture and hold a congressional seat, the public's mandate loses its force and its withdrawal holds no threat. The civic virtues of obligation, statecraft, and concern for the public good are all laudable, necessary qualities in elected officials, well-recognized by the Founders as essential to the proper functioning of a representative democracy. But the framers of the American system put some of their trust in lesser human motives as well. As Madison observed: "Those ties which bind the representative to his constituents are strengthened by motives of a more selfish nature. His pride and vanity attach him to a form of government which favors his pretentions and gives him a share in its honors and distinctions."[7] Madison concluded: "Duty, gratitude, interest, ambition itself are the chords by which they [Representatives] will be bound to fidelity and sympathy with the great mass of the people."[8]

Thus one of the essential conditions for continuing public control over elected officials is pure political ambition. Another is a steady supply of unseen candidates back in the district. In combination, they help hold elected representatives in check. We believe that modern congressional campaigns, which have high costs, complex organizational requirements, and heavy personal tolls, ensure in an almost Darwinian fashion that the public is served by officeholders of sufficient political ambition. We are less certain that the nation's pluralistic, federal arrangement of political power and progressive election rules are capable over the long run of providing a sufficiently predictable supply of strong unseen candidates in each of the nation's 435 congressional districts to keep incumbents on their toes and give voters real choices. By our reckoning, the current system of congressional recruitment is simply too unpredictable to assure that enough of the right people will be in the right place at the right time. Perhaps it is only fair that because politicians cannot pick their time and place, neither can the voters.

7. *The Federalist*, no. 57.
8. Ibid.

Index

Abortion, 22, 52, 56, 156, 157, 177. *See also* National Right to Life PAC; Right-to-Life Party (New York State)
ACLU, 52, 56
Adduci, Pat, 67, 108
Adler, Norman, 205
AFL-CIO, 56
Age of candidates, 142–143, 225
Ambition, 197, 224–228; discontent as catalyst for, 134; importance of, xi, 2–3, 72, 238–239; local setting of, 229–233; nurtured by national parties and PACs, 234; opportunity as catalyst for, 15; popular control of elections and, 235–239; of women, 204n
American Civil Liberties Union, 52, 56
American Federation of State, County and Municipal Employees, 205
American Medical Political Action Committee (AMPAC), 37, 111–112, 115, 117

Baker, James, 213, 216
Balanced-budget amendment, 178
Bastuk, William, 211
Batavia, N.Y., 9, 176
Bausch & Lomb, 9, 62
Berrigan, Daniel, 155
Brighton, N.Y., 61
Broder, David, 151
Bush, George, 213

Caddell, Pat, 185n
Call, Doug, 29, 236, 237, 238; ambition lacking in, 180–181; Conable compared with, 175–176, 178–179; fund-raising problems of, 181–183, 186–187, 189–

190, 191; issue problems of, 192–195; poll conducted for, 183–185; pragmatism of, 177–178; as prospective candidate (1986), 203; strong showing of, 195, 200
Campaign finance: election outcome and, 35n9, 191; incumbents' advantage in, 91; in-kind contributions, 111–112; name recognition dependent on, 181–182; national parties' role in, 36–37, 93–94, 190, 234
Campaign spending: growth in, 35; in open-seat races, 5, 36; on polls, 68–69
Candidates: age of, 142–143, 225; backgrounds of, 1–2, 7; campaigns centered on, xi, 236–237; congressional staff members as, 125n; declining number of, 224; districts compatible with, 237–238; local ties of, 140–144; obstacles faced by, 2; options available to, 3, 122–123, 230; opportunities for, 15–24; prospective, pool of, 7, 20, 138–140, 141, 144, 239; unseen, 1–8; women as, 102–121. *See also* Ambition; Recruitment
Carpetbagging, 63
Carter, Jimmy, 29, 55, 106, 108, 114, 179, 216
Casework, 17n3, 90
Central America, 120, 214
Chamber of Commerce, 3, 56, 64, 123, 129
Changing of the Guard, The (Broder), 151
Citizens for the Republic, 187
Civil rights, 23
Coehlo, Tony, 79, 111, 208, 213
Colgate Rochester Divinity School, 176
Committee on Committees, House Republicans', 201
Committee on Political Education (COPE), 56
Committees, legislative, 17, 88, 95